For Josh —
A great student
and a great force
for good at our
beloved Rutgers.
With best wishes,
WC Tom —
29 April 2008

CONFESSIONS OF A SPOILSPORT

WILLIAM C. DOWLING

confessions of a
SPOILSPORT

My Life and Hard Times Fighting Sports Corruption
at an Old Eastern University

The Pennsylvania State University Press
University Park, Pennsylvania

Library of Congress Cataloging-in-Publication Data

Dowling, William C.
    Confessions of a spoilsport : my life and hard times
    fighting sports corruption at an old eastern university /
    William C. Dowling.
        p.   cm.
Includes bibliographical references and index.
ISBN 978-0-271-03293-1 (cloth : alk. paper)
1. College sports—Moral and ethical aspects—United States.
2. College sports—Economic aspects—United States.
3. Rutgers University.
4. National Collegiate Athletic Association
I. Title.

GV351.D68 2007
796.04'30973—dc22
2007009448

The Pennsylvania State University Press is a member of the
Association of American University Presses.

It is the policy of The Pennsylvania State University Press
to use acid-free paper. This book is printed on Natures
Natural, containing 50% post-consumer waste, and meets
the minimum requirements of American National Standard
for Information Sciences—Permanence of Paper for Printed
Library Material, ANSI Z39.48–1992.

Book design/typesetting by Garet Markvoort/zijn digital

For the alumni, students, and faculty of Rutgers 1000

Contents

Introduction

On July 25, 2003, police investigators found the badly decomposed body of a Baylor University basketball player, Patrick Dennehy, in a grassy field four miles from the Baylor campus. Dennehy had been missing for more than a month. His disappearance had drawn widespread press coverage. Six days after he'd been reported missing, his SUV, a dark blue new-model Chevrolet Tahoe, turned up in Virginia, stripped of its Texas plates. In Waco, rumors were circulating that Dennehy's disappearance was connected to a fight he'd had with another Baylor basketball player, Carlton Dotson. Then Dotson, calling from his home in Maryland, told the FBI he was willing to discuss Dennehy's disappearance. The information he provided led Waco police to the field where Dennehy's corpse, lying exposed to a hot Texas summer sun, had been decomposing for more than four weeks. An autopsy showed that the player had been killed by two bullets to the head, fired at close range from a 9mm pistol.

The story that unfolded after Dennehy's body was found is a parable about Div IA athletics at hundreds of American universities. It's a story of corruption and hypocrisy and self-deception. Of pious claims and brutally cynical behavior. Of frightened faculty and powerful regents or trustees who see winning football and basketball teams as immeasurably more important than academic and intellectual values. It is the story, not least, of thousands of ordinary undergraduates who, brainwashed by years of televised bowl games and "March Madness" hype, have no idea of what a real college education might otherwise be. The Baylor scandal is in this sense all Div IA scandals: academic fraud at Ohio State or Georgia or Minnesota, booster bribery as in Michigan's "Fab Five" case, sex-and-recruiting parties at the University of Colorado, rape and assault and financial fraud at Miami or Virginia Tech, and others too numerous to count.

The Baylor scandal is about the way commercialized college sports, powered by billions of dollars in TV advertising revenues, have permitted a retrograde booster subculture to assert control over institutions of higher learning from coast to coast. Private universities like Baylor and Miami and

Duke. Public universities like Nebraska and Colorado and Ohio State. It's about the academic decline that sets in when the brightest students in a state flee in large numbers to out-of-state schools whose undergraduates value ideas and knowledge over big-time sports. Or when top faculty, sickened by teaching at a school owned and operated by the local boosters' club, leave for institutions whose undergraduates have come to college to use their minds. The Baylor story is in this sense about the triumph of commercial culture and consumerist ideology over higher education in contemporary America.

Most of all, though, the Baylor scandal is about the separate sphere of reality inhabited by everyone involved in Div I A athletics—players, coaches, academic tutors, Athletics Department personnel, sports-friendly trustees and administrators. The great value—perhaps the only value—of the Div I A scandals that have so regularly broken out over the last few years is that they permit those who know nothing about the N CAA or "March Madness" to see what this sphere of reality looks like from the inside. It's increasingly important that they do so. As recently as thirty or forty years ago, Div I A reality was still a self-enclosed subculture within the university. Today, it has expanded its boundaries to become, in many cases, identical with the university as such. This is the context in which the scandals provide, in addition to predictably sordid stories of corruption and moral cynicism, a way of understanding the actual dynamics of sports corruption in American higher education.

Let's return for a moment to Baylor. At Baylor, administrators maintained that Dennehy's death had nothing specifically to do with Baylor athletics. "This is not related to anything Baylor does or doesn't do," a Baylor vice president assured the *Chronicle of Higher Education*. "We're not insulated from society, or from what good or bad happens in the world." By the same token, the rules laid down by the N CAA for treatment of scholarship athletes—tuition money, some help with living expenses, and no special benefits beyond that—really had been scrupulously observed at Baylor. "We followed the rules, however difficult they may be, for thirty years," basketball coach Dave Bliss said at a press conference. Given that Baylor was a Baptist institution with a strong commitment to Christian morality, there was every reason to suppose that he was telling the truth. A Baylor student who organized a prayer meeting during the turmoil surrounding Dennehy's murder called President Robert Sloan "the godliest president Baylor has had." A distraught Coach Bliss told reporters that "all the members of the Baylor family and myself are in tremendous disbelief" at Dennehy's disappearance, because Dennehy was "an unbelievable young man."

Still, there was some concern at Baylor that all might not be quite right with Coach Bliss's basketball program. For one thing, Patrick Dennehy, a talented six-foot-ten center, had transferred to Baylor the year before from the University of New Mexico. NCAA rules require transfer athletes to sit out one playing year at their new school. Dennehy's family was unable to contribute to college costs. Since Coach Bliss had not wanted to give his new center an athletic scholarship that could go to an active player, Dennehy was without university funding to cover his $17,200 tuition bill at Baylor, much less the cost of a brand-new Chevrolet Tahoe. Still, he had somehow managed to pay his bills and drive a late-model SUV. So there were anomalies that seemed to need explaining. The trustees appointed a special investigating committee to scrutinize the program more closely.

After Dennehy's body was recovered, an assistant basketball coach, driven to disillusionment by Dennehy's fatal shooting, took a hidden microcassette into Coach Bliss's closed-door sessions with his team and coaching staff. Listening to the tapes he brought out, committee members heard Coach Bliss urging his players, some of whom were also getting money from undisclosed sources, to collaborate on a cover story that would explain how Dennehy had paid for his own tuition and Chevy Tahoe. The most effective strategy, the coach somberly told the players, would be to portray Dennehy as a drug dealer who'd been killed in a botched narcotics deal. His teammates could testify that they'd seen him with a tray of illegal drugs and a roll of $100 bills. The virtue of the scenario, Coach Bliss told them, was that Dennehy, since he was dead, "is never going to refute what we say." All the team and the other coaches had to do was present a solid front. Police and media attention would soon shift to something else.

The downfall of Bliss's basketball program came when the *Fort Worth Star-Telegram* printed portions of the transcript. The Baylor regents and President Robert Sloan promptly expressed moral outrage. Coach Bliss's attempt to cover up the truth, declared the president, was "a profound betrayal of the trust that Baylor University and our players put in him." "All the Baylor family," echoed the chair of the board of regents, had experienced "a huge sense of betrayal and anger" at the basketball coach's behavior. Viewed against the background of numerous other stories about crimes involving Div IA coaches and players, the Baylor story follows a familiar pattern. There is the utter shock of college officials. There's the decision to establish an investigating committee. Then comes the protest that, regrettable as the current case may be, it is not representative of the true ideals of the institution. Finally, there is a solemn announcement that nothing similar will ever be allowed to happen again. Still, the homicidal violence at Baylor brought into the broad light of day something that remains obscured in many scandals: the dynamics through which big-time athletics can take over an entire institution.

Until recently, the typical Div I A athletic program was presented as being complementary to the educational mission of the university. Coaches were "teachers." Sports involved "learning opportunities" and "discipline" and "character." Athletes took courses, lived in college dormitories, and were, like students who acted in plays or wrote for the student newspaper, simply pursuing a chosen extracurricular activity. Even when the football coach was making four or five times as much as the university president, when special tutors were provided to help athletes with their class work, or when boosters showered expensive gifts upon "blue-chip" recruits, it remained possible for many people, and especially members of the local boosters club, to imagine the sports program as a realm analogous to the university—one populated by individuals who might be larger, stronger, and more physically coordinated than other students, but not essentially different from them. Only when the moral and legal conventions of the everyday world undergo a dramatic collapse, as in the murder of Patrick Dennehy at Baylor, does the repressed question of the connection between athletics and criminality come more insistently into view.

Consider the evidence that Baylor basketball players saw themselves as belonging not to some separate but complementary realm within the university, but to a self-contained reality utterly distinct from it. Three of Coach Bliss's newest recruits were junior college transfers—players who, having failed to meet the NCAA's very minimal academic standards, had been sent to junior college to earn enough credits to qualify for athletic scholarships. In the world of Div I A athletics, "JUCO transfers" are notoriously likely to be what sportswriters and boosters call problem players—young men with a history of violent or antisocial behavior in addition to severe academic deficiencies. Among the Baylor players, personal tensions had built up to the point that Dennehy bought and practiced with a .32 caliber pistol for self-protection. His closest friend on the team, Carlton Dotson, bought a 9mm pistol for the same reason. This was the same gun that, when tensions later developed between the two young men, was used to kill Patrick Dennehy. This background helps explain why Baylor's infractions of NCAA rules, its silent evasion of the university's own standards and procedures—necessary for virtually any "big-time" sports program to remain competitive—were more than mere infractions. They helped to create at Baylor a sense of moral and legal immunity that led to a rotting corpse in a grassy field.

The moral of the Baylor story is not that Div I A athletes imagine themselves to be dwelling in a separate reality exempt from ordinary moral and legal claims. It's that athletes are right to think so. To turn from Baylor to any major NCAA program is to discover that its athletes live inside a sphere in which the duties and responsibilities of the outside world have been suspended. Consider, for instance, the basketball program of Jim Harrick at the University of Georgia. Like Coach Bliss at Baylor, Harrick was an effective recruiter of marginal players. Many did not qualify academically. In some cases, those who did qualify had histories of violent or antisocial behavior. One was Tony Cole, a star point guard Harrick had first recruited when coaching at the University of Rhode Island. When Cole failed to qualify academically for URI, he was sent to a junior college in Rhode Island to pick up the credits needed to qualify as a transfer student. Forced to leave when he was charged by two women in the athletics department with sexual molestation, Cole was then cycled through two other junior colleges—Jacksonville College in Texas and Wabash Valley College in Illinois—before joining Harrick's team at Georgia.

Harrick was unapologetic about recruiting players like Cole. "I believe in young people," he told the *Chronicle of Higher Education*. "When you teach you take a vow to educate all the public's children." The education Coach Harrick's players were getting at Georgia was exposed to public view when Tony Cole, by then a star player on a winning team, ran into trouble with the law. Among the courses Cole was taking at the time was "Coaching Principles and Strategies of Basketball," taught by the coach's son, Jim Harrick Jr. In the burst of publicity surrounding Cole's legal troubles, its final exam became briefly notorious. Some sample questions:

1. How many halves are in a college basketball game?
   a. 1
   b. 2
   c. 3
   d. 4

2. How many points does one field goal account for in a basketball game?
   a. 1
   b. 2
   c. 3
   d. 4

3. How many points does a 3-point field goal account for in a basketball game?
   a. 1
   b. 2
   c. 3
   d. 4

Despite the make-believe character of the final exam, Cole didn't show up to take it. He also never attended class. Still, he received an A for the course.

Tony Cole's charmed life at Georgia changed dramatically in 2002, when he and another player were charged with aggravated assault and rape. The episode says a great deal about the moral epistemology of Div IA athletics. For to view events through the bewildered eyes of Tony Cole himself is to get a sense of shattered reality. A world that always before arranged matters in his favor had somehow dissolved around him. About the alleged rape, Cole repeatedly and disbelievingly protested that the woman accusing him just hadn't understood the prerogatives of star Div IA athletes. "You know how it is in college," he told the *Chronicle* reporter. "You come into my room, you already know what's going on." When Coach Harrick tried to deny all knowledge of Cole's previous history of sexual molestation or his circuitous junior college path to Georgia eligibility, Cole was dumbfounded. "Coach Harrick knew everything," he protested. It was a plausible enough assertion, since Harrick had verifiably been in contact with Cole since high school.

At Georgia, Cole and his teammates experienced Div IA basketball as a magic sphere in which powerful men—Coach Harrick, a network of wealthy local boosters, even, as events would show, Georgia's president—could bestow a cloak of invulnerability upon players in their lives off the court. Now, suddenly and unaccountably, the players had awakened to find themselves stripped of the magic charm. Even Coach Harrick himself was no longer invulnerable. When ESPN reporters made public the bogus grades and make-believe final in "Coaching Principles and Strategies of Basketball," assistant coach Jim Harrick Jr. was fired outright. Harrick Sr., a popular figure with Georgia boosters and legislators owing to his successful program—ESPN's preseason poll for 2002 had ranked Georgia No. 7 nationally—was placed on suspension. Still protesting that his only aim had been to give disadvantaged young men a second chance in life, Coach Harrick subsequently resigned. As with similar scandals, the episode was soon forgotten.

The separate reality created for athletes by Div IA sports was even more on display in the case of Ohio State football player Maurice Clarett, who as a freshman carried OSU to a national championship. On campus, driving a Lexus SC 430, Clarett moved among ordinary mortals as a god, with every desire—money, girls, expensive clothes, breathless adulation from students and adults alike—granted as soon as it was wished. His eligibility, Clarett later reported, had been bestowed by bogus grades and credit for nonexistent courses. Looking up from the field to the hundred thousand adoring spectators in the OSU stands, or at the state legislators, wealthy boosters, and high-level university administrators gazing raptly down from the corporate skyboxes on high, Clarett would have been delusional not to believe that this multitudinous, throbbing, televised spectacle—rather than some ephemeral institution of higher learning—was the real Ohio State. "The only thing that matters at Ohio State," Clarett said, "is football." Yet a bitter break with coach Jim Tressell would soon enough teach Clarett to look back on his football celebrity as a vanished fairy tale. "Ohio State created me," he would tell an ESPN reporter, almost in wonderment at the total change. Then Ohio State had unmade him. In the aftermath, Clarett would undergo something very like a complete psychological disintegration.

The grade changes and bogus credits that Clarett said kept him eligible are a normal feature of big-time college athletics. In Clem Haskins's basketball program at the University of Minnesota, for example, a tutor was revealed to have written some four hundred pieces of work for Haskins's players over one five-year period. Minnesota's president, Mark Yudof, quickly ran through the standard repertory of responses. He displayed shock and outrage at academic fraud in the athletic program. He ordered an immediate investigation. Then he announced sweeping changes that would guarantee academic integrity from now on. Yet the crucial point was never mentioned. It is that the Minnesota tutor who was supplying papers and exams to Haskins's basketball players was not simply an academic convenience. She was a reality principle, a constant reminder of the coach's power over the institution as a whole. Just as at Dave Bliss's Baylor or Jim Harrick's Georgia, Clem Haskins's Minnesota represented to his players a world in which the power wielded by the athletics department could rearrange, to any degree necessary, the environment in which athletes lived their daily lives.

In such a moral climate, there's no mystery about why anything that counts as criminality in the ordinary world should come to seem, for athletes living inside the magic sphere of Div IA reality, little more than harmlessly exuberant behavior. Take the case of Virginia Tech's football team. In a single year during the 1990s, the school had nineteen football players facing criminal charges ranging from rape to assault and battery. To the outside world, it looked disgraceful. But Virginia Tech had built a winning program in a very short time by recruiting problem players turned away by more established programs. Which was likely to seem more powerful to the players, the machinery that had transported them to Blacksburg, Virginia, solemnly presenting them to the world as college students, or the feeble prohibitions of local law? In recent years, as stories of violence and criminality—murder, assault, rape, armed robbery, drug use, illegal gambling, and more—have become commonplace, the question why they so often appear on the sports page rather than in the police blotter is seldom addressed. Still, the reason seems obvious enough: college sports has produced them. Such crimes are the outcome of the separate reality generated and sustained by commercialized college athletics.

The more sordid aspects of Div IA reality were on display in the briefly notorious sex-and-recruiting scandal that erupted at the University of Colorado in 2004. Three women reported to Boulder police that they'd been raped by Colorado football players at a campus party. When the district attorney declined to bring charges, they filed a lawsuit against the university. The suit brought to light police records showing that two other women had reported being raped by Colorado football players earlier that year. In a widening investigation, the University of Colorado was portrayed as routinely using alcohol, drugs, and sex to lure recruits to its highly successful football program. News accounts featured strip clubs and drinking parties. Reports circulated about consensual sex with female students who volunteered as campus escorts for visiting recruits. A football team assistant admitted to using his university-provided cell phone to hire prostitutes and dial up sex-chat lines. All this activity was understood by the recruits, one of them was reported to have told a Colorado campus police officer, as a promise of what you could expect if you came to play football at Colorado. As the firestorm of media coverage grew, crimes and recruiting abuses involving sex were uncovered at Div IA schools nationwide.

To high school athletes looking in from the outside, the magic of Div IA invulnerability must have seemed unusually powerful at Colorado. Six players accused of raping a female student were allowed to play in a New Year's bowl game a month later. A university spokesman explained that, because of a crowded court schedule, their case couldn't be heard immediately. Meanwhile, the athletic department was taking the position that accused rapists were innocent until proved guilty. Colorado's president, Elizabeth Hoffman, stressed that, in the original incident, no recruits had been present. "It was not a recruiting party," she noted. "It was a regular Saturday-night college party." The chairwoman of an investigative panel appointed by Colorado's governor raised the possibility that the women themselves, rather than the accused rapists, were responsible: "The question I have for these ladies is why they are going to parties like this and drinking." How could these young women not realize that they were "putting themselves in a very threatening or serious position"? "You know how it is in college," Georgia basketball player Tony Cole had protested, making much the same point. "You come into my room, you already know what's going on."

At Colorado, President Hoffman's attempt to control public relations damage gave a rare glimpse of the part administrators are today increasingly willing to play in sustaining the magic sphere of Div I A invulnerability. Until recently, the role of presidents at schools like Colorado was to publicly proclaim Div I A athletics to be a realm complementary to the academic sphere of the university. The Colorado scandal showed why this has long since become a sentimental fiction. For it was one thing to hear that a visiting Colorado recruit might have had consensual sex with a female student who volunteered to serve as his campus escort. It was quite another to learn that many other Div I A programs have organizations of female students—news stories mentioned the Bulldog Bells of Mississippi State, the Crimson-n-Cream of Oklahoma, the Texas Angels of the University of Texas—assigned to visiting recruits as a standard practice. A stripper hired for a Colorado recruiting party might represent an isolated case. But when the Denver adult entertainment company that supplied that stripper is reported to have done the same for recruiting parties at other Div I A schools—the University of Houston, Rice, Colorado State, the University of Northern Colorado—another reality begins to emerge.

At Ohio State, we heard Maurice Clarett say, the only thing that matters is football. When the only thing that matters at a university is big-time sports, the symbolic center of the institution has shifted profoundly. Everyone at the university becomes at some level palpably aware of the change. When the athletes recognize that they are virtual demigods on campus, real students come to regard themselves as marginally important to the university, less real in the life of the school. When every institutional resource is dedicated—and known to be dedicated—to the support and celebration of specialized physical skills, intellectual talent and the pursuit of learning come to be disregarded and displaced, even, at many schools, despised. In the world of Div I A institutions, the Maurice Claretts and Tony Coles are real. The student who has come to college hoping to learn about Greek philosophy or Renaissance poetry or molecular biology walks the campus as a ghost.

This is the significance of that curious phenomenon, the undergraduate sports riot. The masses of Ohio State students who broke store windows and overturned automobiles in downtown Columbus after their football team beat Michigan, for instance, or the University of Connecticut students who set fires and passed out drunk in public after a basketball victory, were responding to the hallucinatory reality projected by Div I A sports. Dazzled by the celebrity and media power of their teams, students at OSU and UConn and other schools were doing their best to lay claim through postgame rioting and vandalism to the sphere of moral and legal invulnerability already granted to the athletes on their campuses. They were enacting the belief that professionalized sports are the only thing that matters, in just the terms already enunciated by a university whenever new stadiums are funded while library acquisitions are cut, or the coaching staff is enlarged while the honors program is curtailed.

Wherever this shift in the symbolic center of an institution occurs, the consequences for higher learning are profound. Even at private universities with admissions standards well above those at state schools, a highly visible Div IA sports program works to attract students openly hostile to any higher culture of ideas or learning, as the recent lacrosse scandal at Duke demonstrated. But the situation is most critical at public universities. For consider what bright and intellectually engaged students find upon enrolling at a typical Div IA school. They've imagined college as a time of personal growth and inward development, a world in which Wittgenstein's *Tractatus* or medieval European history or the intricacies of RNA replication are considered as real as—or indeed much more real than—the transitory spectacle of basketball's March Madness or the New Year's Day bowl games. Instead, they find themselves in a dreary educational wasteland. They pick their way through a curriculum largely given over to remedial teaching and learning. Their professors, they come to realize, are faculty members who've been unable to escape to better institutions elsewhere, as their more talented colleagues have done long since.

To be sure, many bright and intellectually engaged students don't need to worry about the way Div IA athletics work to reduce a university to an educational wasteland. The most talented will be admitted to schools like Harvard and Yale and Amherst and Swarthmore, where substantial endowments provide full scholarship aid to anyone coming from a less-than-wealthy background. An Ohio high school student accepted at Harvard or Amherst need never waste a moment thinking about football riots at Ohio State. Students who fall just short of Ivy League standards of selectivity have, if they come from moderately wealthy families, an excellent list of choices among private universities like Tufts, Emory, and the University of Chicago, or smaller liberal arts colleges like Oberlin and Middlebury and Bowdoin. The moral of the story lies in the schools students in both categories choose. Their common denominator is that academic and intellectual values lie at the core of the institution. Athletics, except as an extracurricular activity important mainly to those who participate, remain at the margins.

The single biggest problem in contemporary American higher education concerns bright students who lack these options. For these students—I have come to think of them as America's missing million—the only practical choice is their state university. Here the threat posed by Div IA athletics to American higher education may be seen in its starkest terms. When you teach, Coach Harrick said at Georgia, you take a vow to educate all the public's children. It is precisely through big-time athletics that the university violates its vow to teach the public's children—not just the bright or talented students who are marginalized and neglected in favor of star athletes like Tony Cole and Maurice Clarett, but thousands of others whose own education would be incomparably richer if intellectually talented students were put at the symbolic center of the institution's values. As bright students flee to other colleges and universities because of a school's Div IA sports emphasis, remedial courses proliferate and standards in regular courses begin to sag. When the big-time sports ethos of athletes and boosters breeds drunkenness, violence, and defiant crudity, impressionable young people, joining in because they fear being left out, lose out on an educational experience that could lift their lives to something better.

In the immediate background of Div IA athletics as they exist today, in short, may be glimpsed a violated ideal of democratic education. If we take that ideal to mean that bright and intellectually engaged students from less-than-wealthy backgrounds deserve an education worthy of their talents, the typical Div IA university is something very like its opposite. At public universities, a talented student most often arrives on campus to find that every other bright student who has been able to do so has fled the state to a better institution elsewhere. In the classroom, where a core group of highly talented students would otherwise provide intellectual energy and incentive to more average undergraduates, very bright students find themselves isolated and suspect. Above-average students find themselves absorbed into the mass of unmotivated or disruptive undergraduates who are now so prominent a presence in public university classrooms. Under the regime of big-time professionalized sports programs, any idea of genuine intellectual community—that invisible university that might exist if such bright and motivated students were put at the center of the institutional structure—remains an impossible dream.

The view I've just sketched of democratic education and its demise at the hands of "professionalized" college athletics is not abstract theory. It comes as the result of personal experience. As the following chapters will show, some of that experience was sickening. Some of it was painful. Some of it led to the most treasured moments in my life as a teacher. My awakening to the reality of big-time athletics began when I arrived, wide-eyed and innocent, as an assistant professor of English at the University of New Mexico in the mid-1970s. What I learned at UNM about the pernicious influence of Div IA sports was something I wanted to forget as fast as possible. I thought I'd done that when, some years later, I took up a professorship at Rutgers University in New Jersey. But there, I would find to my dismay that I hadn't left behind big-time sports corruption at all. It had begun to penetrate Rutgers. I let my dismay be known, partly by organizing faculty resistance to the growing power of the Athletics Department, partly by writing a series of op-ed columns for New Jersey newspapers about the dangers of commercialized athletics.

Thus began my career as a spoilsport. Within weeks, Rutgers booster boards on the Internet were flooded with angry denunciations of the mad English professor who for some incomprehensible reason didn't understand that holiday bowl games and appearances in "March Madness" were what made a real university. My observations on Div IA sports, one outraged booster wrote, "insult student-athletes, alumni, and the taxpayers who support Dowling and pay his salary, pension, and benefits." He called for my immediate dismissal. "Not a chance this ass gets fired," another wrote glumly. "One word: tenure. In that one word, you can basically do whatever the hell you want and have no reason to be nervous about your job. It makes me sick." I got death threats, and anonymous threats of physical harm. There were even proposals to organize anti-Dowling chants at football and basketball games. By the mid-1990s, I had become for most Rutgers athletics boosters the Devil personified.

Nonetheless, *Confessions of a Spoilsport* isn't really my story. I happened to become the target of booster outrage because I wrote a few outspoken columns at just the moment when Rutgers was for the first time in its history entering the corrupt world of big-time athletics. But the real heroes and heroines of the struggle that followed were the Rutgers undergraduates who took up the cause as their own. For at Rutgers, the ideal of democratic education that seemed so tragically to have disappeared at other state universities still remained strong. An uncompromising campaign against Div IA athletics was born in the moment a small band of bright and resourceful students decided to dig in and resist, refusing to be marginalized or displaced from the symbolic center of their university in favor of the world of pampered athletes and screaming spectators and corporate skyboxes. Their struggle ended with an amazing apparent victory that then, as through a sudden twist of fate, turned into disheartening defeat. I believe their story contains serious lessons for American higher education. The name of their campaign was Rutgers 1000.

1

Lost in Loboland

I got my first taste of big-time college sports when I began teaching at the University of New Mexico in 1975. At that point, UNM was a national bas-ketball power. The state was convulsed with excitement about the team. A senior colleague, meaning to be kind, invited me to a UNM home game in "the Pit," the university's huge subterranean basketball arena, dug into a nearby mesa. Since faculty tickets were given out by seniority, his seats were excellent, located just a few rows behind the courtside box of UNM's president, William "Bud" Davis, a former football coach. It was an amazing spectacle: fifteen thousand screaming fans, ten very tall young men run-ning around on the brilliantly floodlit floor below, referees getting raucously booed whenever a call went against the home team. Shouting over the uproar, my colleague pointed out the UNM head coach, Norm Ellenberger—blow-dried hair, shiny shirt, lots of turquoise and silver jewelry—who struck me as looking more like a lounge lizard than a college basketball coach. But I put this down to differences in regional style between the colorful Southwest and the more decorous East Coast. Besides, at the opposite end of the bench from Ellenberger was an assistant coach wearing a suit and tie. True, the suit was badly rumpled, but the man had clearly made an attempt to dress for the occasion. Later I'd learn his name was Manny Goldstein.

After that night in the Pit, I didn't pay much attention to UNM basketball. For the next few years I was finding my way as a teacher and beginning to publish as a scholar of eighteenth-century English literature. During that time, a much more pressing concern for me was the steady drop I was seeing in students' ability and the corresponding decline of academic quality at the university. I wasn't alone in noticing these changes. Colleagues in my own department and elsewhere would refer to them guardedly or half-jokingly. I noticed that a number of professors were quietly leaving UNM for other schools. Those who couldn't get out seemed to settle in glumly to wait for retirement, which on the model of the U.S. military was granted after twenty years of full-time service. Soon, however, our most pressing problem in the English Department became urgent: enrollments in literature courses were dropping sharply while the demand for remedial composition was rising.

This was happening in part because of a university rule that any upper-level course that didn't draw a certain minimum number of students wouldn't be authorized. At UNM the critical number was ten. If you were teaching a Chaucer or Shakespeare course and only nine students enrolled, the course was canceled. Then, in place of Chaucer or Shakespeare, you'd be assigned to teach a section of freshman composition, usually English 101 or 102, which were only marginally above the level of the designated reme-dial English course, English 100. It wasn't just Renaissance Poetry or New England Transcendentalism that were being canceled. Literature courses in every period weren't making it. Even when my colleagues stopped teaching long novels and then gave up assigning papers altogether, their enrollments kept dropping. By the time I left UNM, the English major had shrunk to 134 lonely souls, out of a total student body numbering about fifteen thousand.

It would be comforting to report that the low draw in upper-level English courses was the result of poor teaching or unimaginative curricular plan-ning. But this wasn't so. The English Department was one of the strongest in the region. It included highly regarded scholars and gifted classroom teach-ers. The unhappy fact was that by 1980 most students coming to UNM lacked the level of reading comprehension necessary to deal with standard writers like Robert Browning and Henry David Thoreau. By then, ordinary popular fiction—let alone authors like Chaucer and Shakespeare and Henry James— would have represented an insurmountable challenge. In one section of freshman composition I taught, I passed out a questionnaire that revealed a dismaying fact. In a class of twenty-seven students, not a single student had ever read a book on his or her own simply for pleasure. Not in third grade, not in junior high, not in high school. Reading was something my students considered a "school" activity. If you did it, it was only in a spirit of grudging protest, to get the high school credits you needed to go to UNM.

During these years the atmosphere in the English Department grew increasingly gloomy, at times panicky, especially among faculty members still a long way from retirement. I remember one day when I'd just picked up my mail and met one of my younger colleagues coming the other way. She was a woman who'd studied at Oxford, had an Ivy League PH.D., and had recently published a brilliant book on Yeats and literary modernism. She was waving a bunch of student papers from English 100. She had a desperate look in her eyes. "We *can't* go on like this," she said a little wildly. "We weren't *trained* to do this. It's third-grade English." It turned out her course in Yeats and Pound hadn't made the minimum of ten students, and she'd been shifted into English 100. Now she was teaching subject-verb agreement, correct use of the apostrophe, and the difference between *there* and *their.*

Years later I'd come across a personal essay written by a young faculty member in Texas that expressed with a terrible candor the very situation we were all facing at UNM:

I guessed we all sensed, rightly or wrongly, that we were made for better things than this: for students who would come to class prepared, who came from decent high schools, and who could understand what we were saying if we said it clearly. Instead, we had students on the sophomore level who did not know the moon causes the tides or who, halfway into a semester of political science, would ask the instructor, "But what is *government,* anyway?" They weren't questioning authority; they did not know what authority was. . . .

After a few months of trying to get a good discussion going in class, I gave up. . . . I had always prided myself on my ability to get ninety percent of any class to contribute to the flow and debate, but my new job beat me down. It wasn't that my students were mean or bad people; they were mostly friendly and attractive. They just didn't understand. Anything, it seemed.

So I had them write in class much of the time and stopped asking too many probing questions or expecting probing answers. I think this was a good solution, because they certainly need writing practice, but something was lost. What can you do with a college class that doesn't know what *hierarchy* or *enchantment* means (I mean the literal definitions—they've never heard the words)?

My questions in class now have to do with vocabulary and basic reading comprehension. My sophomore literature classes are now all about basic reading skills. Anything beyond that is asking many students to use an analytic thought process beyond their grasp.

Still, what is a university supposed to do when its student body is increasingly made up of such students? UNM's answer was simple. In 1979 it instituted a "basic skills" program for entering freshmen who were still operating at a very low level in reading comprehension, mathematics, elementary science, and general knowledge about such subjects as history and geography. The program was divided into four areas—English, mathematics, natural science, and social science—and students with substandard test scores were required to pass a remedial class before going on to "university-level" work. At that point, UNM found out just how bad the situation had become. For in its first year of operation, the basic skills program revealed that more than 60 percent of the entering class would have to do remedial work in at least one area before they could be admitted to any real university courses. A substantial number would be required to complete courses in two or more basic skills categories before they could go on.

Why didn't UNM simply raise its entrance requirements? Wouldn't that be more efficient than setting up an elaborate and expensive remedial-learning program? I made this argument at the time, in a long series of department and faculty meetings. It wasn't simply, I told my colleagues, that higher entrance standards would do a great deal to shift the emphasis at UNM back toward real college education. Higher entrance requirements at the university would also exert a top-down pressure for higher achievement on every schooling level in the state. Within a relatively short time, the high schools and the grade schools, as well as UNM itself, would show the benefits of higher expectations. Whenever I made this argument, though, I felt as though I'd bumped into some invisible obstacle or medium of resistance. It wasn't that people disagreed with what I was saying. It was more that, whatever I said, impersonal forces were somehow making my argument incomprehensible. Only later would I understand that the invisible obstacle had to do with Div IA athletics.

The best way to grasp the problem posed by higher standards at UNM, perhaps, is to take a look at the test scores that play a major role in college admissions. In the eastern United States, the most widely used measure of student preparedness for college is the SAT. In the American heartland and the West, it's the American College Test, or ACT, a somewhat easier test that is, nonetheless, roughly comparable to the SAT. As the reports that regularly issue from the testing services make clear, both tests are taken annually by a large number of students who show themselves to be unprepared for college. As this is being written, for instance, the latest *Chronicle of Higher Education* features a story—"Barely Half of High-School Graduates Have College-Level Reading Skills, Report Says"—in which the ACT reports that only 51 percent of the previous year's high school graduates taking the test were able to read even at a level assumed at nonselective colleges and vocational training schools. I'm going to be referring a lot to standardized test scores in this book, so let me say why I think they play a crucial role in college admissions.

The SAT verbal section measures a student's capacity for dealing with college-level reading. In this sense, applying to college is a bit like auditioning for a symphony orchestra: the minimum qualification for winning a seat in the orchestra is your ability to read music and play your instrument. If you can't do that much, you're going to impede the performance of the other orchestra members. A basic competence has to be assumed. In this context, a 580 verbal SAT is, roughly speaking, the minimum score needed to demonstrate college-level reading comprehension. Anything below that and a student has virtually no chance of making sense of a college-level reading assignment in the time allotted to read it. The SAT verbal has come under heavy attack in recent years, mainly because these scores keeping bringing the unwelcome news that high school students who have grown up on MTV and video games, and who have never done any reading on their own, aren't ready to enter a college environment where they'll be expected to read and understand Hobbes's *Leviathan* or Thoreau's *Walden*. The roughly equivalent minimum score in math is 550, making a combined SAT score of 1130 the minimum threshold for college work generally.

You'll notice in this analysis that the verbal section is weighted more heavily than the math. That's because a disproportionate amount of the learning one does in college—in psychology and history and anthropology and many other subjects besides English—depends on reading ability. To understand why I've given 580 as the threshold for college-level reading comprehension, though, you need to know a bit more about psychometric testing. If you're interested in the way the SAT verbal section actually measures developed reading ability, let me refer you to my article "Enemies of Promise: Why America Needs the SAT," published in the journal *Academic Questions* (Winter 1999). In it, I provide a step-by-step analysis of an actual SAT verbal test to show how, question by question, it measures competence in a number of areas—logical relations, syntactic relations, recognition vocabulary—needed for college-level reading. A crucial part of the analysis concerns what are called the difficulty levels of SAT test items. Students who operate comfortably at difficulty levels 4 and 5 will have no trouble reading a thirty-page assignment in Thoreau's *Walden* overnight for a college class. To students who consistently miss questions at those difficulty levels, on the other hand, a paragraph from *Walden* will look very much like the opening lines of Homer's *Iliad* to someone who doesn't read ancient Greek.

On the ACT scale, the combined score corresponding to an SAT 1130 is roughly 25. At the time that UNM instituted its basic skills program, however, its average ACT for entering students was 18. So the question becomes, why didn't UNM just raise its ACT admissions requirement to 25? Obviously, some weaker students would be kept out, and the faculty would have to be reduced through attrition to a size commensurate with a smaller undergraduate population. But wouldn't the level of UNM education then very quickly rise spectacularly? The explanation is shockingly simple. A study commissioned by the UNM regents showed that raising the ACT minimum merely to 20 would exclude nearly 65 percent of New Mexico's high school graduates. Even though an ACT score of 20 represented only the twenty-ninth percentile nationally, two of three New Mexico students were unable to reach that level. Set the ACT standard at 20, that is to say, and two-thirds of the buildings on campus would go unused. Set it at 25 and UNM as a whole would dry up and blow away. Even the most modest increase in admissions standards would quickly leave New Mexico with no state university at all.

I understood all this on an abstract level. Still, I didn't see how desperate our situation had become until I took on an administrative assignment in the English Department. For some years a colleague and I had talked about setting up honors sections of freshman composition. The idea was to get the tiny number of entering students who really did have higher developed verbal ability out of regular Comp courses, which by now had pretty much become a remedial grind. Our solution was, we thought, simple and elegant. Most students entering UNM took remedial English courses taught by graduate students. By contrast, our small honors sections would be taught by senior faculty and would—alone among 100-level English courses—have genuine intellectual content. They'd be real college courses, taking as their center either great literary works or other works having major importance in Western thought. In the section I taught, for instance, the single text I assigned was Plato's *Republic*.

What my colleague and I found was that almost no matter how low you set the ACT bar, UNM didn't have enough entering freshmen to run a real English honors program. Ultimately, by setting the ACT threshold for honors seminars very low indeed, we managed to scrape up two sections of "honors" English for a couple of semesters running. This was only a few years before I left UNM, so I don't know what happened to the program after that. What I do know is that a former chair of the English Department and I undertook some informal research into UNM admissions, focusing specifically on reading comprehension. Could it really be that the state of New Mexico was producing *no* high school graduates who were able to operate—not at a Harvard or Yale level, obviously, or even at the level of a good liberal arts college like Oberlin or Hamilton—but at the level of the very weakest students at better public institutions like Berkeley and William and Mary? The answer turned out to be that, yes, the state of New Mexico was producing a substantial number of such students. It was just that most bright New Mexico high school students never considered for a minute going to UNM.

But why? This was the moment I first glimpsed the underlying connection between academic decline and commercialized Div IA athletics—in UNM's case, between Norm Ellenberger's highly visible basketball program and the flight of New Mexico's best high school students to out-of-state schools. For when I later got to know a number of young people who had chosen to leave for out-of-state schools, I found that they perceived UNM as not caring about the education of bright and intellectually engaged students. When I sensed that sports were playing a role in shaping that perception, I began to ask questions that put academic values in direct opposition to an emphasis on athletics. The answer came through loud and clear. In the eyes of New Mexico's top high school graduates, all anybody cared about—the regents, the legislators, the average New Mexico resident and taxpayer—was how this year's Lobo team was doing. If a New Mexico kid wanted to go to a university where students were valued for their intelligence, he or she would have to go out of state.

It's easy enough to understand why bright New Mexico high school seniors should regard UNM this way. Every newspaper and TV station in the state was effectively telling them that "UNM" was really a basketball team with some incidental classroom space attached. At public universities especially, a winning Div IA team has enormous glamour to a large population that knows nothing and cares less about the university as an institution of higher learning. The excitement of ideas or the revelations of the chemistry lab are negligible to this huge audience, compared to "March Madness" and the "Final Four." Norm Ellenberger was a winning coach. Not only had he taken UNM to a top-ten ranking in the national polls, but in 1978 he would come within a single vote of being named Coach of the Year by the U.S. Basketball Writers Association. Like the talented Ohio high school students who grew up hearing about the hundred thousand people who crowded into OSU stadium to watch Maurice Clarett, a gifted New Mexico student went through high school acutely aware that the fifteen thousand roaring fans who filled the Pit were doing more than just screaming their support for the Lobos. They were projecting in symbolic terms their sense of what was important at the university.

The same bright high school students would also have sensed, if only subliminally, that the players running back and forth on the floodlit floor of the Pit were an alien presence in the university conceived as an institution of higher learning. For Ellenberger's basketball players were very obviously persons imported, purely on the basis of physical skills, into a setting—classrooms, laboratories, libraries—where they moved uneasily, like bewildered tourists in a foreign country. From the outside, the actual system sustaining them as "college students" remained invisible. The machinery keeping them eligible—special admissions procedures, spurious courses open only to athletes, bogus grades and credits—was being assiduously kept out of sight. But that machinery would be unexpectedly exposed in the scandal known as "Lobogate." Suddenly, as if a magic veil had been torn aside, the cynicism and deceit endemic to "big-time" Div 1A programs were laid bare to public view. Even the most impassioned Lobo booster could no longer plausibly deny that UNM had sunk deep into the pit of college sports corruption.

Ellenberger's coaching career at UNM ended as a result of a bizarre accident. Just as Patrick Dennehy's murder unexpectedly brought to light wrongdoing that finished Dave Bliss's coaching career at Baylor, so would Ellenberger be undone by evidence discovered in an apparently unrelated investigation. The FBI, looking into illegal gambling in New Mexico, had placed a wiretap on the telephone of a major Lobo booster. Visiting this same booster on November 17, 1979, Ellenberger happened to take a call from his assistant coach, Manny Goldstein, on the tapped phone. The brief conversation between Goldstein and Ellenberger would ultimately lead to the coach's federal indictment on seven counts of fraud and forgery of academic transcripts. Goldstein would get a reduced sentence in exchange for turning state's evidence. Here's what the FBI agents heard:

GOLDSTEIN: I got him a degree, an A.A.

ELLENBERGER: You got him a degree?

GOLDSTEIN: Yeah, they're gonna put sixteen more hours on the transcript. This is the way they want it. . . .

ELLENBERGER: And he'll do that?

GOLDSTEIN: Yeah, he's doing that. I mean we got to give him a little money, but he's doing it.

ELLENBERGER: Yeah?

GOLDSTEIN: You know, I bought the guy and that was it.

ELLENBERGER: Who was that, this Maruca?

GOLDSTEIN: No, this is Dr. Wooley, the head guy.

ELLENBERGER: Uh huh.

[A bit later]

GOLDSTEIN: I'm leaving for a recruiting trip. I'm gonna be in New Jersey Monday, get an envelope, mail it myself, special delivery, air mail, and it's being shipped out there.

[Then]

GOLDSTEIN: Is everything else okay the way I handled them?

ELLENBERGER: Ah, yeah, whatever, you know, you know.

GOLDSTEIN: Yeah, I told you, I'm protected.

Goldstein was telling Ellenberger that he'd arranged for a Lobo player named Craig Gilbert to receive a bogus Associate of Arts degree ("an A.A.") from Oxnard Junior College in California ("out there"). He had needed only to bribe a dean ("Dr. Wooley, the head guy") while seeing to it that sixteen course credits from another junior college ("in New Jersey") were transferred to Gilbert's Oxnard transcript. Goldstein's so-called recruiting trip would let him mail to Oxnard a fake transcript bearing a New Jersey postmark. Backed by the evidence from this wiretap, the FBI got a search warrant for Goldstein's apartment. There they found a trove of incriminating items—academic transcripts for Gilbert and another Lobo player named Andre Logan, plus something more interesting still: an apparently official embossing seal from Mercer County Community College in West Windsor, New Jersey, the kind that imprints a raised pattern on paper.

Goldstein's testimony gave the story behind the seal. A year or so before the FBI-wiretapped conversation between Ellenberger and Goldstein, the UNM coaches had been trying to solve the eligibility problems of a player named Andre Logan. When Manny Goldstein recruited him for UNM, Logan was nine hours short of the academic credits needed in order to play under NCAA rules. At first Goldstein had tried to get the credits by enrolling Logan in summer courses at Mercer County Community College. But because Logan had cut so many classes, he didn't have passing grades. The necessary credits were still missing. After a hurried consultation with Ellenberger, Goldstein hopped a plane to New Jersey. At Mercer, he told each instructor who had flunked Logan that only his one grade stood in the way of Logan's eligibility. If the teacher would just change the failing grade to passing, a deprived inner-city youth could realize his dream of becoming a Div IA basketball star. Five of the six teachers agreed to change their grades.

At this point, the hero of the story, for anyone honoring notions of academic integrity, becomes one Donald A. Beach, the vigilant registrar of Mercer Community College. Noticing a flurry of grade change forms for Andre Logan, Beach undertook inquiries, forwarding the results to the dean of Mercer. "I'm convinced," this dean responded, "that the coach from the University of New Mexico placed undue pressure on our instructors. He led them to believe that it was only their individual course that was keeping Logan from getting a scholarship." As a result, all but two of the grade changes were denied. In a letter to the UNM registrar, Fred M. Chreist, Beach complained that Goldstein had also tried to pressure a Mercer secretary into making other changes in Logan's transcript before sending it to UNM. "Had I been aware of it at the time," Beach told Chreist, "I would have thrown him out. This type of behavior is inexcusable and dishonest. Mr. Goldstein is not welcome ever again on this campus."

Back at UNM, however, Beach's letter set off no alarm bells. Neither Fred Chreist nor any other UNM administrator was reported to have seen any serious problem with Goldstein's machinations at Mercer. The only problem concerned the Lobo basketball team. Logan was a key player, and he still didn't have the necessary credits. Goldstein testified that he, Ellenberger, and another coach then held an anxious conference at the Village Inn Pancake House at San Mateo and Central. There Goldstein saw a way out. Out in his car, he told the others, he had a blank Mercer County Community College transcript that he'd lifted from a secretary's desk at Mercer. Since athletic eligibility was just a bunch of marks on paper, couldn't they fill out the blank transcript, award Logan the needed grades, forge the name of the Mercer registrar, and hand the document over to the UNM registrar's office? Why wouldn't that work?

Ellenberger immediately spotted a reason it wouldn't work. "That piece of paper is no good because you still need a seal," Goldstein reported him as saying. "You have to get a seal to make him eligible, somehow." What Ellenberger understood, Goldstein's testimony clearly implied, was that even the UNM registrar's office, permissive as it might be about accepting athletes' grade reports, would balk at taking an obvious fake: if only for his own protection, the UNM registrar would need an officially embossed transcript. But how to get a Mercer seal? Goldstein was no longer welcome on the Mercer campus. To solve this problem, they called on a loyal Lobo booster, an Albuquerque printer named Bill Blackstad. After examining the blank Mercer transcript form, Blackstad assured them there would be no difficulty in producing a convincing forgery. As for the seal, Valiant Printing, located right there in Albuquerque, specialized in embossing seals. Armed with a picture of the Mercer seal cut out of a catalog, Goldstein paid Valiant Printing a visit. Shortly thereafter, he found himself in possession of an official-looking Mercer County Community College seal. By then, Blackstad had produced a fake transcript for Logan. Duly signed and sealed, the new transcript was delivered to the UNM registrar, whereupon Andre Logan instantly became a "student" eligible to play basketball for the UNM Lobos. He would play the entire season.

By the time the FBI put a wiretap on the phone of the Lobo booster, the UNM coaches were worried about the eligibility of another Lobo player, Craig

Gilbert. But now Goldstein's embossing seal could work its magic a second time. Armed with the seal, Goldstein could simply manufacture eligibility without any further trips to Mercer. For, as we've already heard, he'd made some useful contacts at Oxnard Junior College—two coaches, Lee Porter and Bob Maruca, and, most important, the dean, Dr. John Wooley. (Goldstein: "Maruca came to me and said, 'It will cost you four hundred dollars, man. It's not for me. It's for Wooley." Why so much? the trial transcript reports Goldstein as having asked. Maruca: "He has a cocaine habit.") Dean Wooley would supply Gilbert with an Oxnard A.A. degree if Goldstein could supply an academic transcript showing that Gilbert had been awarded sixteen credits from another junior college. With his Mercer seal and blank transcripts in hand, Goldstein had no difficulty in coming up with the credits.

But why, the prosecuting attorney at Ellenberger's trial wanted to know, did Goldstein imagine that Oxnard would go along with so flagrantly dishonest a scheme? Goldstein's answer is deeply revealing. Anyone who wants to understand the world of Div IA football and basketball should pay close attention. For what it reveals is not simply the hidden world of phony credits, fake degrees, nonexistent courses, fraudulent test taking, and bogus "academic support" systems that keeps big time college athletics afloat. What it reveals is how fully the entire world of American higher education, right down to the level of obscure junior colleges, has entered into complicity with Div IA sports.

PROSECUTOR: Were you a little worried about Mr. Gilbert's being eligible or having grades or whatever?

GOLDSTEIN: No. Because I felt Oxnard was a fishy school.

PROSECUTOR: Fishy school. What do you mean?

GOLDSTEIN: Well, Gilbert wasn't going to classes.

PROSECUTOR: He wasn't even going to school?

GOLDSTEIN: Not after the basketball season. He never attended a class, and he had a three point four index.

PROSECUTOR: Three point four?

GOLDSTEIN: Cumulative.

The 3.4 grade point average Goldstein is referring to is based on a four-point scale. While genuine students were juggling jobs and family obligations trying to keep up their GPAs, officials at Oxnard were handing out a B/B+ average to Craig Gilbert for not going to class.

Lobogate would ultimately reveal that a great many UNM athletes had never been students at all. On December 6, 1979, for instance, the UNM Academic Council learned that six Lobo "student athletes" had been kept academically eligible through credits they'd earned in an extension course called "Current Problems in Coaching Athletics," plainly a variant on Jim Harrick Jr.'s "Coaching Principles and Strategies of Basketball" at Georgia ("How many points for a three-point goal?"). The extension course was advertised as being "held under the auspices" of Ottawa University in Kansas. It turned out, however, to have been held under the auspices of an instructor named Durley, freelancing on his own out of Van Nuys, California. For the six UNM student athletes kept eligible by the course, a disconcerting problem was that they'd never heard of it. In a press release prepared by their lawyer, the players declared they "did not attend such a course, and have no knowledge of how they became enrolled. The players were unaware until today that they had received credit for this course. They are also unaware of how the Ottawa University records were transmitted to the University of New Mexico, or who was responsible for their transmission."

Still, it was Ellenberger's testimony at his federal trial—on, it will be recalled, seven counts of fraud and forgery—that sheds the clearest light on how Div I A athletics expand their sphere to take over an entire university. At first, under the adroit prompting of an Albuquerque defense attorney named Leon Taylor, Ellenberger threw up a smokescreen of incomprehension about all matters relating to academic conduct. He didn't know anything about credits or courses or majors or transcripts. He was just a basketball coach. He didn't set UNM's academic policies. No more did he set the academic policies of Oxnard Junior College or Mercer County Community College. Then, still prompted by Taylor, and sounding uncannily like Jim Harrick at Georgia, Ellenberger explained in poignant detail that the purpose of his basketball program had been, from the very outset, to provide opportunities for deprived inner-city youth. How did it happen, some people were asking, that UNM basketball was seemingly played by so many young men who appeared unable to read and write?

ELLENBERGER: Now and then in our recruitment of athletes, in order to get the type of athlete that we need, football, basketball, whatever, at the University of New Mexico, to make that program good, to make that properly fill the seats, to make that program pay the bills of the university, we will go find a downtrodden young man, and some of my best friends, some of the best people I know, have come from down in the gutter someplace.

Q: When talking to people at Oxnard, what had Ellenberger meant by asking, "Can you get it done" or words to that effect?

"A juror assured reporters that she and the others 'had the impression that Norm didn't know what was going on.'" Norman Ellenberger in the Lobo locker room in the late 1970s. Photo courtesy of University of New Mexico Office of Sports Information.

ELLENBERGER: Are they going to take care of Craig, so that he can enter into the University of New Mexico and do the only thing that he ever wanted to do in his life, and that's play basketball and have a chance to be a human being.

Q: What persuaded Ellenberger to go along with the forging of the transcript and the manufacture of a false Mercer Community College embossing seal?

ELLENBERGER: One of my assistants, or both, or whoever was involved, said, "Hey, we have got a deal that we can fix this thing. We are going to have a seal made." And I can remember that. I can remember that because it—that—that thing right there, that appalled me. . . . The idea that you could manufacture something to do an act like that, that—appalled me, and I said, "Hey, whoa," I said, "Absolutely not." And talking about making, manufacturing a transcript. Well, the thing went on within the next hour or whatever, and through the insistence and through them bringing it down to the cold facts that, hey, we can help Andre. We can give him his opportunity.

To anyone reading the trial transcript, Ellenberger's testimony comes across as an excruciatingly crude attempt to give self-interested actions a sanctimonious gloss of altruism and philanthropy. He had admitted under oath that he'd been fully aware of the Mercer embossing seal. He knew that Logan's forged transcript had been handed in and accepted by UNM's registrar. He knew that Andre Logan had never become legitimately eligible to play Div IA basketball. Nonetheless, twelve New Mexico citizens were moved by Coach Ellenberger's humanitarian zeal. A jury in Roswell found him not guilty on all seven counts. One juror serenely assured a reporter that she and the others "had the impression that Norm didn't know what was going on." Her willingness to turn a blind eye to sports corruption was widely shared across the state. Even the UNM president and regents had been unwilling to see what was going on while the Lobos rose in the national rankings at the same time that UNM was rapidly sliding downhill academically. Nor did they see any connection between Ellenberger's Lobo team and the university's decline.

To see why, you have to look closely at the way those responsible for university governance had come, under the influence of big-time athletics, to understand the nature and purpose of institutions of higher learning. Take, for instance, Calvin Horn, the head of the UNM Board of Regents during this period. Horn owned a local oil company. Many UNM faculty members disliked his tendency to regard the university as a business, and especially his habit of viewing professors as "employees" much like his oil company workers. But Calvin Horn had his virtues. An amateur historian of the Southwest with several self-published books on Territorial history, he had a historian's respect for archival preservation. Many primary materials for the chapter you're now reading—including the complete court transcript of Ellenberger's federal trial in Roswell, plus a large file of internal university documents—come from the Calvin Horn Collection preserved in the UNM Library.

Horn had graduated from UNM. He felt a sharp sense of personal anguish at seeing his university slip into academic decline. In a 1973 talk to an athletics group called the Alumni Lettermen, he tried with some urgency to get across to them his own dismay at seeing the brightest high school graduates in New Mexico flee the state. As early as 1967, he told his audience, more than 50 percent of the state's National Merit finalists had begun leaving for out-of-state institutions. "We are not consistently getting the best students," Horn said. "We should. We need them just as a football or basketball team needs the best students it can get." Though he wouldn't have seen why, Horn's phrasing unwittingly lays bare the connection between Div IA sports and academic mediocrity. His proposal for solving the problem of the top students' flight from UNM was better recruiting and more advertising. UNM alumni, he told the Lettermen, should "join in an intense recruiting effort for top New Mexico high school graduates in every community of the state." All alumni and administrators needed to do was make such students "aware of the University of New Mexico and what it has to offer them." If that job was done properly, "the numbers will take care of themselves."

It might be thought that Calvin Horn was merely choosing language he thought would suit an audience of ex-athletes. But that's not the case. Again and again in the personal records included in his archives, Horn gives every sign of believing that when top students are avoiding their state university, the answer to the problem is "recruiting," "getting out the news," "showing them what we've got to offer." This is an actual belief widely held at lower-tier institutions across the country. Part of Horn's message is shaped by assumptions about "image" and "public perception" widely shared in a consumerist society—if you've got a "product" that's not "selling," the answer is to do more advertising. But the other part of Horn's message comes from a Div IA sports model of universities as institutions of higher learning. If football and basketball programs produce winners by recruiting top high school athletes, can't a university improve itself by recruiting more top students?

The short answer is no. Understanding why is essential for comprehending the problem of Div IA athletics at public universities. Interestingly enough, Horn could have seen this himself if he'd carried his sports analogy all the way through. Every Div IA booster in the country understands why a weak team—a team with a series of incompetent coaches, untalented players, and a long history of losing seasons—has little chance of attracting top recruits. The average "blue-chip" recruit may not read and write at a college level, but he's a close student of recruiting magazines like *SuperPrep* and *Hoop Scoop*. He's extraordinarily knowledgeable about which teams will give him the most TV exposure, be most likely to get him into a postseason bowl game or the NCAA playoffs, and give him the best shot at making the NFL or the NBA. Very occasionally coaches can build a winning program by recruiting problem players that more established programs won't touch, as Miami and Virginia Tech did in football and Jerry Tarkanian did in basketball at the University of Nevada at Las Vegas. But the one thing that won't work is trying to draw top players by "getting out the news" about a losing program.

The same thing is true in higher education, where the same principle is known as the "theory of peer effects." Developed by a group of educational policy analysts at Williams College, the theory itself is complicated, a mix of rational choice theory and economics. Still, its two main points, which provide the single most important key to understanding the problem of Div IA sports corruption, can be stated simply enough. They are (1) that no college or university can be better than its students, any more than an orchestra can be better than its musicians or a team better than its players, and (2) that bright students, when considering where they'll go to college, are wholly aware of this fact. Note that none of this involves mere social exclusivity. The main reason gifted musicians want to play in a top orchestra isn't money or prestige but the chance to develop their musical gifts by playing with others just as talented. As every booster knows, the same holds true in sports, where no star athlete wants to play on a team made up of second- and third-rate players. What most Div I A administrators and regents fail to understand is that the same principle holds when bright students are choosing a college.

Let's go back for a second to a revealing slip Calvin Horn made when talking to the Alumni Lettermen. A university, he said, needs top students "just as a football or basketball team needs the best students it can get." What Horn meant, obviously, was "just as a football or basketball team needs the best *players* it can get." A Div I A football or basketball team that recruited its members from among the best students in the country would never win a game. He was right, though, to be worried about UNM. With the academic level plummeting almost week by week, it was only a matter of time before no top New Mexico student who had a choice would think twice about going there. To see why, one need only look at institutions like UNM from the viewpoint of a talented student. If you were bright and intellectually engaged, if you were looking forward to late-night arguments and discussions with students as bright as yourself, if you wanted to take classes with professors who could help you understand Plato's *Republic* or Nabokov's *Pale Fire,* how would you view a school where the students sitting beside you in class had never read a book on their own?

It was then that I saw the relation between UNM's academic decline and Norm Ellenberger's basketball program. Bright New Mexico high school graduates weren't fleeing the state simply because UNM had a winning basketball team. Instead, consciously or unconsciously, they were responding to what might be called a symbolic declaration of institutional purpose. The enormous popularity of a coach like Ellenberger, the attention lavished on recruited players like Andre Logan and Craig Gilbert, the thousands of screaming Lobo fans who crowded into the Pit to cheer and jeer the action on the floodlit floor below, the endless stream of *Albuquerque Journal* sports stories and weekly Associated Press rankings, were being taken as a clear and unmistakable declaration of the only real purpose the state could perceive in having a state university. The results—academic decline, faculty flight, second- or third-rate administrators, a board of regents heavily under the influence of the local boosters club—were merely unintended consequences. Only many years later, when I'd been involved for more than a decade in the struggle against college sports corruption at Rutgers, would I come to perceive the more general principle revealed by my UNM epiphany. It is that the damage done to higher education by commercialized sports always takes place at the hidden point of intersection between the theory of peer effects and Div IA athletics.

As Lobogate receded, UNM's slide began to accelerate. Since the university was funded on a crude "body count" formula, the administration grew more and more desperate about getting more bodies onto campus. I still remember my shock when it dawned on me that UNM had begun busing in prisoners from the state penitentiary to take classes. The first convict I had in a course seemed to be a pleasant enough fellow—late twenties, well spoken, brown goatee, arms covered with crude tattoos. Only halfway through the semester did he say something that made me realize that after class he'd be returning to his cell in the state pen. When I talked to him later about his crime—it involved both sexual assault and theft—he made a point of explaining that he'd been totally innocent. His conviction had been a bizarre case of mistaken identity. There were other students who were compelled to miss class to meet with their parole officers. One, I remember, sniffled continuously. It took me a while to figure out that she had a cocaine habit—no mere head cold could possibly last four months—and to learn that she was still active as a prostitute.

My chance to leave UNM came in the mid-1980s, when my wife was offered an attractive appointment at a university in the Great Lakes region. The day I went into the chairman's office at UNM to turn in my letter of resignation, I felt as though an enormous weight had been lifted from my shoulders. I said goodbye to my friends and, as I then thought, put New Mexico and its Lobo basketball program out of my mind forever. It was only some years later, when I'd begun teaching at Rutgers University in New Jersey, that I'd find my mind turning suddenly and insistently to the lessons of Lobogate.

The Birth of Rutgers 1000

When I arrived at Rutgers, I was working on an edition of David Humphreys's *Life of Israel Putnam,* an early biography of the Revolutionary War hero who had famously left off plowing his Connecticut field when the call to arms came. Humphreys's book tells the story of Washington's perilous campaign in the winter of 1776, a struggle fought in part over the very ground I now crossed every day on my way to class. My route took me past a bronze historical marker in what is called the Old Queen's quad. Placed by the class of 1899 at the top of a small rise, the marker says: "Here, in early December 1776, Alexander Hamilton (graduate of King's College), with his battery of horse artillery, covered the ford of the Raritan, delaying the advance of the British while Washington withdrew through Princeton to Trenton." I felt a ghostly shiver when I realized that two hundred years ago, a handful of soldiers in a desperate rearguard action had held this very ground, keeping up a steady artillery fire across the Raritan River just long enough for the Continental army to escape.

The bronze marker made vivid what I already knew in a general way: Rutgers was a colonial college. Like UNM, it was the flagship public institution of its state. But unlike most state universities, Rutgers's history stretched back hundreds of years. Founded in 1766 as Queen's College, Rutgers was one of only nine American colleges and universities in existence before the

Declaration of Independence was signed. After the Revolution, British kings and queens not being greatly in favor in the young American Republic, Hamilton's King's College became Columbia. Queen's College, taking the name of a Revolutionary War hero, became Rutgers. Today, most of those prerevolutionary schools—Columbia, Harvard, Yale, Princeton, Dartmouth, Brown, Penn—are private institutions. Only two—Rutgers and William and Mary—are public. In fact, Rutgers has been a fully public institution only since 1956. Until then the university had received New Jersey state funding but had been governed by a board of trustees operating under the original colonial charter.

That's why Rutgers seemed to me from the outset to represent the best of all possible worlds. It was an old university with a distinguished academic and intellectual tradition, but also a public institution representing the democratic ideal in education. As a kid from a working-class Irish Catholic family, I'd been fortunate enough to win a full four-year scholarship to Dartmouth. At Rutgers I found that thousands of talented young people from modest backgrounds were getting a similar opportunity. Rutgers undergraduates were bright and intellectually engaged. Because the English Department had been particularly strong for the preceding twenty years, English was still at that point one of the most prestigious majors on campus, attracting some sixteen hundred students in the year I arrived. Rutgers English majors were kids who'd read all the time while they were growing up, so high SAT verbal scores were taken for granted. Unlike the English majors I'd taught at UNM, these students didn't look blank when you mentioned Vladimir Nabokov or Wallace Stevens.

What mattered even more to me was that unlike the pampered products of upscale suburban high schools, these Rutgers students had won their way to intellectual accomplishment on their own. They hadn't taken expensive SAT prep courses. They didn't have parents who hired consultants to groom them for admissions interviews. They hadn't attended college essay camps. They'd been too busy earning the money to go to college. A large percentage of my Rutgers students were the first members of their families to go to college. Many of them were immigrants' kids or immigrants themselves—from Russia and Korea and Romania and the Indian subcontinent. Lying just a few hundred yards off the Jersey coast, Ellis Island no longer served as a gateway for new immigrants. But the democratic ideal symbolized by the Statue of Liberty still pulled them toward New Jersey. Foreign-born or native, with parents who might only recently have earned citizenship or permanent residency, these Rutgers students were tracing the same path my own family had followed in the early twentieth century. Ambition, talent, hard work, and luck would open the golden door for them, as it had for my own relatives and so many others. Surrounded by fellow students who shared their talent and drive, Rutgers students could win for themselves an education that rivaled those found at private institutions costing two or three times as much. Within my first two weeks of teaching at Rutgers, I knew I'd wound up where I'd always wanted to be.

After UNM, it was an exhilarating experience. In my first years at Rutgers, I was still in a state of bliss, marveling at having undergraduates who were not only able to read *Paradise Lost* and *Hamlet* but actually loved Milton and Shakespeare. I must have done a bit of marveling out loud, because students kept asking me why I found it so astonishing to have English majors who liked reading Chaucer and Dryden and Trollope and Browning. Why else, they asked, would anyone *be* an English major? I did my best to explain to them what it felt like to come to Rutgers from a place like UNM. As you'd guess, a lot of what I told them had to do with Lobo athletics, including much of what you've read in the preceding chapter—forged transcripts, counterfeit embossing seals, "student athletes" who couldn't read and write, a state where fifteen thousand screaming fans crowded into a place called "the Pit" to cheer for a group of imported basketball players, but where nobody noticed, or cared, if the university had become a remedial learning operation.

The UNM I told them about couldn't have been more remote from the ideal of democratic education that was still vital at Rutgers in the early 1990s. It wasn't just that I was getting students who had grown up reading books, or that the high-SAT kids in my classes were setting a pace that encouraged more average students to extend their reach, but that everyone seemed to share a common sense of intellectual purpose. Part of this, no doubt, had to do with the courses I teach. When you make your living teaching Dryden's *Absalom and Achitophel* or Pope's Horatian satires or Samuel Johnson's *Rambler* essays, you're likely to get highly motivated students if there are any on campus. But part of it, too, was that Rutgers had such students in what seemed to me amazing abundance. There were Irish kids and Jewish kids and Italian kids, Asians whose parents spoke Cantonese or Korean or Vietnamese at home, students from India perfectly bilingual in Bengali and English, African Americans who, having felt isolated and lonely in their high schools, had now arrived in a world where other people, too, loved reading and talking about what they'd read.

The man who most clearly enunciated this ideal of democratic education at Rutgers was Mason Gross, the president who had guided Rutgers's transition from private to public status in the 1950s. A philosopher who studied with Alfred North Whitehead at Jesus College, Cambridge, he came from a patrician family. He'd been educated at a series of private institutions—the Taft School, Cambridge, Harvard. Against the clamor for open admissions during the 1960s, Gross firmly maintained that only high academic and intellectual standards were consistent with a true ideal of democratic education. For all his patrician background, however, Gross struck people as having been born for the new world of ethnic and educational diversity that emerged during the '60s. He came out of that contentious period, when the struggle over civil rights and the Vietnam War turned American campuses into battlegrounds, as one of the most popular figures in the state. As I'd hear again and again from alumni who knew him personally, his popularity was due to moral character.

All through the campus demonstrations of the '60s, for instance, Gross made clear that his sympathies were solidly with the students who were going south to break down the system of racial segregation, and later with those who were opposing the Vietnam War. Yet he did so without alienating New Jersey citizens whose views on these issues opposed his own. When Gross took a stand, people sensed that, whether or not they agreed with him, his conclusions were the honest product of deep moral reflection. Throughout his years as president of Rutgers, he taught at least one undergraduate class each term. Stories abounded about important visitors being kept waiting for Gross the president while Gross the philosopher finished debating a point in Plato or Spinoza with one of his students. When he stepped down from the Rutgers presidency, the New Jersey Democratic Party begged him to run as a candidate for governor. Polls indicated he would have won by a mile.

Nonetheless, in reading the speeches given by Mason Gross during his presidency, one sees that the transition from private to public university had begun to put a severe strain on his ideal of democratic education. President Gross was clearly and uncomfortably aware of a mounting pressure to move Rutgers in the direction of big-time college athletics. Nor was the pressure coming mainly from alumni athletics boosters. As alumni who attended Rutgers in the Gross era would later tell me, much of the pressure was coming from New Jersey politicians and local businessmen. When I thought back to my UNM years, this made perfect sense. In Albuquerque, the Lobo boosters club had been dominated by local beer distributors and building contractors and car dealers. Many of these men had not graduated from UNM. A good percentage of them had never gone to college. But all of them got a sense of enhanced personal importance from having a connection to Norm Ellenberger's Lobo basketball program. In New Jersey, the pressure for big-time athletics was coming from the same types, but here they worked for companies like Prudential Life instead of Coors Beer. One group of Prudential employees would later emerge as prominent members of "Scarlet R," the Rutgers athletics booster club.

The best expression of Mason Gross's response to outside pressure is an address on college athletics policy included in his collected speeches. At its center is an ideal of participatory athletics that seems today to have come from another world. For Gross himself had been a college athlete, a member of the Jesus College crew all during his undergraduate career. "I rowed throughout my four years," he told his audience, "in singles, pairs, fours, and eights, six days a week the year round, in intercollegiate competition and at regattas all over England. It was for me a tremendously exciting and important part of those undergraduate years." It's true, Gross admits, that Cambridge athletics had none of the elaborate machinery that had come to dominate Div I A sports in America even by the time he was delivering this speech in 1960. The English universities were without professional coaches, recruiting, or athletic scholarships. Still, he and his classmates had found competition supremely worthwhile. In later life, Gross remained steadfastly loyal to this ideal of a broad-based and genuinely participatory college athletics. Throughout his years at Rutgers, he would donate his public speaking fees to the underfunded Rutgers crew.

In stressing genuinely amateur athletics for his students, Gross was leading from Rutgers's strength as an old university. For, though sports had long been part of its institutional life—the first college football game in America was played between Rutgers and Princeton in 1869—its traditional opponents over the next hundred years would be the schools that today make up the Ivy and Patriot Leagues: Columbia, Colgate, Princeton, Lafayette, Bucknell, Lehigh, Yale, and Brown, along with the military academies at West Point and Annapolis. All were schools that did not give out athletic scholarships, and so had been able to resist the degradations of commercialized sports in the late twentieth century. In this sense, Gross's address on athletics policy reads like a gentle but firm reminder that Rutgers had belonged to a world where college sports were played by real students at the college—undergraduates who went out for the football or basketball team in the same spirit as others of their classmates went out for the *Daily Targum*, the student newspaper, or the Glee Club or orchestra or a college production of *Othello* or *A Midsummer Night's Dream*.

The man who followed Mason Gross as president, Edward Bloustein, was entirely different in personality and outlook. The Rutgers campus lies on the Raritan River. With his keen interest in undergraduate education, the good-natured joke about Mason Gross had always been that he saw Rutgers as

"Amherst on the Raritan." By contrast, his successor set in motion a radical reorganization of the university, emphasizing research and a high-powered faculty. So the joke about Bloustein was that he saw Rutgers as "Berkeley on the Raritan." Still, both men shared a strong commitment to high academic standards. By the early 1980s, for instance, Bloustein had already spotted the decline in secondary education that over the next twenty years would turn so many state universities into diploma mills. "Too many high school graduates are coming to college inadequately prepared for college level study," he warned. "We cannot continue to ignore this problem." His own answer was to keep a sharp watch on the Rutgers admissions policy, which throughout his presidency would remain highly selective.

Although Bloustein reportedly took little personal interest in sports, his weakness as Rutgers's president would turn out to lie on the side of college athletics. The 1956 legislation that turned Rutgers into New Jersey's official state university set aside a number of seats on the university's board of governors as political appointments. So it unexpectedly came about that the small group of local alumni boosters whose demand for big-time athletics had been so stoutly resisted by Mason Gross would find themselves, under Edward Bloustein, receiving powerful support from a Trenton political culture whose model of public universities was sports-centered schools like Nebraska and Oklahoma and Ohio State. In addition, the campaign for big-time athletics was spearheaded by Rutgers alumnus "Sonny" Werblin, an entertainment impresario and NFL team owner to whom, as a major donor to the university, Bloustein felt he had to pay due attention. After a series of private conferences with Werblin, Bloustein eventually announced that Rutgers would be jettisoning its historic rivalries with Princeton and the other traditional opponents to enter the world—not of big-time but, as he put it, of "bigger-time" athletics.

By the time President Bloustein dropped dead of a heart attack in 1989, Rutgers was already launched on the path to big-time Div IA athletics. The state legislature had authorized a $25 million bond issue to finance a large modern football stadium in Piscataway, across the river from the Old Queen's campus. The amount given out in athletic scholarships—it would eventually reach $2.7 million annually—was steadily rising. The board of governors, at this point increasingly dominated by a core group of Scarlet R boosters, was casting about for a major football conference that would provide Rutgers teams with the sort of national television exposure taken for granted at schools like Nebraska and Oklahoma. With Bloustein's death, his intermittent resistance to the athletics buildup, based on fears that even "bigger-time" sports had already begun to undermine academic and intellectual values, no longer presented them with an obstacle. The problem now was to choose a president wholeheartedly committed to the vision of a Rutgers able to get TV exposure in holiday bowl games.

The man the board chose was Francis L. Lawrence, an administrator at Tulane University in New Orleans. Although Tulane had had problems with its Div IA teams—the basketball program had grown so irretrievably corrupt that Eamon Kelly, Tulane's president, had abolished it for a time—it was incontestably a school with a big-time athletics orientation. As important, Francis Lawrence was a tireless advocate of big-time college sports, able to recite readily and with evident conviction the list of reasons typically given for trying to produce winning teams in football and basketball: stronger funding from the state legislature, increased alumni giving, revenue from gate receipts that could be used not simply to support other sports but for worthy purposes such as library acquisitions, and the prospect of increased applications—the so-called "Flutie factor"—from high school seniors who had seen the school's teams on TV. At Rutgers, he would prove to be a fervent fan of football and basketball, at times even venturing into the locker room to give pep talks to the football team.

By 1994 the ambitions of the Scarlet R boosters on the board of governors seemed well on their way to being realized. The new Piscataway stadium, capable of seating more than forty thousand spectators, had been completed. Over the next few years, millions of dollars more would be spent on upgrading other facilities to attract "blue-chip" recruits, as with the basketball locker room complex, which would feature a sunken theater with oversized leather seats for watching films, stereo speakers in the showers, and hand-carved cherrywood lockers for individual players. The first of a long series of high-salary coaches had been hired in football and men's basketball. In women's basketball, Rutgers hired a head coach for a salary exceeding that paid to the president of Harvard. With Francis Lawrence at the institutional helm, Rutgers was invited to become a full member of the newly expanded Big East conference, featuring such perennial basketball powers as Georgetown and Syracuse and, in football, the redoubtable Hurricanes of the University of Miami.

In the beginning, faculty doubts about Rutgers's entry into the Big East didn't concern sports as such. Instead, we were concerned that in removing the university from its ancient rivalries with schools like Colgate and Lafayette and Princeton, the board of governors had at a single stroke erased a great part of Rutgers's centuries-old institutional identity. With my own UNM experience painfully fresh in my mind, I noted that some Big East schools—West Virginia, for example, whom Rutgers would now be playing annually in football—had standardized test scores that put its students in the same extremely low academic range as those I'd taught at New Mexico. A few faculty members who followed college sports closely were worried about the influence of what they called Div IA sports corruption. They reminded us that a few years earlier, when the University of Miami had played Notre Dame in football, Notre Dame students had worn "Catholics versus Convicts" T-shirts as a sardonic allusion to the notoriously shady recruiting practices Miami had used to turn itself into a football powerhouse. Now Rutgers would be associated with Miami in the public mind.

Still, sports did not yet play a major role in faculty dissatisfaction with the Lawrence presidency. Nor did most faculty members take very seriously a notorious verbal blunder Lawrence made, early in his term, in referring in a public speech to the disadvantage of African Americans in higher education due to their "genetic hereditary background." The real problem was that Rutgers seemed to have entered a period of serious academic and intellectual decline. In March 1996 the *Chronicle of Higher Education* ran a story about a growing faculty initiative to remove Lawrence from the presidency. "More than 100 senior professors," reported the *Chronicle,* "have sent a petition to Rutgers's Board of Governors calling him unqualified to run a major university." One faculty member made it clear that it was Lawrence's ineptness—"ineptness" is the word quoted in the *Chronicle* story—and not his controversial remark about genetic disabilities, that was at issue. Lawrence's problem, said this man, was his being "an inarticulate spokesperson for the university." Other senior faculty members were more outspoken still. "'For people who have been so much a part of the effort to make Rutgers better, President Lawrence is terribly disappointing,' said a noted senior professor of urban planning and policy development. He 'does not exert intellectual leadership,' said Prof. Susan S. Fainstein, pointing to Lawrence's recent commencement address. 'He has no ideas, no views, and there is no substance to it.'"

As faculty opposition to Lawrence mounted, I joined it, but for a different reason. Alerted by my experience at UNM, I was well aware of how quickly shifts in institutional emphasis could affect the academic atmosphere. At UNM, I had become convinced, Norm Ellenberger's basketball program had played a role in driving the brightest and most intellectually engaged students out of state. Thus far Rutgers's newly "big-time" athletic teams had been no better than mediocre, so it was possible to hope that the corrosive effect of commercialized athletics wasn't going to affect things anytime soon. Still, I was concerned. What struck me forcibly was a single marked similarity to the UNM situation I'd known before: top students were going out of state for their college education. By the time Lawrence was several years into his presidency, more than 70 percent of New Jersey's top students were fleeing the Garden State. True, New Jersey had an applicant pool immeasurably richer in intellectual talent than New Mexico. It was also true that Rutgers had been doing well by drawing a substantial share of the remaining 30 percent of the top students who did stay in the state for their schooling. Still, such massive out-migration of the state's most intellectually talented students was deeply worrisome. I knew from my days in Loboland that the brightest students were always the first to detect a change in the intellectual atmosphere. Like the canaries nineteenth-century coal miners took down with them into the mines, these kids sensed when the oxygen was giving out.

Even more alarming was my discovery that Rutgers's share of that remaining 30 percent of top students was beginning to shrink markedly. I had done some research showing that a very high percentage of my own students were drawn from this cohort. So once again, my UNM experience set off alarm bells for me that were inaudible to the rest of the faculty. For Rutgers has a high-powered faculty. Most of my colleagues had either spent their careers at Rutgers or, if they had come from elsewhere, had previously taught at selective colleges or universities. Up to 1996 Rutgers had a director of admissions, with a Rutgers College honors program as selective as many Ivy League schools. When I took my turn at serving on the honors selection committee, I came away powerfully impressed with the time and attention committee members gave to the applicants' dossiers. It wasn't simply a matter of comparing SAT scores and reviewing records of extracurricular achievement. These senior faculty members were reading and rereading college essays written by New Jersey's top high school seniors. That's why it seemed so ominous in 1996—the seventh year of Lawrence's presidency—when the office of the director of admissions was abolished in favor of an "office of enrollment management" that admitted applicants through a largely automated process. Several years after that, the highly selective admissions process for the honors program would also be abolished.

Was Rutgers on its way to the open admissions policy I'd known at UNM, a "body count" policy designed only to fill empty seats in the classroom? To see why I found the prospect so disheartening, you have to understand why earlier Rutgers presidents like Mason Gross and Edward Bloustein had viewed selective admissions as essential to any meaningful ideal of democratic education. From the outside, the notion that any high school graduate should have an automatic right to enroll at his state university seems appealing, something like saying that every resident in a town should have access to its public beach. But universities are not public beaches. A university consists of its students, and no university can be better than the students it admits. When every student is prepared to do college-level work, and when the very brightest students are setting the pace in the classroom, education becomes a rich and rewarding process of personal development for all concerned. At Rutgers, I'd so far been lucky enough to encounter just this situation in virtually every class I taught.

Once again, in short, I'd encountered the theory of peer effects. The same theory helped me understand why Rutgers's declining share of the academically gifted students who stayed in New Jersey was so ominous. A few, of course, were going to Princeton. Others were going to in-state public and private colleges for purely personal reasons. But there was a more alarming reason that these students were staying in New Jersey but bypassing Rutgers. A colleague explained to me why: the most talented New Jersey students had begun to enroll at The College of New Jersey. Formerly known as Trenton State College, TCNJ had been all but unheard of thirty years before. By 1996, however, it was overtaking Rutgers in student selectivity and student test scores. In a few more years it would be ranked as one of the top public liberal arts colleges in the nation. With a very talented student body, it had been able to attract exceptionally strong younger faculty. The New Jersey state legislature, impressed by its rise to national prominence, had funded a lavish building program that, based on a harmonious style of Georgian architecture, had given TCNJ an idyllic rural campus.

Just as the theory of peer effects predicts, bright and intellectually engaged New Jersey students wanted to live and take classes with students like themselves. And increasingly they were choosing The College of New Jersey. But why was the theory of peer effects working at TCNJ and not at Rutgers? The reason had to do with TCNJ's farsighted president, Harold Eickhoff. In the 1970s, in the very midst of a national dearth of college-age students, at a time when other small colleges were scrambling to fill their beds or closing their doors entirely, Eickhoff had defied conventional wisdom by raising admissions standards. Moved by "the belief that bigger is not necessarily better, that institutional growth could be calculated in quality as well as size," Eickhoff persuaded his trustees that Trenton State, as it was still called, could become a model institution. Its rise was dramatic. As recently as 1985 Trenton State had had entering classes with a 1070 combined SAT. (All pre-1994 SAT scores in this book have been converted to present-day equivalents.) Tightening admissions standards not only did not shrink applications, it increased them. It also greatly raised the percentage of very bright students in the pool. By 2004, even while accepting almost fourteen hundred more students than twenty years previously, TCNJ was able to enroll a freshman class with a combined average SAT of 1270. Had Rutgers's SAT scores risen at the same rate, its average SAT in the same year would have been 670 verbal, 690 math, for a combined SAT of 1360.

At first, I was interested in TCNJ's remarkable story simply as a lesson for educators. But I soon found out that New Jersey students were exquisitely sensitive to such shifts in academic prestige. I was startled when one of my students told me that TCNJ was now harder to get into than Rutgers. Soon I grew used to hearing my students' stories about bright high school classmates whom they no longer saw because they'd chosen TCNJ over Rutgers. A student of mine named Joseph Mersinger was distressed enough about the change to try to warn the Lawrence administration. "Everyone who goes to Rutgers," Mersinger wrote in an op-ed for the student newspaper, the *Targum*, "has heard some other student talk in a dispirited way about Rutgers as a 'school of last resort.' The point isn't that you can't argue against this perception. You can. The point is that it's self-fulfilling. A few more years during which Rutgers is perceived as a 'school of last resort' and . . . top New Jersey students who currently stay in-state will be going elsewhere. Nobody wants to go to a school of last resort."

Another Rutgers student, a recent graduate named Rob Stevens, was alarmed at the university's decline in the national college rankings. At a time when The College of New Jersey was doing very well, rising steadily in the *U.S. News & World Report* rankings and gaining a spot in the "Top 10 Best Buys"—no. 1 in the Northeast—in *Money* magazine, Rutgers was sliding inexorably downhill. By 2001 it could only manage a tie with the University of Maryland for twenty-fifth place in the *U.S. News* ranking of major public institutions. Many professors—I'm one of them—see these magazine ratings as pernicious in their effects. Ranking colleges in the way *Consumer Reports* ranks refrigerators or automobiles reinforces a commodity model of education that in my view is doing immense harm to American universities. Rob Stevens, however, emphasized another point about the *U.S. News* rankings. He focused on a Lawrence administration press release expressing delight that the university "continues to be ranked among the top 50 public schools in the nation."

That claim, Stevens pointed out, was exactly like boasting that New Jersey continues to be ranked among the top fifty states. For when you cancelled out the states too thinly populated or too poor to support a major research university, there were only about fifty public universities with which Rutgers might reasonably be compared. But Stevens went further. He'd taken the trouble to analyze the *U.S. News* ratings carefully, correlating numerical rankings in various categories to determine where Rutgers really stood in the overall hierarchy of American universities. If you consulted the "National Universities" category, for instance, you'd find that Rutgers hadn't even managed to get listed among the top fifty institutions in the country: it had been consigned to the group called "Tier 2" schools, ranking behind such places as the University of Kansas and Iowa State. Within Tier 2, it had been listed as twenty-third in the "Academic Reputation" category. Put all this together, Stevens wrote in a *Targum* op-ed, and what you found was that Rutgers under Francis Lawrence could do no better than claim to be the seventy-third-best university in the United States.

Increasingly concerned by the palpable academic slide and institutional drift under the Lawrence administration, the Rutgers faculty now began to focus on the role of Big East athletics in diverting institutional attention and resources away from the university's primary mission of teaching and research. "I saw him at football games," said Benjamin Barber, a distinguished political scientist who would eventually leave Rutgers after thirty-two years, largely because of his openly declared dissatisfaction with Lawrence's governance. "I saw him at basketball games. I never saw him at lectures or seminars." A professor in the History Department, James Maaschaele, undertook an exhaustive study of recent funding for the library system, the beating heart of any major university. His report was filled with statistical analyses too elaborate for inclusion here, but their import was clear. "The data presented in these tables," said Maaschaele in an introductory note, "show clear and unambiguous evidence of a severe decline in the Rutgers University Library system over the past decade, relative to peer institutions. . . . In 1989, Rutgers ranked 24th in terms of library expenditures per number of teaching faculty; by 1999 it had fallen to 59th."

As another historian, John Gillis, pointed out in the *Targum,* Rutgers faculty and students were being starved of academic resources under the Lawrence administration at a time when the Athletics Department was gorging at the trough of legislative largesse. The athletics budget, at $30 million, was now an astounding 45 percent larger than it had been just four years earlier. Half of that total came from university general funds. "The subsidy this year," Gillis wrote, "is $13 million, up from $7.9 million just three years ago. The astronomical salaries paid to coaches like football coach Greg Schiano ($500,000), women's basketball coach C. Vivian Stringer ($300,000), and men's basketball coach Gary Waters, the expensive training facilities maintained for a handful of scholarship athletes . . . affect the lives of only a small proportion of students. Except for the tiny group of people at Rutgers who make their living from big-time athletics, nothing could be less essential to our core values as an institution of higher learning."

Yet, as an article in the *Chronicle of Higher Education* pointed out—"A Shaky Football Conference Fears Defections and Collapse" (June 6, 1997)—even these vast sums might not be enough. For in joining the Big East conference, Rutgers found itself in a realm conceived entirely in terms of marketing and advertising, where teams were chosen for membership, as *Chronicle* reporter Mike Waller put it, "on their access to large television markets." To Princeton, Rutgers had been a traditional opponent with a shared competitive history reaching back to their first football game of 1869. To such Big East teams as Virginia Tech and the University of Miami, Rutgers meant little more than access to two large media markets, New York City and Philadelphia. The per-team expenditure in Big East football, Waller pointed out, was second-highest among major Div IA conferences: "on average, each of its teams spent about $4 million on football in the 1995–96 academic year, not counting salaries and the cost of facilities." Even if Rutgers were generating no revenue at all from its Big East sports, it would be expected to spend as if it were a national champion.

Aware that football powers like Miami and Virginia Tech might desert the Big East for a conference where packed stadiums, postseason conference championship games, and holiday bowl appearances would yield more TV exposure and advertising revenue, Rutgers was responding by spending frantically on facilities and coaches' salaries. The amount the university was actually spending is difficult to determine. For every Div IA program has innumerable ways of "hiding" athletics costs in the general university budget, as economist Andrew Zimbalist, author of *Unpaid Professionals: Commercialism and Conflict in Big Time College Sports,* has demonstrated. A conservative estimate of the cost of Big East membership to Rutgers would be $100 million. Just totting up the stadium upgrade ($25 million), athletic scholarships ($29.7 million), and the admitted deficit for one six-year period ($50.6 million) puts the figure well over that amount. Given complete access to the university's books, a sharp-eyed auditor would almost certainly come up with a total between $200 and $300 million.

Still, extravagant as the spending on athletics was, many Rutgers faculty were even more disturbed by the university's association with schools like Miami and Virginia Tech, where domination by an entrenched booster subculture had long since led to unrepentant cynicism about the recruiting practices that give Div IA programs an edge. Shortly after Rutgers joined the Big East, for instance, a member of the Miami Athletics Department was sent to the penitentiary for having illegally steered nearly $700,000 in federally financed scholarship aid to athletes, mainly football players. Unrelated investigations would disclose that the positive results of Miami drug tests had been mysteriously "lost," permitting athletes to remain eligible when the evidence against them unaccountably disappeared. Meanwhile, Miami boosters were reported to have paid football players substantial sums in cash for big plays made in key games. In the larger world of Div IA sports, none of these episodes attracted more than momentary attention.

At Rutgers, though, where faculty memories of Mason Gross and a long tradition of participatory athletics persisted, association with Miami could hardly help being felt as a matter of institutional disgrace. The same was true of association with other Big East schools like Boston College, where thirteen football players were suspended in a gambling scandal tied by the Middlesex County district attorney to organized crime. Or, even more discouragingly, the seemingly unending series of criminal episodes at Virginia Tech, where football players would be faced with charges ranging from rape and sodomy to assault and battery. By July 1997, only three years after Rutgers had been invited to join the Big East, some nineteen Virginia Tech football players would have been implicated in criminal activities. As news reports of such episodes continued to come in, the simpler world in which Rutgers had taken the field against opponents like Colgate and Princeton and Lafayette on autumn afternoons began more and more to seem the dream of a golden age.

I wasn't surprised by the mounting faculty opposition to Francis Lawrence and his pursuit of Div IA glory. But I never expected Rutgers students to take any interest. As at most universities, even our brightest students normally remained oblivious to issues of university governance. It's the sort of thing that concerns deans, provosts, and faculty senates. Students are usually too busy trying to get their latest lab report or Shakespeare paper done to pay attention to educational policy. So I was amazed when three of my most talented English majors came to my office one day to ask about Big East athletics. I'd talked to them, quite incidentally, about how much better things were at Rutgers than at my old university. Now they'd drawn their own conclusions. We've heard you talk about athletics at UNM, they told me—the Lobo Club, and Lobogate, and that coach Ellenberger, and the level of students at the university. You've told us that the best professors left for other universities as soon as they could get out. You've said that the top students in New Mexico left for out-of-state schools. Do you think that could happen at Rutgers?

Some Rutgers faculty, I admitted, had begun to think so. The three students, Chris Cram, Greg Tuculescu, and Sean Murphy, nodded, as though this confirmed what they'd been saying among themselves. With the purely intuitive sense of bright students sensitive to shifts in academic distinction or prestige, they'd hit upon their own version of the theory of peer effects. They knew that in their own high schools, top students were thinking about Columbia and Colgate and Brown, with NYU and Hamilton and Wesleyan as fallbacks. If they needed a "safety school" in the state, they were applying to The College of New Jersey. Increasingly, top students weren't wasting a moment thinking about applying to Rutgers. The reason, my students had decided, had a great deal to do with the new forty-thousand-seat stadium in Piscataway and football coaches making half-million-dollar salaries. It had to do, they thought, with a perception among the brightest students that Francis Lawrence and the board of governors were trying to turn Rutgers into a Tennessee or Ohio State.

By now our athletics discussion group had grown to eight people, with Eli Levin, Dan Greenberg, Liz Hronkova, Dale Osofsky, and Brian Edgar joining the original three. They were convinced that much of what was being written about in the state press as the "Lawrence decline" really was due to the message Big East membership was transmitting to New Jersey's top students. But so what? I countered. The Scarlet R coterie on the board of governors that had appointed Francis Lawrence wasn't about to be swayed by the opinion of eight undergraduates. How many other students agreed with their analysis? For that matter, how many of the most recent students thought that Rutgers was even in a state of decline? When people were saying that the university was going rapidly downhill, it was likely to come as unwelcome news, I pointed out, to students whose own mediocre academic credentials provided evidence of the decline.

The group agreed. If there was to be any hope of turning the situation around, they'd have to find out how many undergraduates shared their own perception that membership in the Big East was driving away top students and giving Rutgers a reputation as a school of last resort. They came up with a simple plan. They'd run a box ad in the *Targum* inviting undergraduates to sign a petition asking the board of governors to (a) resign from the Big East, (b) abolish athletic scholarships, and (c) either join a Div I AA nonathletic-scholarship league or conference like the Patriot League, or compete, as did certain large and estimable private universities like NYU, at the Div III non-athletic-scholarship level. My own contribution was to draw up a petition for Rutgers faculty, so we'd present a united front against Div I A sports corruption within the entire Rutgers community.

The name "Rutgers 1000" was born when the students decided that their petition shouldn't be open-ended. It would be more effective to announce that the petition would be presented to the board of governors when it had gained one thousand signatures. Shortly afterward, they published the petition in a Thursday issue of the *Targum*. I don't remember what sort of response the RU1000 organizers hoped for. I do know the results were deeply discouraging: exactly seven signatures. For that matter, the response I got from the Rutgers faculty, who rarely read the *Targum,* was scarcely better: just thirty-six sent in their names. At that point I was ready to advise the students to throw in the towel. The response to RU1000's petition had given it an organization consisting of exactly fifty-one members, scarcely enough to take on the juggernaut of Div IA athletics, with its billions of dollars in TV advertising revenue and its huge NCAA marketing apparatus. Running more *Targum* ads was unrealistic for a tiny organization with a nonexistent budget. With an all-out membership drive, the students might pick up another fifty signatures or so. That would leave them some nine hundred short of their very modest target number.

The students were undaunted. The *Targum* ad doesn't mean anything, they told me. We're going to take our campaign to the Web. Today, it seems impossible to believe that I had no idea what they were talking about. But it's true. In 1994 I had a home computer that I used for word processing—it was, as I conceived of it then, simply a sort of magical typewriter that could put my footnotes in books and articles into MLA format with a single keystroke. At that point, I was still several years away from even being on e-mail. My first venture onto the Internet wouldn't come until a year after that. Now, a decade later, the world before the Web seems impossibly distant, something that must have existed around the time of the Napoleonic wars. But to the RU1000 students, already moving freely in a cyberspace that I'd never personally experienced, it was clear that the means to take on even a juggernaut like Div IA athletics was already there, waiting to be deployed. Over the next ten years, watching as they mounted an increasingly effective campaign that would eventually remove Francis Lawrence from the presidency, I'd come by degrees to understand why they'd been so optimistic about what I'd been unable to see as anything but a setback. They were already living in the future. I'd been living in the past.

Fairly or unfairly, the ills that appeared to be dragging Rutgers down toward the lowest tier of American higher education tended to be identified in the public mind with the presidency of Francis Lawrence. For by the mid-1990s, the separate elements of Rutgers's downward slide—association with schools like Miami and Virginia Tech, the slippage in the *U.S. News* and other rankings, the extravagant spending on the so-called revenue sports at a time when academic facilities at Rutgers were in a woeful state of decay, the move away from selective admissions to "enrollment management"—seemed to be converging into a single dismal story of institutional decline. In 1998

"They were already living in the future. I'd been living in the past." Original RU1000 Steering Committee, 1996. Photo: Rutgers 1000 Archives.

New Jersey Monthly magazine ran a list of the twenty-five most powerful people in the state. Lawrence, the president of Rutgers, wasn't on it—he was listed among the "Outs," people who should logically have been candidates but who, for whatever reason, failed to command general respect—and his absence was widely remarked. How, in the midst of so general an atmosphere of institutional failure, was Lawrence managing to hold on to his job?

The question was asked most pointedly in a series of outspoken opinion columns by a former New Jersey newspaper editor named Arthur Z. Kamin. As an undergraduate in the 1950s, Kamin had been editor of the *Targum* and a member of Rutgers's oldest senior honor society, Cap and Skull. As an active and prominent alumnus, he'd served as chair of the board of trustees. In retirement he served as a member of the Board of Overseers of the Rutgers Foundation. With his deep knowledge of state and university politics, Kamin was among the first of Rutgers's older alumni to perceive that Francis Lawrence, brought to the university by a small coterie on the board of governors, was surviving in office thanks only to the unwavering support of that same coterie. Under presidents like Mason Gross and Edward Bloustein, wrote Kamin in a 1996 *Star-Ledger* column, Rutgers had been moving into the company of schools like "the University of California at Berkeley, all with noble traditions as publicly supported universities. It was a heady time. Now all that has changed."

Even with Kamin's spotlight focused on Francis Lawrence, however, it wasn't easy to catch a glimpse of the personalities and motives of those whose support was keeping him in office. The board of governors had eleven members. A simple majority was enough to keep Lawrence in office. By the year 2000 it had become painfully evident that Lawrence's only real support in the state of New Jersey had dwindled to six unidentified members of the board of governors, who had the statutory right to keep him on as president so long as they thought he was carrying out what they regarded as the central mission of the university. But who were they? What, exactly, was the mission they perceived Lawrence as having successfully carried out? The answer became clear when two major Scarlet R boosters, the chair of the board of governors and the chair of the board of trustees, provoked by the fusillade of criticism now coming from all sides, wrote a widely discussed op-ed. They insisted that Francis Lawrence, for all the contumely he had earned in the state of New Jersey, was held in high regard in the wider and more consequential world of Div IA athletics. "Lawrence's stature among his presidential peers," they wrote, "is evidenced by his election as Big East conference chairman and Big East representative to the National Athletic Association Board of Directors."

Faculty, alumni, and student readers of the op-ed were wholly unimpressed by Lawrence's standing in NCAA athletics circles. To many, it confirmed their worst fears. At the same time, some faculty began to see that the athletics issue might provide the leverage to bring Lawrence's presidency to an end. The students agreed. Rutgers 1000 would concentrate on opposition to Lawrence and his Scarlet R supporters on the board of governors. It was the right strategy. Under mounting pressure, Lawrence would finally be compelled to resign several years later. There would be general agreement that the athletics issue, more than any other, had brought him down. Most observers would further agree that Rutgers 1000—the student-faculty-alumni campaign to get Rutgers out of the Big East, abolish athletic scholarships, and return the university to its older tradition of participatory athletics—had played a major role in bringing about that triumphant conclusion. But the story of Rutgers 1000 would not end with their triumph. In a strange turn of events, Rutgers 1000 would learn that it had won a hollow victory. The tale of this final reversal carries, as we shall see, a somber moral for all those who care about real college education and honorable college sports.

The Friedman Statement

Effective as the students' campaign on the Internet would be, it was the *New York Times* that put Rutgers 1000 in the national spotlight. In late September 1997 I got a call from a senior *Times* sportswriter, Robert Lipsyte. He was coming to campus to speak to a journalism class taught by an old friend. He'd heard there was some sort of student campaign pushing to get Rutgers out of the Big East and abolish athletic scholarships. Was this true? Well, yes, I said, but only if you considered fifteen students and a few professors a campaign. I ran through the story of the *Targum* ad and the seven signatures from a student body of more than twenty thousand. That hardly counted as massive undergraduate support, I told him. That didn't matter, said Lipsyte. What intrigued him was the simple existence of student opposition. It was a new thing in college sports. Could I arrange for him to interview some members of Rutgers 1000? Several steering committee members were going to be in class, but Chris Cram and Greg Tuculescu were free. They arranged to talk with Lipsyte over coffee in the student center.

Lipsyte's story appeared in the national edition of the *Sunday Times*. The response was amazing. But it didn't come from students. Instead, thousands of Rutgers alumni across the country read the column. Chris and Greg had described the sharp disconnect they felt between the traditional Rutgers and the new sports factory type of university demanded by the Big East. Chris said he'd chosen Rutgers for an intellectual experience centering on books and ideas. He and his friends spent far more time arguing about their favorite writers or problems raised in their philosophy classes than about how Rutgers football was going to do against Virginia Tech. Greg made a different point. His idea of college sports, he told Lipsyte, was watching teams made up of students like himself, kids who lived down the hall in the same dormitory and sat beside him in his ancient history class. Both young men were dismayed to see Rutgers's long tradition of participatory athletics being traded away for semiprofessional football and basketball teams that had no organic connection with the student body. Their anger struck a nerve among Rutgers alumni.

In Lipsyte's column, my name was mentioned in passing. A few days after it appeared, I began to get alumni letters in my departmental mailbox. Not knowing how to contact the students directly, they'd written me instead. Over the next several weeks, more came in, most of them variations on an identical theme: many alumni had fallen out of touch with their alma mater in recent years, convinced that the Rutgers they'd known as undergraduates had vanished, swallowed up in the morass of cynicism and corruption that Div I A athletics had so notoriously become. They were thrilled to hear that today's undergraduates thought there was an older, more honorable Rutgers worth trying to preserve. From Alabama there came a letter from a retired state judge, now partially disabled. His senior honors thesis had been directed by Mason Gross, who remained for him a model of intellectual integrity. The judge had been a southern conservative at a time when segregation reigned as a social and legal system in the South. Gross had been an eastern liberal. But thanks to Gross's intellectual openness, their disagreements had always remained rational and civil. Gross's deepest concern was not to convince his students that they should accept this or that ideological position, but to think for themselves. The very existence of Rutgers 1000, the judge concluded, seemed to be evidence that Gross's spirit remained alive at Rutgers.

A Texas alumnus wrote, "I strongly support your efforts to get Rutgers out of pro athletics before we get entrenched. I have a deep feeling that there are a lot of other alumni like me who are deeply concerned but didn't know there was anything going on to fight this problem. Let me know if there is anything I can do." "I support the effort to rein in big time sports at Rutgers," said an alumnus from North Carolina, "and to maintain the high academic standards for which Rutgers is known. I salute Rutgers 1000, and hope you can bring back some sense to the boosters, students, and administration."

"I know the students of the 70s had more fun playing Princeton, Lehigh, Lafayette, and Columbia," remarked a former Rutgers class president, "than the students of the 90s have had watching RU in the Big East." "From down here in South Carolina," a South Carolina commissioner of higher education wrote in a letter addressed to the students, "we applaud your work! We have the same problems in our institutions but very few to stand up as you have done."

A surprising number of the letters came from alumni who had played sports. "I was co-captain of the varsity swim team," wrote an alumna from Connecticut. "I treasure my years at Rutgers and the strong intellectual foundation I gained. Rutgers should return to its roots as a strong academic institution." "I now watch Ivy League football, which is medium-to-lousy with occasional sparkles of brilliance," said a former Rutgers football player who had gone on to become a coach. "If I want to watch really excellent football, I turn on an NFL game. I've given up watching college football as long as it is peopled by illiterates." "I was a member of the crew," wrote a Pennsylvania alumnus. "I'm disturbed by seeing Rutgers admitting unqualified students to play football and basketball. 1000 signatures seems inadequate: 5000 to 10,000 would have a much greater impact." "As an 'ex-jock,'" wrote a Georgia alumnus, "I've always maintained an interest in athletics, but I recall the words of Rutgers All-American Bill Austin that 'at Rutgers football is a part of college; college is not a part of football.' As a historian, I have a strong sense that Rutgers 1000 is not a flash in the pan."

One of the most important letters Rutgers 1000 would ever receive was addressed not to the campaign but to Francis Lawrence. The alumnus who wrote it, Richard Seclow, sent me a copy. In it, Seclow told President Lawrence that he'd known "Sonny" Werblin personally. He was aware that Werblin was an extraordinary salesman. But the owner of the New York Jets was not, Seclow suggested, the best person to set policy for an institution of higher learning. I sent a brief note of thanks but, in the flood of letters, paid no more attention to Seclow's letter. Several weeks later, my office phone rang. It was Richard Seclow. Had there been any response other than his own to Lipsyte's *New York Times* column? Yes, I replied, an astounding response: my mailbox was stuffed with letters from alumni all around the country. What about the students, Seclow wanted to know. Was there an uprising against professionalized college sports on the campus? I told him about the seven student signatures. If a tiny group of undergraduates who'd drawn certain conclusions about Rutgers athletics from hearing me talk about the University of New Mexico counted as an uprising, then we had one. Otherwise, given that 99.9 percent of the student body had no idea that Rutgers 1000 existed, prospects were poor. The really amazing response had been coming from alumni like himself. "Then let's organize the alumni," said Seclow.

So that's what we did. From then on I forwarded alumni letters to Richard Seclow in Connecticut. A month or so later, I visited him to plan strategy. The total number of alumni letters was just over forty. Seclow had contacted the writers. With the contributions he received from them he had opened a bank account in the name of the Rutgers 1000 Alumni Council. Given the fifteen students who'd signed the petition and the thirty-six faculty who returned the cards I'd sent out through campus mail—I'd now formally registered these as the Rutgers 1000 Faculty Council—that gave us a total membership of about ninety. Stationery had been printed up, so it all looked very official. But Seclow, who'd been a partner in a high-powered New York advertising agency, wanted more. "It's a Potemkin village," he said, meaning the prosperous-looking false-front settlements built by the chief minister of Catherine II when the empress was to tour the Russian countryside. I did my best to console him. Ninety people were ninety more than were opposing Div I A athletics at Miami or Virginia Tech, I pointed out.

Still, how exactly were we going to develop alumni support? I'd already thought about this problem a good deal. What we really need, I said, is a distinguished Rutgers alumnus whose endorsement of the campaign would show that opposition to Big East membership and Div I A athletics at the university was serious. But the difficulty might be coming up with anyone from Rutgers with the necessary stature. I'd always been uncomfortably aware that my own alma mater had in two centuries managed to produce only one really distinguished alumnus, Daniel Webster. The only celebrated Rutgers alumnus I knew about was Mr. McGoo, the cartoon character whose fierce attachment to Rutgers had been a hilarious send-up of raccoon-coated old school loyalty in the 1940s and '50s. Seclow smiled. Then he went inside the house, only to reappear a few minutes later, riffling through the pages of his Rutgers alumni register. "How about Milton Friedman?" he asked. "Class of 1932."

It was too good to be true. I knew a fair amount about Milton Friedman. One of the things I thought I knew was that he'd gone to the University of Chicago. But no: he'd taken a graduate degree at Chicago and had taught there for many years, but Friedman was a Rutgers alumnus. "Do you think he'd be too controversial?" asked Seclow. I knew what he meant: to liberal Democrats of Seclow's generation, Friedman was associated with free-market economics and school vouchers and, more generally, with conservative politics. It was true that he was universally acknowledged to be a brilliant economic theorist, especially in monetary policy, the area for which he'd won the Nobel Prize in 1976. He was also the founder of the Chicago School of Economics, which had produced several other Nobel Prize winners, and which in the era of post-Soviet collapse was having an enormous influence on economic policy at the international level. But Friedman had always been a controversial thinker.

We argued the pros and cons. I'd myself gotten interested in Friedman's theories many years before when I'd read Daniel Patrick Moynihan's book proposing a guaranteed annual income for all American families—a program combining the best elements, I thought then and think now, of free-market economics and something very like Scandinavian socialism, with its concern for the welfare of the less fortunate in a society of material abundance. The originator of the idea had been Milton Friedman. Friedman had also begun his career as a committed Keynesian in the era of the New Deal. His critique of centralized economic planning wasn't based on any doctrinaire attachment to conservative ideology but to his sense that the unintended consequences of well-meant social policies—such as welfare dependency, which had created a bleak and hopeless inner-city culture with brutalizing effects on the children born into it—had been little short of tragic. Friedman seemed to me, I said, to be neither Democrat nor Republican, as those terms are usually understood. He was what he sometimes called himself, a classical liberal.

The more I thought about it, the more convinced I became that Milton Friedman was an ideal symbol of the older Rutgers that we wanted to preserve. He'd been born into a working-class Jewish family in New Jersey. His parents had been immigrants from the Ukraine. Seclow had already told me that his own class at Rutgers had been filled with undergraduates from a similar background—Irish and Jewish and Italian kids, many of them going to school on the G.I. Bill, whose parents had never gone to college. As I looked out at my own classes today, I was seeing the same miracle of upward mobility that had taken Milton Friedman from the tenements of Rahway, New Jersey, to the Nobel Prize. The mix had changed—my students now were as likely to be Chinese or Pakistani as Irish or Italian—but the underlying principle was the same. Mason Gross's democratic ideal—a Rutgers able to provide first-class education to bright students from every social group and background—was precisely what was being destroyed by the university's headlong plunge into commercialized Div I A athletics.

Nor was this all. Friedman was identified in the public mind with the University of Chicago. In 1939 Chicago had famously declared its independence from big-time athletics by dropping football under its farsighted president, Robert Maynard Hutchins. Most people no longer remember that the University of Chicago once had been a national football power, winning seven Big Ten titles and in 1935 producing such players as Jay Berwanger, the first-ever winner of the Heisman Trophy. After Chicago decided to withdraw from the Big Ten conference entirely in 1946, the university went on to become renowned for its core curriculum, based on the so-called great books, and for the Socratic method in teaching—preparation, as Hutchins would say in his various writings on educational policy, not simply for gainful employment but for a future lifetime of learning. Today, when the *Princeton Review* regularly ranks Chicago as providing the "best overall educational experience" for undergraduates among all American colleges and universities, it's the Hutchins legacy that lives on. Wasn't that precisely what we wanted for Rutgers?

We agreed that I'd write a letter to Friedman, explaining the goals of the Rutgers 1000 campaign and asking if he'd be willing to publicly endorse its petition to the board of governors. I thought Friedman was almost certain to agree, given his fierce independence as a thinker. He'd never shown any nervousness about going against received ideas or the established machinery of power and influence. Seclow wasn't so sure. Ever since Friedman's retirement from Chicago, he'd been a fellow of the Hoover Institution at Stanford. He was also a Nobel laureate. He moved in the rarified circles of international policy populated by cabinet members and diplomats. How likely was it that he'd take a personal interest in the campaign of a tiny group of students and alumni against Div I A sports at a university from which he'd graduated more than half a century earlier? For that matter, how likely was it that he'd even see my letter? Nobel Prize winners were hedged round by secretaries and assistants whose job was to screen their mail, making sure that only important letters—from the World Bank, say, or the secretary-general of the UN—got through.

For a month and a half, it looked as though Seclow was right. I didn't hear from Friedman. I never even got an acknowledgment from the Hoover Institution. Then, suddenly, when I least expected it, everything changed. I went out one day to find a letter in my mailbox:

Dear Professor Dowling:

I thoroughly share your and the Rutgers 1000 campaign's views about the undesirability of professionalizing athletics. As a graduate student at the University of Chicago when Robert Maynard Hutchins was president, I have a long background in believing that professionalized athletics have no place at a university. Accordingly, I shall be glad to serve as a spokesman for your campaign. Herewith a brief statement that you asked for:

"Universities exist to transmit knowledge and understanding of ideas and values to students, and to add to the body of intellectual knowledge, not to provide entertainment for spectators or employment for athletes.

"The proper role of athletic activity at a university is to foster healthy minds and healthy bodies, not to produce spectacles.

"When I entered a much smaller Rutgers sixty years ago, athletics were an important but strictly minor aspect of a Rutgers education. I trust that today's much larger Rutgers will honor the tradition from which I benefited so much."

I am enclosing a proper picture for you to use. Wish you luck.

Sincerely yours,
Milton Friedman
Senior Research Fellow

P.S. Excuse my late answer but I was out of town when your letter arrived and have only just received it in the past few days.

I raced to the phone to call Richard Seclow, finally tracking him down in California, where he was on a visit to his grandchildren.

"We've gotten the Friedman endorsement," I told him in a rush of words.

"Could you repeat that?"

"Milton Friedman has endorsed Rutgers 1000." I read him the letter twice straight through.

Seclow gave a soft whistle.

"This changes everything," he said.

The Friedman statement did change everything. With Friedman's letter in hand, Seclow set about getting in touch with the alumni who had written Rutgers 1000 after Lipsyte's *New York Times* story. He also called some of his own Rutgers classmates whom he knew to be concerned about the "big-time" athletics buildup. Within days Seclow's outreach effort turned into a remarkable educational campaign. Lulled by the endless upbeat articles about Big East athletics carried in official Rutgers publications, many alumni were amazed to be given the full details about the outbreaks of criminality at Virginia Tech, or Miami's long history of shady dealings in making itself over as a Div I A football power. Fewer still had thought about the longer-term consequences of Rutgers's being associated in the public mind with schools widely regarded as sports factories. Others, without thinking much about it, were still living mentally in a world where Rutgers athletics meant rivalries with schools like Princeton and Colgate. Appearing as a full-page ad in *The Daily Targum*, the Friedman statement prompted a second column—"An Eminent Voice Pleads for the Soul of Rutgers" (April 12, 1998)—by Robert Lipsyte in the *New York Times*.

In 1932, Milton Friedman graduated from Rutgers University

In 1976, he was awarded the Nobel Prize

In 1998, he's concerned about academic and intellectual values at his alma mater.

"Universities exist to transmit knowledge and understanding of ideas and values to students, and to add to the body of intellectual knowledge, not to provide entertainment for spectators or employment for athletes.

The proper role of athletic activity at a university is to foster healthy minds and healthy bodies, not to produce spectacles.

When I entered a much smaller Rutgers sixty years ago, athletics were an important but strictly minor aspect of a Rutgers education. I trust that today's much larger Rutgers will honor the tradition from which I benefited so much."

— Milton Friedman

Like many other distinguished Americans, Milton Friedman is the son of immigrants. He was born in New York City in 1912. His father died when he was 15. He nonetheless managed to graduate from Rutgers with a B.A. in 1932 and to earn an M.A. from Chicago one year later. He received a Ph.D. from Columbia in 1946, and went on to become the author of such seminal works as *A Theory of Consumption* and *A Monetary History of the United States*. The *Dictionary of Economics* says about Milton Friedman that "in effectiveness, breadth and scope, his only rival among the economists of the 20th century is John Maynard Keynes." He received the Nobel Prize in Economics in 1976.

Photo courtesy of the Hoover Institution.

Publication of the Friedman statement brought together a group of alumni who would serve on the executive committee of the Rutgers 1000 Alumni Council. Three among them would become its core members. One was Howard Sands, a biochemist who had graduated from Rutgers in 1960 and lived in Delaware. After reading Lipsyte's second column, Sands sat down to compose a letter to *Rutgers Magazine.* "I am very pleased that my daughter, a first-year student at Rutgers College, received the Kramer Scholarship from the Rutgers Alumni Association," Sands wrote. "But I would like to point out that she chose Rutgers because of the high ranking of the English department, not the ranking of the football team. It is by the quality of its students and academic programs that Rutgers will benefit the State of New Jersey, the United States, and the world." Over the next three years, Deborah Sands would become a student of mine in eighteenth-century English literature, as well as a key member of the RU1000 student steering committee. She would be our first example of two Rutgers generations working together in the common cause—a living example, as one of her classmates remarked, of the older Rutgers traditions threatened by commercialized sports.

Another alumnus who would play a major role was Rudolph Rasin from Chicago. At first glance he seemed a perfect example of the "white-shoe" Rutgers of the 1950s—J. Press suit, Brooks Brothers shirt, summer home on Lake Michigan. Yet beneath the impeccable attire beat the heart of a radical social idealist. Rasin had always been a Republican. But he was a Republican who had backed civil rights activism in Chicago from its earliest days, not just by contributing money but by working energetically to develop political support for Martin Luther King. He opposed the Vietnam War at a time when, in Republican circles, doing so was considered tantamount to treason. I once asked him once about the apparent contradiction between his outward appearance—private school background, white-shoe Rutgers, old and wealthy family—and his tendency to identify with unpopular causes. Given the circles in which he moved, I remarked, doing that must surely take some courage. "It doesn't take courage," he told me. "I have very little to lose. It's the people who don't enjoy the freedom that goes with material means who show courage when they speak out. They have everything to lose—their jobs, the security of their families, their standing with their co-workers. They're courageous. I'm not." It was, I reflected, exactly the sort of answer one might have gotten from Mason Gross.

A third remarkable alumnus was an attorney living in Lebanon, New Jersey, Mark Mattia. As with Howard Sands and his daughter Deborah, Mattia's ties to Rutgers spanned two generations. In his case, they also involved a family tie to Douglass, the women's college that is to Rutgers what Barnard is to Columbia, an all-female residential college that functions as an integral part of the university as a whole. Though Mark Mattia would contribute money, legal expertise, and strategic thinking to the Rutgers 1000 alumni campaign, his most memorable contribution came about when Rutgers dropped precipitously in the *U.S. News* rankings. An opinion column he wrote for the *Daily Targum*—"Alumni Without a Country"—would galvanize alumni who had never before taken seriously the struggle against Div IA sports corruption at their school. Written more in sorrow than in anger, "Alumni Without a Country" was less an op-ed than an elegy for a Rutgers that Mattia felt was now slipping almost irretrievably away.

He had grown up in a Rutgers family, he told *Targum* readers. His uncle had played football for the university, winning the Coursen Award as the outstanding male athlete in his graduating class. His father had entered Rutgers in 1941, where he met the attractive Douglass coed who would become Mark's mother. Mark's father had been a top student at Barrington High School in Newark, earning grades that got him into Rutgers, Columbia, and Princeton. As an Italian American kid from Newark, Mattia Sr. would have liked to break what was then still called the "color line" at Columbia or Princeton. The problem was money. Tuition at Columbia and Princeton was $400 more a year—a substantial sum in those days—than at Rutgers. His family was not wealthy. Mark's father enrolled at Rutgers.

Then history intervened. War was declared against Germany and Japan. Mark's father was plucked out of Rutgers by the navy, which enrolled him at Princeton, where he wound up spending most of the rest of his undergraduate career. Having felt at home at Rutgers, he soon came to dislike Princeton intensely—so much so that in later years his friends could always get a rise out of him by calling him "Tiger," after the Princeton athletics mascot. When the war ended and it came time to graduate, he could have taken his degree from either university. He chose Rutgers, getting his degree at a ceremony in Kirkpatrick Chapel. Years later, after his father's death in 1971, Mark Mattia would get married in Kirkpatrick Chapel, partly to honor his father's memory. "I remember thinking," he wrote in his *Targum* column, "that Dad had the best seat in the house."

Among the many voices raised in opposition to big-time athletics at Rutgers, Mark Mattia's testimony communicates perhaps most poignantly the loss that occurs when a university abandons its core values for the empty pursuit of Div IA advertising revenue and TV exposure. For Mark's father, after graduation from Rutgers, had devoted himself heart and soul to his alma mater. He was one of the founders of the medical school. He served on the board of trustees, resigning only when the governor appointed him to the State Board of Higher Education. He took his son to Rutgers football games, including every home game during Rutgers's undefeated 1961 season. Today a residence hall on the Rutgers campus bears his name. That's why, Mattia wrote in "Alumni Without a Country," he was sometimes almost glad that his father never lived to see the day when Rutgers would be ranked as a "second-tier" university.

By the time Mattia wrote his piece, it was clear to most close observers that Francis Lawrence's days in the presidency were numbered. Even with the staunch support of the Scarlet R faction on the board of governors, the pressure was mounting from many directions—from FAR, the Faculty Alliance for Rutgers, from Rutgers 1000, from state legislators who had begun to perceive that the university was in decline, from journalists who saw that Old Queen's had become, as Arthur Kamin remarked in an op-ed, "a bunker under siege." So Mattia's essay ended with a warning that would reverberate long afterward:

President Lawrence would like to believe that a post season bowl appearance would somehow restore Rutgers' prestige. That seems to me badly misguided. It's true that a tiny number of selective universities have big time football teams, but no university is prestigious because of athletics. If there were a correlation, we'd be mentioning Oklahoma and Oxford in the same breath. Is Stanford what it is because it went to the Rose Bowl 30 years ago? Columbia went over 60 years ago. Has it been living off that ever since?

Many of my friends graduated from leading public universities. They never mention athletics when talking about their degrees. One of my close friends went to Rutgers and never mentions his school. It's like he never went there. My friend got his graduate degree at Wisconsin. It's Wisconsin's logo that's on his mugs and bookends. His kids wear Wisconsin T-shirts and sweatshirts.

My friend's silence about Rutgers stands for a lot of Rutgers alumni these days. We're not people "without a country," just without a college. The Lawrence era is ending, finally, but an enormous amount of work will have to be done before Rutgers is Rutgers again. We've slid a long way down towards oblivion since the days when my Dad turned down a Princeton degree to be able to say that he graduated from Rutgers.

With public sentiment coming over to its side, the RU1000 Alumni Council decided to take the initiative. Their plan was to run a paid advertisement in *Rutgers Magazine,* a publication going out to 105,000 alumni and friends of the university. If only 5 percent of the readership chose to join, the Alumni Council would gain a membership of more than five thousand. By design, the first ad placed in the magazine would be small and unobtrusive, to be followed by larger and more pointed advertisements as membership grew.

I still have a mock-up of the original advertisement. It was understated in the extreme. There were no denunciations of Div IA sports corruption, no lamentations about Rutgers's association with such acknowledged sports factories as Miami and Virginia Tech. There was simply a heading that read, "For Rutgers Alumni, a Time to Choose," with a picture of Milton Friedman and a short excerpt from his statement about Rutgers and big-time athletics. There was a form for alumni to fill out and return with their name, address, and Rutgers class, plus a box to check for making a donation.

I thought, myself, that the Alumni Council ad might have had just a bit more urgency, if only to get across a sense that Div IA athletics were already doing serious damage at Rutgers. Still, there was an obvious advantage to a low-key approach. With a statement so uncontroversial, there could at least be no objection on the part of *Rutgers Magazine* to running it. So it came as a shock when Seclow called me one afternoon to say that the magazine had rejected the ad. At first I thought there must have been some sort of mix-up. Then Seclow faxed me a copy of the letter he'd received just that morning:

Dear Mr. Seclow:

I have been advised by Lori Chambers, editor, that you wish to place an ad in the next issue of *Rutgers Magazine*.

Rutgers Magazine accepts a limited number of paid advertisements promoting events or offering goods or services to alumni, faculty/staff, and other readers. *Rutgers Magazine* does not sell space for letters, opinion articles, or advocacy advertising of any sort.

A review of your proposed ad indicates that it falls into a category that is not allowable under our standard practice. Therefore, we will not be able to accept it.

Sincerely,

William W. Owens

Editorial Director

I couldn't believe my eyes. I'd been getting issues of *Rutgers Magazine* in my departmental mailbox for as long as I'd been at Rutgers. Some months the entire magazine seemed like little more than one large advertisement for Big East athletics. How could anyone reasonably claim that *Rutgers Magazine* didn't allow advocacy?

When I called Seclow back, he'd already spotted the contradiction. "They're not saying they reject advocacy," he agreed. "If we'd put in an ad saying we wanted to organize charter flights to away games, they'd have taken it in a minute. They're saying that they reject advocacy by alumni who don't want to see Rutgers become a sports factory." "A great point," I said. "Somebody ought to make that argument." "We mean to," Seclow said grimly. "In court." That was the beginning of the landmark *Rutgers Magazine* case. For the American Civil Liberties Union would decide that there was a major constitutional issue at the center of the dispute. Keeping a group of concerned alumni from being heard in their own alumni magazine represented, the ACLU concluded, "viewpoint discrimination," a special instance of a violation of free speech. The ACLU agreed to represent the RU1000 Alumni Council pro bono. The Lawrence administration, using state funds to hire expensive outside counsel, made a motion for summary dismissal. But, having reviewed the arguments on both sides, Judge Joseph Messina of the New Jersey State Superior Court denied the motion. "It will be a very interesting case," he was quoted as saying, "and I'm looking forward to it."

Rumors reached us that the Lawrence administration was contemplating the trial without anxiety. President Lawrence's lawyers had assured him that the university stood no chance of losing. Nor was their confidence entirely misplaced. In conventional terms, the Rutgers 1000 lawsuit didn't represent a free speech issue. Just a year earlier the ACLU had defended the *Miami Herald* against a suit by a reader whose op-ed pieces it had repeatedly turned down. The case was superficially similar to that of *Rutgers Magazine*. The reader claimed that the *Herald* had suppressed his views. In that case, the ACLU had taken the newspaper's side. In its successful defense, the ACLU had argued that a privately held newspaper had no obligation under the First Amendment to run any material with which it was in editorial disagreement, so long as the plaintiff had alternative means of making his views public. This was precisely the ground on which the Lawrence administration's lawyers would stake their own case. The apparent similarity between the two cases explained why the ACLU had hesitated for some months before agreeing to take on the *Rutgers Magazine* case.

When the ACLU did agree to represent Rutgers 1000, its reason for doing so would be brilliantly formulated by ACLU lawyer Grayson Barber. A Pomona College and Rutgers Law School graduate, she proved to be the heroine of the *Rutgers Magazine* case, both for those opposing President Lawrence and the board of governors and for others concerned with First Amendment rights. The *Rutgers Magazine* case, Barber argued, was radically different from that of the *Miami Herald*. As a publication of Rutgers University, it was not a privately held periodical but what in legal terms is called a "state actor." Because *Rutgers Magazine* was taxpayer-supported, it couldn't make its pages available only to the views of the Lawrence administration. A *Rutgers Magazine* that relentlessly promoted Big East athletics while denying Rutgers 1000 a voice in its pages would inevitably become, argued Barber, little more than a taxpayer-subsidized house organ for Francis Lawrence and the Scarlet R Club.

The way Grayson Barber constructed her argument that *Rutgers Magazine* was a "state actor" would give the Rutgers 1000 case landmark status in First Amendment doctrine. At a level closer to home, it would also make clear that the Lawrence administration had been made extremely nervous by precisely the vision of burgeoning Rutgers 1000 membership that had inspired our Alumni Council to place the ad. In a searching cross-examination, Barber got William Owens, the magazine's editorial director, to admit under oath that there had never been any explicit policy against "advocacy advertising" before Richard Seclow submitted "A Time to Choose." Accurate or not, the impression was inescapable: the magazine's policy against dissent was something that had been cooked up only after President Lawrence and his Scarlet R allies unexpectedly found themselves having to defend professionalized college athletics against a group of dissenting Rutgers alumni.

In her closing statement, Grayson Barber also dwelt with great effectiveness on the special responsibility of a university publication to welcome dissent and free inquiry as part of its very mission. Judge Messina agreed. A university, he declared, is nothing if not an institution devoted to the free exchange of ideas, even or especially on controversial issues. In a phrase that Rutgers 1000 would subsequently adopt as one of its own slogans, Judge Messina said that the RU1000 Alumni Council fit the classic mold of a "loyal opposition." Furthermore, the judge decreed, the concept of viewpoint discrimination was clearly an essential part of free speech under both the U.S. and New Jersey constitutions. When a publication serves a specific constituency, he said, and only a small governing group within that constituency is permitted to support its position, "you're giving the reader only one side of the story, and that is constitutionally prohibited."

Judge Messina's decision was, as Richard Seclow declared to the media, a home run for both RU1000 and free speech. In New Jersey, newspapers were unanimous in celebrating the decision. Reading the commentary, it was hard to escape the sense that contempt for the Lawrence administration had been building for years. Now steam had built to a head. In an editorial—"Rutgers Prefers Rah-Rah"—the *Trenton Times* treated the episode with barely concealed disdain: "For four years, Rutgers University fought Rutgers 1000, a group of its own alumni that wanted to place an advertisement in the alumni magazine criticizing the school's pursuit of big-time football status. It was not an inspiring position for an institution dedicated to the free market in ideas." A *Home News Tribune* editorial commented that "*Rutgers Magazine* tried to pass itself off as neutral in its views, but it never was. Though it claimed to serve all alumni, it served only those who agreed to agree with its limited—and one-sided—content. The shame is, it didn't have to be that way. Allowing the alumni group to express its critical views could create even greater support for the university, as ACLU lawyer Grayson Barber noted, because those views are born of loyalty and enthusiasm—not the desire to tear down an institution."

In the aftershocks of the *Rutgers Magazine* case, the university's lawyers protested that their arguments hadn't been properly understood. The administration promptly appealed the court decision. It would be another year before the New Jersey appellate court ruled that Judge Messina's position on viewpoint discrimination was constitutionally sound. There was talk of an appeal to the next level. At this point, though, the public had had enough. In New Jersey, newspaper after newspaper took the position that the silliness had gone too far, and had been much too expensive to the taxpayers, to be carried any further. In fighting the case to the degree it did, the Lawrence administration had spent $376,149 on outside legal counsel, research, and other costs. When you added the billings of the university counsel and his staff, the cost could be estimated at well over half a million dollars. Then, to add insult to injury, the court ruled that the Lawrence administration was obliged to pay fees amounting to $77,182 to Grayson Barber and her ACLU staff—a standard outcome in cases where governmental entities are found to have violated the constitutional rights of the party that has brought suit. Big-time sports at Rutgers was getting more expensive all the time.

With its victory in the *Rutgers Magazine* case, the RU1000 Alumni Council became one of the most authoritative voices in the country for mounting resistance to Div I A sports corruption, not simply at Rutgers but throughout American higher education. This was entirely an unintended consequence. "We only set out to save our own school from being devoured by the sports monster," Richard Seclow remarked to me later. "It's sad to see us getting all this national attention. There should be alumni groups like ours at a dozen universities." Still, after publication of the Friedman statement, Seclow and other members of the Alumni Council would devote a great deal of time and energy to carrying the message about Div I A sports corruption to the outside world, making television and radio appearances, writing op-eds when asked to do so by editors in North Carolina or Texas or Oregon, making guest appearances in university classes on sports sociology, and debating NCAA representatives in public forums. For better or for worse, the Friedman statement had put Rutgers 1000 at the center of a growing national debate about commercialized college athletics. As we'd soon find out, it was a contentious place to be.

Warriors on the Web

While the Alumni Council was defending the principle of "viewpoint diversity" in court, the RU1000 students were setting up a Web site that put the principle into action. It's difficult today to remember just how revolutionary the Web seemed in the early 1990s. I remember hearing my own department chairman say, "We've got to get a Web site up right away. If we don't, we'll have ceased to exist!" Apparently we were among the last few English departments in the country without one. I had no idea what he was talking about then. I was still thinking about the Web as a sort of post-television pastime among my students, something like the video games they'd played in high school. I'd learn to think otherwise. Over the next few years the RU1000 Web site would come to be recognized as a major force in the national struggle against sports corruption. Tens of thousands of outside visitors would browse the site for arguments and evidence to use against big-time college athletics.

Rutgers 1000 was fortunate to have several HTML programmers in its group. The other students called them the Web elves. Within a few weeks the elves had set up a system allowing them to collaborate on Web design and content from widely scattered computers. Later, when Web technology had grown more advanced, they'd be able to send in material from Internet cafés as far away as Japan and Australia. Their work gave the campaign a tremendous strategic advantage. As thousands and then millions more people came onto the Internet during the 1990s, the RU1000 site was already there, making the case against commercialized Div IA sports in every mode—statistical tables, opinion articles, news updates, parody, satire—that a resourceful group of bright undergraduates could come up with. Then too, the Web elves' expertise meant that RU1000 response time could be measured in nanoseconds. Often, after a board of governors meeting dealing with some major athletics issue, board members would discover that the RU1000 Web site had posted an analysis of the vote and its implications while they were still driving home.

In the beginning, the Web site included a response board where the RU1000 students could respond to arguments and questions as they came in. There were two problems. One was that many responses were abusive or obscene. The other was that if they weren't, they kept repeating the same arguments to defend commercialized college sports. Quickly growing impatient with these repeated arguments—always trumpeted as if no one had ever made them before—the RU1000 response team began to give them shorthand names. So, for instance, when someone wrote in to say, "Sports are great because they give a university valuable exposure," the response team dubbed it the "Everybody Knows O. J." argument. When somebody objected, "Hey, places like Michigan and Duke combine high-quality academics with big-time sports programs. Why can't Rutgers?" the kids took to rolling their eyes and chorusing, "It's the 'What About Duke?' argument." It wasn't long before the Web team simply took down the response board and replaced it with a page entitled "Pro & Con: The 'Standard' Arguments."

Though festooned with attention-getting headings like "Here Come the Frosh" and "The Big Rock Candy Mountain," the Pro & Con page was filled with the results of serious research. The point of Pro & Con, as the Web team saw it, was to show why each of the standard arguments was based on either faulty empirical evidence or logical error. A good example is the "Big Rock Candy Mountain" argument, which came in two versions. In its simplest form, the claim is that a winning football or basketball program generates money for what are called nonrevenue sports: when twelve thousand fans pack the Taco Bell Arena at Boise State University to watch a basketball game, the money they pay is going to support swimmers and wrestlers and cross-country runners on Boise State's other teams. The more grandiose version of the argument asserts that "revenue sports" like football and basketball generate large amounts of income for library acquisitions, laboratory equipment, and classroom construction. Even if they care nothing about sports themselves, this argument goes, Boise State students, alumni, and faculty ought to be grateful to any basketball program that can fill the Taco Bell Arena.

What the RU1000 response team found was that the Big Rock Candy Mountain argument had long since been exploded. Economists who had carefully examined the balance sheets at Div I A universities discovered that not only do most major athletics programs lose money, but among the few that do turn a profit, the money goes right back to the program. So if the University of Nebraska football team, say, generates a substantial profit in any given year, the money will go for more assistant coaches, more elaborate weight-training equipment, more lavish hotel accommodations at away games, and similar purposes. Not a penny will go for more seminar rooms for undergraduates, more subscriptions to scholarly journals for the library, or more laboratory space for biochemists. As it happens, Nebraska is a particularly salient example of the Big Rock Candy Mountain fallacy. In one recent year, Nebraska football coaches were given across-the-board raises while the university itself, pleading financial exigency, was firing tenured professors.

One of the books the Web team consulted in composing its answer to the Big Rock Candy Mountain argument was Murray Sperber's *College Sports, Inc.,* a pioneering investigation of Div I A athletics as they actually operate behind the deceptive veil of the NCAA's myth of college amateurism. "If profit and loss is defined according to ordinary business practices," Sperber reported, "of the 802 members of the National Collegiate Athletic Association's Division I . . . only 10 to 20 athletic programs make a consistent albeit small profit, and any given year another 20 to 30 break even or do better. The rest . . . lose anywhere from a few dollars to millions annually." Sperber's book cast a harsh new light on the annual $3.3 million deficit admitted by the Rutgers Athletics Department. Reading Pro & Con, people were able to see that Francis Lawrence's Big East buildup was not only a current drain on academic resources but was likely to remain one in perpetuity. Even worse, the real figure, if you applied standard accounting practices, would be closer to $11 million a year.

Still, even with the evidence provided by Sperber and sports economists like Andrew Zimbalist, the RU1000 response team sensed they hadn't overcome one objection perennially raised by Rutgers sports boosters. What about their dream that one big triumph—winning the Bowl Championship Series, finishing in the Final Four—would redeem all the costs spent on the athletics program in the years before? If Rutgers 1000 were only able to expose the logic that was driving spending on "big-time" sports, one of the students pointed out, you could show how the vast majority of Div I A schools were shortchanging their real students by lavishing resources on athletics. Then one day a student read an article for an economics class on rational choice theory. The essay treated college athletics as an exemplary case of what in game theory is called the dollar auction game. It's an exercise in which an auctioneer gets bidders to offer extravagant sums for an ordinary U.S. dollar bill. The article, by Fredrick H. Murphy of Temple University, appeared in *Interfaces* (June 1996), a publication of the Institute for Operations Research.

How do you get bidders to offer more than a dollar for a dollar bill? The whole notion sounds so bizarre that it seems wrong to call it a problem in rational choice theory. But it seems less irrational once you know the rules of the dollar auction game. Here they are: (1) the highest bidder wins the dollar, (2) both the highest bidder and the second-highest bidder pay what they bid, but (3) the second-highest bidder wins nothing. The rules look innocent enough, but look at them closely and you'll see why they lead to wildly irrational behavior. When he runs the dollar auction game in one of his classes, Professor Murphy starts off by asking one student to make a very low bid, ten or twenty cents. He then gets a second student to bid thirty cents. The first student then comes back with a bid just below a dollar, usually ninety-nine cents. The second bidder then offers a dollar, and the class assumes the auction is over. But now Professor Murphy points out to the second bidder that he or she will lose less if the bid is raised to $1.10. As soon as they have grasped the point, both players then begin raising the ante in a steady upward spiral.

To understand how the dollar auction principle works in Div I A, you only need to put yourself in the position of the second bidder. Under the rules, he or she still has to pay ninety-nine cents. So a bid of $1.10 now means that he or she can magically "save" eighty-nine cents. But now the first bidder, who suddenly faces paying $1.00 if he loses the auction, has a huge incentive to bid $1.11. The second bidder, now looking at a loss of $1.10 and hoping to shut the auction down by preemptive action, bids $1.50 or $1.75. Soon the bidding spirals out of sight. If you try the dollar auction game at a party where everyone has had a few drinks, says Professor Murphy, you'll make a nice profit and have something to kid your friends about later. But don't kid them too much, he warns, or they won't be your friends much longer. His conclusion: "College athletics is a classic dollar auction game. Each school draws up its athletic budget at the beginning of the season. They spend all of the money they have budgeted, but only a few are winners. The next year, the losing schools either opt out of the game—which rarely occurs—or, hope springing eternal, they up their budgets trying to win the next round. After all, last year's money is a sunk cost."

The Web team developed their answer to the "Everybody Knows O. J." argument after they noticed a post on a Rutgers sports board by a Virginia Tech booster boasting about his team's quarterback, Michael Vick, and its high ranking in the national football polls: "here I am bitching, with MV and #6 ranking, best damn coaches in the country, and more magazine covers and unheard-of publicity than any other 20 schools put together. What's my problem, huh?" Such gloating may seem crass, but if publicity is in and of itself a valuable thing, weren't Virginia Tech fans right to glory in the publicity their highly ranked football team had brought to the school? The RU1000 students attacked the problem logically. First, they pointed out, there were a substantial number of universities, such as Harvard, Yale, Princeton, Columbia, Brown, the University of Chicago, and NYU, that never got publicity from televised bowl games—in the case of the first five, because Ivy League rules prohibit postseason play, in the case of Chicago and NYU, because they compete at the Div III nonathletic-scholarship level—and yet rank among the best academic institutions in the nation. Second, Virginia Tech had earned at least as much publicity for the criminality of its football program—the nineteen players up on charges of rape, assault, and other felonious acts—as for its won-lost record. Wasn't the notion of "publicity" invoked in such arguments somehow spurious?

The error, the students concluded, was a failure to distinguish between mere name recognition and something more substantial and valuable, which they called earned prestige or reputation. The name they gave to this particular argument came from the example they used to illustrate the distinction: "Mere 'exposure' is worthless. One of the most-discussed events of recent years was the O. J. Simpson trial. Those whose name recognition increased as a result do not seem to us models to be envied or imitated. On the other side, 'reputation' very often comes not from exposure but from a long-term commitment to genuine intellectual attainment. At the institutional level, for instance, Harvard enjoys a reputation as a good university. Not because it has a winning football or basketball team, but because it has remained committed to academic and intellectual values over a long period." The debate about Div IA athletics at Rutgers, they suggested, was ultimately about whether Rutgers should be aiming for "exposure" or reputation.

A similar error lay behind what the RU1000 Web team dubbed the "What About Duke?" argument. The site excerpted a letter to the *Targum* that analyzed this particular argument: "It consists of this: in trying to defend professionalized athletics at your school, you (1) pick one of the tiny handful of institutions in the United States that has managed to sustain a decent level of student selectivity while playing Division IA football or basketball, (2) pretend that this handful is representative of 'sports factory' schools generally, and (3) end by asking 'Why can't Rutgers do the same?'" Going through a standard logic text, one member of the Web team discovered that this argument was a version of a logical fallacy called *per enumerationem simplicem,* or arguing by counting only examples favorable to your case. As they demonstrated, the tobacco companies in the 1950s could have shown, on the same grounds, that smoking wasn't dangerous to your health by producing one or two healthy octogenarians who had smoked a pack a day for sixty years. Such people do exist, but they're not an answer to the argument that smoking causes lung cancer, emphysema, heart attacks, and similar diseases on a very large scale.

The Pro & Con page analyzed and provided evidence against other arguments typically used by Div IA boosters. The "Here Come the Frosh" argument, for instance, was their name for what boosters like to call the "Flutie factor," based on the reported increase in applications seen at Boston College after a popular quarterback named Doug Flutie had taken the school's football team to a holiday bowl game. In this case, their research consisted of examining the similar rise in applications—the "Rose Bowl bump," as it was labeled in admissions circles—experienced by Northwestern when its football team unexpectedly won a Big Ten championship. What they discovered was that the additional applications had come from students with very poor academic records, simply multiplying the number of rejections sent out by the admissions office. "The kind of students who apply because your football team is winning," a member of the Northwestern faculty told the RU1000 Web team, "aren't the kind of student you want in your freshman class."

The RU1000 Web team was indefatigable in its research. Its members absorbed the results of empirical studies like Sperber's *College Sports, Inc.,* Sack and Staurowsky's *College Athletes for Hire: The Evolution and Legacy of the NCAA's Amateur Myth,* Bowen and Shulman's *The Game of Life: College Sports and Educational Values,* and Andrew Zimbalist's *Unpaid Professionals: Commercialism and Conflict in Big-Time College Sports.* In addition, they did research on the Web, compiling statistical tables from the *Kansas City Star*'s NCAA database and using the *Chronicle of Higher Education*'s powerful search engine to dig out detailed records of the evolution of Big East programs like those at Miami and Virginia Tech. After watching the Web team busily discussing and researching materials for the Web site, I found that some of my colleagues and I had been struck by the same thought. "These students of ours," I remember one professor saying, "are creating their own college."

It was true. A Rutgers that valued low-SAT recruits more than talented students had paradoxically catalyzed the emergence of Rutgers 1000 as a center of intellectual vitality. Constantly vilified by Scarlet R boosters, and even by a new type of boorish undergraduate that Div IA athletics had begun to attract to campus, the students had responded to Rutgers's academic decline by making Rutgers 1000 an invisible college within the university, one that couldn't be destroyed by Big East sports funding or open admissions policies. This seemed to me wholly admirable. My own undergraduate education had come as much from late-night arguments with my friends about philosophy and history and literature as from lectures or classroom discussions or writing essays for courses. At Rutgers in the 1990s, the same purpose was being served by the campaign against Div IA athletics. Still, there was something wrong about the need to do all this in opposition to their own university. What President Lawrence and the board of governors didn't seem to grasp was that at a better Rutgers these bright and resourceful students would be at the center of university life.

If the RU1000 Web site made a notable impact on the commercialized sports debate at Rutgers, it had a longer-term influence on the Rutgers 1000 students themselves. At first it was instructive for the kids simply to see that they had to deal with nothing more than a limited list of endlessly repeated assertions. Then, as they analyzed these, the students began to realize that they weren't in fact arguments at all. When you scrolled through the entire list—"Big Rock Candy Mountain," "Here Come the Frosh," "What About Duke?"—you couldn't help being left with the impression that they were at bottom little more than an empty litany of justifications that boosters could repeat, as much to each other as to the outside world, should anybody ask why Scarlet R, having no discernible interest in intellectual pursuits, should be exerting so strong a sway over Rutgers University. The arguments boosters gave for commercialized college sports were meant to paper over the crevasse that lay between Div IA athletics and the real life of universities. "If you take away their mantras," a member of the RU1000 Web team said to me one day, "they've got nothing left. They haven't ever really thought about college sports."

As they grew more expert at logical analysis, the RU1000 Web team turned their attention to the pro–Big East statements periodically released by President Lawrence. The most famous page on their Web site was simple but devastating. It focused on a single statement. Answering a reporter from the *Home News Tribune* who'd asked for his response to Rutgers 1000's claim that the university's academic decline was due to its venture into Big East athletics, Lawrence declared, "The combined pursuit of academic excellence and high-level athletic competitiveness has been successful at Rutgers' peer institutions nationally, and there is no reason to believe it cannot succeed here." The Web team led off with that "peer institutions" quote and repeated it all the way down the page, followed each time by a news report about drugs or fraud or bribery or gambling or criminality at Big East schools: "Newspaper says Miami Football Players Got Cash." "6 Men Indicted in Boston College Gambling Scandal." "Football players at Miami were paid hundreds of dollars for making big plays in important games, the *Miami Herald* has reported . . . $500 for a touchdown, $200 for an interception, $100 for a hard tackle."

Still, it was the graphics layout that was most devastating. As you scrolled down the page, you'd see the president's "peer institutions" remark with a photo of a benignly smiling Lawrence, followed by a "Gambling Scandal" quotation with the president looking infinitely sad. Then, once again, the "peer institutions" quote with the cheerful Lawrence. The alternation of quotes and images was so rapid, and the page was so long, that the president's oscillation between pride and shame, hope and despair, seemed manic, almost demented. Every time the words "peer institutions" and "success" and "excellence" flashed on the screen, they seemed more and more obviously detached from reality. I came to see that this is what the Web elves had meant when they tried to explain to me that in the world of the Web, layout is in itself a form of argument. Later we'd hear that the famous "peer institutions" page had turned many previously neutral Rutgers alumni against membership in the Big East.

Although the RU1000 students occasionally manned sign-up tables and handed out petitions, they put their greatest efforts into the Web site. When news stories appeared about a lavish locker-room-and-lounge complex for the Rutgers men's basketball team, for instance, the Web team saw an immediate opportunity. They pored over the newspaper coverage to glean the details. From William Rhoden of the *New York Times* they learned that Rutgers had been spending money on "spacious dressing areas and custom-designed, handmade cherry wood lockers with the players' names and numbers. There are speakers in the showers and seven televisions, two satellite dish hookups, five VCR's and a tiered theater with 23 giant leather seats." From an article in the *Sporting News* they discovered that there was "a theater with state-of-the-art acoustics, a 63-inch screen, 23 cozy movie-style seats. . . . There's a players' lounge, a 52-inch color TV, four more 19-inchers (all with satellite access), 10 preset lighting settings, and high-tech speakers in every corner of the room. Even in the showers."

But how was Rutgers 1000 to make this extravagant spending stand out against the university's woeful neglect of academic facilities? You couldn't do this simply by giving budget figures. Undergraduates at public universities can always be moved to protest tuition hikes, but they tend to regard the university budget as a mass of abstract millions being spent in some distant bureaucratic galaxy. "It's like talking to them about the space program," said one RU1000 student who was trying to bring home the colossal waste involved in Rutgers's $25 million Piscataway football stadium. "The figures are huge, and nobody cares that much about the price of rocket fuel." So how were they to make the basketball team's lounge area, with its hand-carved cherrywood lockers and satellite TV hookups, into a symbol of the Lawrence administration's grotesquely distorted priorities?

Fortunately, the dilapidated state of the Rutgers campus provided an answer. Rutgers has what many of our older alumni have come to call, with some asperity, a slum campus. Though there are some beautiful isolated spots, the dominant impression the campus conveys is one of sprawling confusion and general deterioration: cheaply constructed buildings, traffic-choked streets, weed-infested blacktop parking lots, curbsides strewn with broken glass and crushed aluminum cans, sidewalks awash in a swirling litter of candy bar wrappers, plastic bottles, and styrofoam fast-food containers. Every year, my students tell me, high school seniors making a campus visit to New Brunswick look around, take in the situation, and decide not to apply. Others, who've toured The College of New Jersey's bucolic campus twenty-five miles away, decide to enroll there. While "blue-chip" basketball players were lolling in their leather-upholstered lounge chairs, real students found themselves sitting in linoleum-floored classrooms with flimsy room dividers, or making their way to classes along a dreary streetscape that looked, as one student said to me, like a Wal-Mart parking lot with shuttle buses.

The issue they chose to dramatize the point was toilet smells. Three large resident halls on the Rutgers campus—Campbell, Hardenbergh, and Frey-lingheusen—have classrooms on their lower levels. Erected shortly after Rutgers became a public university in 1956, the so-called river dorms had been thrown up in a spate of shoddy construction due, we repeatedly heard, to politically influenced contracts. I myself had taught in these classrooms. I'd experienced firsthand the effect of the toilet smells on teaching and learning. As hundreds of students in the dorm rooms above got up, showered, and flushed their toilets, there was a sewage backup on the lower levels, creating an odor so strong that it was impossible to ignore. In cold weather it was usually possible to make it through the class period. On warm days the smells were so overpowering that you had to call off class early. It was, one of my colleagues bitterly remarked, like trying to teach in a cesspool.

The Web team's response was their famous "Slum Classroom Contest" page. It featured a down-and-out hobo with a scraggly beard and ragged clothing beside the descriptions of the new basketball lounge area, with its cherrywood lockers and satellite TVs. Students were invited to nominate the slummiest classroom at Rutgers and were given a helpful checklist—"Is the floor 'utility grade' linoleum? (10 pts)," "Is the blackboard pitted and fissured? (5 pts)." Reaction to the contest was immediate and angry. "The classrooms are a disgrace," one freshman in the honors program wrote to the campaign. "I read on your Web site about backed-up toilet smells. I've been in three classrooms like that. They were noisy and dilapidated. The smell was horrible. How can pres. Lawrence justify spending three quarters of a million dollars on 'athlete tutoring services' when real students are struggling to learn in rooms like that?" The Web team posted a sampling of such responses on the Slum Classroom page. Shortly afterward, the team also learned that *Princeton Review* had ranked Rutgers the worst university in the country in its "Dorms Like Dungeons" category. That item, too, went up on the Slum Classroom Web page.

The Slum Classroom Contest struck a nerve in the outside world—especially among New Jersey legislators—unmatched by anything else on the RU1000 Web site. Clearly the nerve in question was olfactory. Broken classroom windows and holes in the ceiling, cheap linoleum floors and pitted blackboards, are one thing. Toilet smells are something else. One spring afternoon I got a call in my office from a state legislator. He knew nothing about Rutgers 1000. He was unaware of any campus opposition to Div 1A athletics. He'd tracked me down because he'd heard that I was advisor to some student group protesting classroom conditions at Rutgers. "Is this true," he asked me, "about the toilet smells?" Indeed it was, I assured him. I'd had to teach in those conditions myself. But the students' real point, I told him, had to do with the millions being spent on athletics. "Why?" he asked, honestly puzzled. "What's that got to do with anything?"

Shortly after my conversation with the legislator, a reporter from *University Business* magazine, John Palatella, called to ask about the RU1000 Web site. He knew about the campaign. He'd read about it in the *New York Times* and the *Wall Street Journal* and *Sports Illustrated*. He thought it was interesting. He was more interested, though, in the way the students were using the Web to mobilize opposition. Were the students aware that they'd been doing something entirely new in the annals of student activism? I thought about it. Partly yes and partly no, I finally answered. Yes, in the sense that they knew they were having an impact in a sphere that extended far beyond Rutgers, one that would have been unimaginable in the previous age of marches and demonstrations and bullhorns and printed flyers. They were getting mail from faculty and fellow students at other universities, correspondents who knew

"Were the students aware that they'd been doing something entirely new in the annals of student activism?" RU1000 Steering Committee, Spring 2001. Photo: RU1000 Archives.

of their existence only through the Web. No, in the sense that, having grown up with the Internet, they could hardly imagine a time before it existed.

Palatella and I had a long conversation. What had been the effect, he wanted to know, of the specific pages he'd gone through on the RU1000 Web site? For instance, the page about classrooms with toilet smells. Had the Lawrence administration responded to that? Yes, I told him, in two ways. First, they'd assigned an upper-level administrator to write a letter to the *New York Times* saying that Rutgers was, contrary to popular opinion, spending money on classroom maintenance—though his letter to editor omitted to mention that not a cent so far had been spent on eliminating toilet smells. Second, during the summer after the Slum Classroom page went up, construction teams had been sent to Campbell, Hardenbergh, and Freylingheusen halls to install new plumbing. So if future generations of Rutgers students were able to take classes without holding their noses, they could thank the RU1000 Web team. But that wasn't exactly a victory over big-time athletics. It was more a victory over toilet smells.

What about public opinion, Palatella wanted to know. Had there been any large shift in the way New Jersey looked at big-time athletics at its state university? This was harder to gauge. The main effect, I told him, seemed to me that, inside Rutgers and beyond, you didn't hear the "standard" arguments any more. Even the Scarlet R boosters didn't try to make the claim that publicity or name recognition from Div IA sports was somehow valuable in itself. The "Everybody Knows O. J." rejoinder seemed to have scotched that one. The "Flutie factor" argument wasn't one you heard much any more. By now, everyone had been made aware that New Jersey's top students were increasingly fleeing to out-of-state institutions, or, if they were staying, were choosing The College of New Jersey over Rutgers. This, too, was something the Scarlet R boosters had learned not to claim would be altered by a winning football or basketball team.

What about student opinion at Rutgers, Palatella asked. Were there now a lot of undergraduates who thought that Rutgers would be better off leaving the Big East and joining a nonathletic-scholarship conference like the Patriot League? Or following the major university Div III model, like NYU? Here I could only guess. My own sense was that the RU1000 Web site, through which most students had become familiar with the campaign, had polarized campus opinion in a salutary way. Before Rutgers 1000, nobody in the student body knew what anyone else thought about big-time athletics. Most hadn't thought about the issue at all. Now you had, at one extreme, a hardcore group of "party animal" students who were vocal supporters of big-time athletics. At the other extreme, you had a group of bright and intellectually engaged students who wanted to see Div IA sports abolished. In between, you had a large mass of students still making up their minds. But that, I told him, seemed to me a victory of sorts. At Rutgers, as at no other public university in the country, Div IA sports were an issue of lively and continuous debate.

There was something else, I told him. It seemed to me that the RU1000 Web site had taught students at the university to see their surroundings. It wasn't just the toilet smells issue, or even the whole slum classroom problem. Before Rutgers 1000 took its campaign to the Web, the attitude of the undergraduates toward their littered and deteriorating campus had been almost fatalistic, as though they somehow deserved to be punished for having wound up at a lower-tier public university. Now you could hear undergraduates talking over coffee at the student union about the possibility of ripping up College Avenue, the noisy and traffic-choked main thoroughfare that runs through the middle of campus, and planting it with grass and trees. You could hear students asking why there was only one seminar room for the thirteen thousand undergraduates on the central campus. If nothing else, Rutgers 1000 had taught students to see that they were second-class citizens at their own school.

University Business, as its name implies, is a magazine devoted to economic and organizational issues in higher education. Palatella was especially interested in whether or not the RU1000 Web team had taught students to think of athletics versus academic spending as a zero sum game—that is, that if $100 or $200 million was going to stadium construction and athletic scholarships and coaches' salaries, it wasn't being spent on classrooms and lecture halls and theater space for student productions. Again, my answer was yes and no. Yes, in the sense that Rutgers students had learned to compare the lack of these things at the university with the lavish facilities for a tiny handful of recruited athletes in Piscataway. No, in the sense that even Rutgers 1000 didn't pretend that it was entirely a zero sum game. At a university that gave zero priority to teaching and learning, I pointed out, taking money away from big-time athletics didn't necessarily mean that a cent more would be devoted to academic purposes. I mentioned the University of Nebraska, which had without apology fired tenured professors at a time when coaches were getting substantial raises.

When the *University Business* article appeared, it focused on the RU1000 Web site as a new mode of student activism. Early on, Palatella had asked me about the authors of certain pages on the site. In fact, the Web elves' collaboration had been so seamless and continuous over the years that it was now impossible to identify any individual hand. To me, I said, the site resembled a medieval cathedral, built by nameless workers—some straining to pull a massive building block up a hill with ropes, others carving a gargoyle for the lintel or croft—whose very anonymity was meant as a gift of their devotion. In that sense, I said, the Web site stood in symbolic opposition to the fleeting celebrity now and then bestowed for a moment or two on some football or basketball player by Div I A sports. Palatella liked the analogy, and he used it in his article. I still like it myself. In an age of flickering images and momentary celebrity, it's cheering to recall that the RU1000 Web team had been able to construct, in the paradoxical irreality of cyberspace, a monument to enduring intellectual values.

The Coca-Cola University

The RU1000 Web team scored a signal success with its Slum Classroom Contest. Rutgers continued to have slum classrooms—most of them were still in a state of advanced deterioration—but at least the toilet smells were gone. More important, undergraduates were brought to see that the tens of millions of dollars lavished on Big East sports showed that the vast majority of students at Rutgers had become second-class citizens at their own university. As long as football and basketball players were getting million-dollar locker rooms while students went to class in decaying surroundings, Rutgers 1000 would have a point of moral leverage against the Lawrence administration, the Scarlet R boosters on the board of governors, and the new athletic director hired in 1998, Robert E. Mulcahy III.

Mulcahy came to Rutgers from the "Meadowlands"—a shorthand name for the New Jersey Sports and Exposition Authority—where, fairly or unfairly, he was increasingly being spoken about as a reckless spender of the taxpayers' money. The sports complex was hemorrhaging money. Routinely mentioned in newspapers as "the failing Meadowlands," it plainly needed new management. But Mulcahy, a skilled and genial backslapper, was protected by a dense network of personal relationships with New Jersey politicians. It occurred to Christine Todd Whitman, New Jersey's governor, that Mulcahy might be detached from the Meadowlands by giving him a soft landing as

Rutgers's athletic director. At first, Francis Lawrence, who'd wanted to name his own A.D., balked at her choice. He meant, he told reporters, to choose his own A.D. New Jersey politicians, many of whom had been Mulcahy's guests at the Meadowlands, were perplexed. Either the Rutgers president was brave, Senate minority leader Richard Codey was quoted as saying, "or he's just stupid." After a second conversation with Governor Whitman, the president decided not to be stupid.

When Mulcahy arrived at Rutgers, he brought his Meadowlands spending ways with him. Virtually his first move as athletic director was to solicit funds from New Jersey legislators to upgrade the offices of himself, his staff, and his coaches. Then he set out to get more. "Rutgers Athletics Getting $7.5 Million for Expansion," reported Sarah Greenblatt in the *Home News Tribune.* Mulcahy would spend this money on the three-story Hale Center, part of the Rutgers football stadium complex, to accommodate "football locker rooms, a weight room, training facilities, meeting rooms, classrooms, administrative and medical offices, and a multipurpose room that overlooks the stadium."

A story in *Rutgers Magazine* celebrated the arrival of the Mulcahy era of legislative largesse. A staff writer, Bill Glovin, followed the new athletic director around during his first days on campus, listening as Mulcahy chatted with the director of the Scarlet R boosters club, Brian Crockett. Within minutes, Glovin reported, the men were "exchanging thoughts on all kinds of issues: seating arrangements for donors at football games, potential corporate sponsors, . . . new marketing strategies." When Crockett told Mulcahy that the men's basketball team had stayed at a Marriot in Manhattan during the Big East Tournament, Mulcahy suggested "moving to the more upscale Plaza Hotel on Central Park South in 1999. 'I want us to do everything first class,' he says. 'If we don't have the money, I'll get it.'" First class, Glovin emphasized, was "an important concept to Mulcahy. Almost from scratch, he turned the Meadowlands Sports Complex into a first-class facility. . . . Now he's determined to do the same for Rutgers athletics."

Other journalists were more skeptical about the cost-benefit ratio involved in Mulcahy's conception of a first-class, Plaza Hotel–type sports program. In the *Newark Star-Ledger,* columnist Fran Wood pointed out the risk involved in giving the ex-Meadowlands chief broad access to an effectively bottomless supply of public money. At Rutgers, she wrote, Mr. Mulcahy had opted "for the aggressive route: spend big bucks on a top coach, put money into the program. Like many Scarlet Knights fans, he presumably envisions first a winning team and then a happy trickle-down effect: more people in the stadium, a higher profile, some TV dollars. . . . Up front, of course, this plan will cost. Never mind that $500,000, probably the minimum he will have to pay his top coach, is two and a half times what our governor makes and more than three times what we pay the chief justice of our Supreme Court. Never mind that, with perks, a $500,000 base is really closer to $700,000. It's still only the tip of the iceberg."

With the arrival of Mulcahy's new football coach, a man named Greg Schiano, Fran Wood's estimates turned out to be right on target. Schiano would not only be paid $500,000 a year but would be surrounded on every side by an upsurge in spending that transformed Mulcahy's Piscataway complex into a miniature version of the Meadowlands. In a *Star-Ledger* story— "Rutgers: Price Tag for Athletics Has Reached $30 million a year"—Matthew Futterman gave some of the details: "It is an era that comes with high-priced coaches such as Schiano, irrigated practice fields, a new weight-training center, a larger academic support staff, a slick new office complex, and even the occasional free cap to spread the word that the sports program is on the move. It is also an era with a price tag of nearly $30 million per year. The $30 million for 2001–2 comes from student fees, money a handful of teams brings in, support from booster clubs, and a growing chunk the university pays so the athletic department can balance its budget. On top of that, the state has given the athletic program a total of $12.5 million during the past four years to renovate facilities."

With Mulcahy pouring $30 million a year into the athletic program, the Rutgers 1000 students thought they'd found the issue that might at last get Rutgers out of Div IA. Since several belonged to CAP, the College Avenue Players, they decided to focus on the impoverished condition of undergraduate theater on the Rutgers campus. Every year CAP struggled to put on first-rate productions of everything from Shakespeare to Tennessee Williams. But the odds against them were tremendous, for there is no student theater on the Rutgers College campus. Not a small experimental theater like the Loeb at Harvard. Not an intimate two-hundred-seat theater like the Murray-Dodge at Princeton. Quite simply, nothing at all. Instead, a talented group of young people are compelled to put on all their shows in Scott 105, a dismal lecture hall with harsh lighting, cheap carpeting, deteriorating seats, and, worst of all, miserable acoustics. I myself had taught large classes in Scott 105, and I found that even for a single lecturer equipped with a good microphone, it was difficult to penetrate the dreary space. Performing a play there must have been all but impossible.

Just a portion of the $30 million Mulcahy was spending annually on athletics would give the College Avenue Players and similar groups a theater that would serve Rutgers—actors, directors, students working on lighting and set design, audiences—for a century. This time, though, the RU1000 Web team wasn't going to just point to the enormous outlay on Big East athletics. They had a better plan. "The alumni got Milton Friedman to endorse RU1000," they reminded me. "We want to do the same thing, except with an actor who graduated from Rutgers. Someone who could help make us make the plea for decent theater facilities instead of more athletics spending." Okay, I said, who do you have in mind? "James Gandolfini," they told me. "He's in a TV series called *The Sopranos,* about a New Jersey Mafia family." Remember, I cautioned them, you can never tell how someone in Gandolfini's position is going to react. He might want to stay out of anything controversial. Gandolfini, they assured me, would speak up. "He graduated from Mason Gross," said one CAP member, referring to Rutgers's highly selective school of the arts. "He's got to be loyal to the cause of theater at Rutgers. It's impossible that he'd side with a huge waste on athletics when students don't have a theater. Besides, he's not scared of controversy. *The Sopranos* is controversial. That's one of the reasons it has high ratings." Well, I conceded, an endorsement from Gandolfini won't get you a student theater in the short term, but it might put some useful public pressure on Lawrence and Mulcahy.

So the students drafted a letter to James Gandolfini, explaining about CAP and Rutgers 1000 and the huge expenditure on athletics. The day after they composed the draft, I ran into a CAP member on campus. When was the letter going in the mail? "It's not," he said glumly. Why? I asked him. It sounded like a great idea. It's got to be worth a try. "No, it isn't," he said. He pulled out of his notebook an AP story that had just appeared in the *Home News Tribune* about a huge billboard that the Rutgers Athletics Department had leased on the road to Miami International Airport in Florida. Looking at the accompanying photo, I saw why the CAP student was downcast. It showed the billboard, with a giant picture of James Gandolfini, identified as a "Rutgers Alumnus," at one end, a giant picture of football coach Schiano at the other, and "SEASON'S GREETINGS FROM RUTGERS FOOTBALL" in enormous letters in the middle. Mulcahy had checkmated the students' move before they even made it. Focusing on his history as a spender of public money, they'd failed to realize that Mulcahy's access to marketing machinery would give him resources they'd never have.

Marketing was one of the reasons Mulcahy had been hired. Professional sports as played at the Meadowlands—the Giants and Jets in NFL football, the Nets in the NBA, the New Jersey Devils in the NHL—were no longer essentially different from the money sports as played at Rutgers's "peer institutions" in the Big East and elsewhere—Miami, Ohio State, Tennessee, Virginia Tech. New Jersey politicians and Rutgers sports boosters alike were convinced that "Bob" Mulcahy would bring much-needed promotional savvy to the Rutgers athletics operation, which had floundered under its previous athletic director, an aging golf coach named Fred Gruninger. "If you think of the A.D.'s job only as an A.D.'s job," Michael Rowe, president of the New Jersey Nets and a personal friend of Mulcahy's, told the *New York Times,* "maybe it's a step down. But if you want to raise funds, work with legislators, and establish Rutgers as a premier entertainment option with sports as a basis, Bob can do it."

Rowe's phrase—"*Rutgers as a premier entertainment option*"—became a sardonic battle cry among the RU1000 students, the clearest expression they ever found for everything we were up against. For the whole struggle against Div IA really boiled down, as one of them said to me, to the penetration of the university by commercial forces using professionalized college sports as the weak point in its defenses. Rowe's phrase came to mind when the *Daily Targum* devoted a story to a Rutgers faculty member in the Communications Department who moonlighted as a basketball announcer. He was, reported the *Targum,* celebrated for the way he incited the crowd to chant "ALWAYS RUTGERS, ALWAYS COCA-COLA" during timeouts. This professor was "more than just a voice," declared the *Targum* reporters. "He embodies the spirit of the university." "We've got to do something," said one of the RU1000 steering committee kids, bursting into my office with a copy of the *Targum.* I tried to calm him down. "The faculty is taking care of this," I told him. Ever since the story appeared my phone had been ringing, and I already knew that FAR, the faculty organization opposing Francis Lawrence, was sending a delegation to the communications professor to ask him to stop chanting about Rutgers and Coca-Cola, for the dignity of the school if not for his own. "You can tell the other students that it's going to stop," I assured him.

It didn't stop. When I ran into a FAR member a few days later, he was glum. "What happened?" I asked. "He didn't see anything wrong with it," my colleague told me. "He told us, 'It's only a sales pitch. It's in the contract.'" This, it turned out, was true. Chanting the slogan at games, specifically linking the brand name with the university, was part of a larger deal the Lawrence administration had signed with Coca-Cola. All Rutgers had to do was give Coca-Cola exclusive rights to have its product advertised at university sporting events and sold in campus vending machines, and Coca-Cola would display the Scarlet Knight athletics mascot, newly designed by a firm specializing in commercial logos, on all the Coke machines around campus. "Now we've really got to do something," the RU1000 students said, when I told them the news.

They did do something. The semester before, an energetic undergraduate named Rob Stevens had started SAUCE—Students Against University Commercialization and Exploitation—to protest, among other things, the

"That spring, RU1000 and SAUCE joined forces to organize marches and demonstrations outside Old Queen's." Photo: RU1000 Archives.

sale of the university's name to Coca-Cola. Now they saw that, as one of the RU1000 students said to me, "We're up against the same enemy." That spring, RU1000 and SAUCE joined forces to organize marches and demonstrations outside Old Queen's, the handsome old building housing the Rutgers administration. Everywhere you turned, colorful stickers mysteriously appeared on campus Coke machines denouncing the sale of the university's name to a soft drink brand. But the campaign's most effective weapon was a striking T-shirt in Rutgers red. On the back, in the trademark retro-looking Coke script, "Always Rutgers, Always Coca-Cola." On the front, in tastefully small print, the simple phrase, "Rutgers, a Wholly Owned Subsidiary of the Coca-Cola Corporation." With the onset of warmer weather, hundreds of these T-shirts blossomed all over campus, on view everywhere as thousands of students changed classes. There was a story about the campaign in the *Chronicle of Higher Education.* With the end of the semester, the Lawrence administration decided to cancel its contract with Coca-Cola.

It was the Coca-Cola campaign, I think, that did most to teach us that the issue of Div IA sports was inseparable from the more general issue of university commercialization. In recent years, this issue has come to be a good deal discussed. Yet, typically, the focus has been on the "corporate university"—the intrusion of corporate marketing, along with a corporate model of organization, into an institution whose essential form and values go back to the early Middle Ages. Here, for instance, is former Harvard president Derek Bok in *Universities in the Marketplace,* describing the myriad influences at work to create the modern corporate university: "Apparel firms offered money to have colleges place the corporate logo on their athletic uniforms or, conversely, to put the university's name on caps and sweatshirts sold to the public. Faculty members began to bear such titles as Yahoo Professor of Computer Science or K-Mart Professor of Marketing. . . . One enterprising university even succeeded in finding advertisers willing to pay for the right to place their signs above the urinals in its men's rooms."

Yet Harvard and private schools like it, blessed with substantial endowments and a long tradition of academic distinction, are not the best places to look for signs of commercial penetration. For various reasons, public institutions have proved to be most vulnerable to the contagion of corporate marketing. Consider, for instance, the case of Boise State University in Idaho. Boise State's basketball games were once played in an arena called the Pavilion. Then the university was approached by representatives of Taco Bell, the national fast-food chain. All Boise State had to do was agree to rename the Pavilion the "Taco Bell Arena," and the company would make a sizeable contribution to university coffers. It was a win-win proposition: Taco Bell would write off the contribution as an advertising expense, and Boise State would have money it would never otherwise see.

Faced with so blatant a move to commercialize their university, professors at Boise State mounted a short-lived protest. After some debate, the faculty senate was persuaded to pass a resolution opposing the Taco Bell deal. Boise State's president struck back immediately. The faculty, he declared, were harming their own university. If Boise State wasn't permitted to sell the name of the Pavilion to Taco Bell, other corporate donors might be discouraged from making similar offers. An anthropology professor named Robert McCarl answered the president in the student newspaper, "If students, faculty, and community members cannot protest a significant decision like this without 'harming the university' . . . then Boise State is well on its way to becoming a corporate-controlled university." The very purpose of a university, Professor McCarl declared, "is to open up debate and create discourse about the issues of the day," placing them in a "wider intellectual and cultural context." Then, having flickered for a moment, the faculty protest at Boise State died out.

Stories like this made it clear that Div IA athletics had at least one peculiar virtue: they put a spotlight on the otherwise invisible forces working to transform American universities into marketing vehicles. Until relatively recently, universities had been exempt from such commercial intrusions. The universities' emphasis on the life of mind and the pursuit of truth for its own sake had always before made marketing, advertising, and commerce seem distinctly out of place within their precincts. That's why, until very recently, commercialized college sports could still seem somewhat anomalous. This is what gives a satiric edge, for instance, to a column by Will Leitch in the college magazine *U*. "When we look through our national heritage," observes Leitch with deadpan irony, "it's impossible to ignore the storied heritage of the Insight.com Bowl or the Carquest Bowl. Don't forget the Tostitos Fiesta Bowl, or the dearly departed Poulon Weed Eater Bowl. And where would we be without the AFLAC Trivia Question, the McDonald's Game Break, or the Chevrolet Players of the Week? . . . And it's not just the North Carolinas and the Michigans, either. Small schools like Valparaiso U. are equally peppered with logos."

Over nearly a decade of struggle, Rutgers 1000 would come to understand that the threat of Div IA sports to academic values went far beyond athletics. The real enemy was commercialization: the erosion and then finally the extinction of the university as the last remaining social space in which learning—that is, ideas and knowledge as a sphere of human consciousness valuable in itself, one providing an essential perspective on the wider world of practical concerns—had been able to hold out against marketing and advertising forces. In his brilliant novel *Infinite Jest*, David Foster Wallace describes an America completely transformed by advertising and consumption into what Wallace calls "an entertainment market of sofas and eyes." The university, from its origins in the Middle Ages to the middle of the twentieth century, had stood apart from that world, preserving what Ann Matthews in her book *Bright College Years* calls a core of transcendental values.

At the outset, it seemed a bit melodramatic to regard Scarlet R or the Touchdown Club as the local representatives of a TV-revenue-driven behemoth existing solely to establish *Infinite Jest*'s vast entertainment market of sofas and eyes. How could anyone take seriously the notion of genial "Bob" Mulcahy as an emanation of an abstract and impersonal system of market relations? Yet hadn't a close friend assured people in New Jersey that "if you want to . . . establish Rutgers as a premier entertainment option with sports as a basis, Bob can do it"? We already knew in an abstract sense that the stakes involved in Div IA sports and university commercialization were high. Before long, however, we would learn in a direct way how high the stakes really were, and how reasonable it was, after all, to regard "Bob" Mulcahy as the agent of an alien culture of marketing and consumption.

We first began to suspect that we were confronting the juggernaut of corporate marketing when Sean Murphy, a member of the RU1000 steering committee, received an unexpected invitation to visit Mulcahy in his athletics empire across the river in Piscataway. Sean was co-editor of the *Rutgers Review*, a student publication then known as a staunchly independent voice of undergraduate opinion. A week earlier, he'd written a long piece about the danger posed by Big East athletics to academic and intellectual values at Rutgers. Sean was at that time studying the history of socialist theories, and he'd absorbed something of their perspective on a world driven purely by commercial forces. In a *Review* article, he'd remarked that Div IA athletics were only the spearhead of a more general assault on the university as the last remaining sanctuary from consumerist ideology. Then one morning his phone rang. It was the athletic director, inviting him over to the Louis Brown Athletic Center for a chat.

Rutgers University is made up of four widely separated colleges. Students as well as faculty normally use a system of shuttle buses to travel between their campuses. Sean first sensed that he was no longer dealing with ordinary second-class Rutgers reality when, a day before his meeting with Mulcahy, the Athletics Department called to say that a car and driver were being sent for him. Where would he like to be picked up? Sean did his best to decline the ride. He knew exactly where the Louis Brown Center was. He'd taken a campus bus right by it a million times. No, said the person at the other end of the line, Mr. Mulcahy insists on sending a car and driver. But why? Sean protested. "Because," said the voice at the other end of the line, "Mr. Mulcahy likes to do things first-class."

Afterward, Sean dropped by my office. "What was it like?" I asked. "Well," said Sean, "he talked a lot about the corporate boards he's served on, and all the politicians he knows in Trenton. Whenever I tried to talk to him about Rutgers athletics, he'd turn the conversation to the Meadowlands." I saw immediately what must have happened. Sean was one of the few freshman I'd met who had actually read Virgil's *Aeneid* in Latin. He knew a great deal about European history and international relations. But he knew nothing and cared less about professional sports. So all Mulcahy's talk about coaches like Bill Parcells and the NBA and NFL stars he knew personally was utterly wasted on Sean, who hadn't recognized their names. Their whole conversation had been a comedy of mutual incomprehension.

When he'd finished, I asked, anything else? "Yes," said Sean. "He asked three times if Rutgers 1000 had heard anything from Collegiate Licensing. He kept smiling this little smile when he said it." Sean looked at me, puzzled. "What's Collegiate Licensing?" I had no idea at the time, but we were shortly to find out. To understand what happened next, you need to know that at the very beginning of the campaign, a sportswriter named Jerry Izenberg had attacked Rutgers 1000 in what the students considered abusive terms. The Web team responded by creating a page announcing the "Herbie Husker Award," to be given each month to the New Jersey sportswriter who had "contributed most to helping Rutgers resemble the University of Nebraska." The page was illustrated with a cartoon drawing of Herbie Husker, Nebraska's mascot: a farmer in overalls, mud boots, and cowboy hat, with an ear of corn sticking out of one pocket, a football cradled under one arm, and a hand raised with an index finger in the "we're number one" gesture. Izenberg was the first winner of the award.

The Web team found the Herbie Husker cartoon on a Nebraska booster page. Since the booster site not only encouraged visitors to download the image but gave instructions for turning it into a computer screen saver, the students assumed that it was in the public domain. They were to find out differently. The campaign received in its mailbox one day a registered letter from the Collegiate Licensing Company, bearing the ominous heading "Unauthorized Use of University Trademarks." It bore the signature of Bruce B. Siegel, vice president and general counsel of CLC. "The Collegiate Licensing Company (CLC)," wrote Mr. Siegel, "is the authorized licensing representative of the University of Nebraska." His company, he explained, represented Nebraska in connection with "the licensing, protection and enforcement of names (including acronyms), logos, slogans, and other proprietary rights." The unauthorized use of the Herbie Husker cartoon on the RU1000 Web site, he said, "constitutes trademark infringement and unfair competition."

The students held a meeting, which they asked me to attend. "Now we know who we're really fighting," I remember Chris Cram saying, once the letter had been read aloud to the group. "What do you want to do?" I asked them. There was a long discussion. Most of the students wanted to ignore the letter and leave Herbie Husker up. This wasn't simply youthful bravado. Their argument was that there were, logically, only two possibilities. Either Collegiate Licensing would send a few more threatening letters and then drop the issue, seeing that they were getting nowhere, or they'd sue. In that case, the students thought, the University of Nebraska, if only out of a sense of institutional self-respect, would have to call a halt to CLC's harassment of Rutgers 1000. "Nebraska's a university," I remember one student saying, "not a Jiffy Lube franchise. They can't afford to have some licensing company sue a student anti-sports-corruption group over property rights and trademark infringement. They'd be proving our point about commercialized sports."

I wasn't so sure. Remember, I told the students, that outfits like CLC don't know how to think in anything but commercial terms. They're not likely to see this as a free speech issue. Wouldn't it be simpler for the campaign to write a letter explaining why it doesn't think that CLC's objections apply to its use of Herbie Husker? They reluctantly agreed. "Your letter makes clear," RU1000 responded to Mr. Siegel, "that the interest of the University of Nebraska in its various 'trademarks, service marks, trade names, designs, logos, seals and symbols' is purely commercial—concerned, as your own letter puts it, with 'products, promotions, and advertising.' Rutgers 1000, however, has no commercial purpose or interest. Indeed, the whole purpose of the campaign is to *prevent* Rutgers from becoming involved in commercialized college sports. So the relevance of 'unfair competition' as raised in your letter is not at all evident to us." If CLC could provide a convincing argument that use of Herbie Husker on a site protesting commercialized Div IA sports constituted "unfair competition," the letter concluded, the campaign would be happy to take him down.

The answer from Collegiate Licensing was peremptory. Either Herbie Husker came down or they'd sue. "Our legal position," CLC wrote, "based upon federal and state trademark laws . . . is that Herbie Husker functions as a legally protected trademark of the University of Nebraska." At this point, I decided to call the University of Nebraska directly, to see if anyone would be willing to talk about giving Rutgers 1000 permission to use the Herbie cartoon satirically in what most people would regard as a constitutionally protected debate about commercialized college sports. I wound up talking to a pleasant fellow named Chris Bahl, a marketing person in the Athletics Department. I did my best to make him see that the University of Nebraska could come out looking very bad on this issue. It was one thing to have a huge football marketing operation and to hire outfits like CLC to write threatening letters. It was quite another for a university, supposedly dedicated to the value of vigorous debate, to use trademark legalisms to try to suppress any hint that Nebraska might be involved in commercialized college sports.

Mr. Bahl said he was sympathetic, but there was nothing he could do. Collegiate Licensing represented Nebraska on marketing, trademarks, and commercial competition, and they'd made up their minds to sue. That ended the episode. The Web team kept the image on its site, changing the name to the Hubie Cornpone Award. (It still went to the New Jersey sportswriter who had done most that month to help Rutgers resemble the University of Nebraska. That, apparently, didn't constitute trademark infringement.) We heard nothing more from Collegiate Licensing. But, interestingly enough, I'd learned during my conversation with Chris Bahl that Nebraska and CLC had been notified about the Herbie Husker Award by someone in the Rutgers Athletics Department. This was puzzling. It didn't seem likely that the average Scarlet R booster knew enough about trademark law to have alerted Nebraska. Notice must have been sent by someone thoroughly at home in the world of marketing and promotion. Then I remembered Sean's account of Mulcahy's having asked him, three separate times, whether Rutgers 1000 had "heard anything from Collegiate Licensing." A light dawned.

The most useful consequence of the Collegiate Licensing episode was that Rutgers 1000 learned a great deal about the commercialization of college sports. We'd known, of course, about the multibillion-dollar contracts paid by TV networks to televise spectacles like "March Madness." We knew about corporate sponsorship of bowl games. Still, the notion of Div IA sports as a commercial juggernaut hadn't fully come home to us until, wanting to know more about our antagonist in the Herbie Husker affair, the Web team undertook a bit of research on Collegiate Licensing. CLC wasn't, they discovered, just some kind of trademark enforcement operation. It was a multimillion-dollar marketing enterprise. In the campaign's files, for instance, choosing virtually at random from its Collegiate Licensing folder, I found an Associated Press story about CLC's pride in having placed in Wendy's hamburger outlets, on behalf of the University of Tennessee, forty thousand Smoky mascot dolls wearing Lady Vols championship T-shirts. Production of Lady Vols merchandise, a CLS spokesman happily announced, had "doubled, tripled, maybe even quadrupled" in the previous year.

In one advertising industry publication, a story about Collegiate Licensing reported that, owing to CLC's efforts, "65 per cent of Division I-A football teams wore a decal of the NCAA Football program on their helmets, authenticating the brand through television broadcasts of college football action." "Collegiate properties," the president of CLC is quoted as saying, "compete against a lot of different entities—entertainment licensors, the pro leagues, branded companies and more." Collegiate Licensing's strategy had therefore been to link Div IA schools together as a single identifiable brand. "When you look at Disney or professional sports property," the CLC president goes on, "you see a very organized, orchestrated approach, where there is singular control, which makes it easier to go out and win a lot of battles. I think the collegiate market sees that it really has to get its act together and get organized to do that on a national basis." No wonder somebody like Mulcahy's friend Michael Rowe had been able to talk with a straight face about Rutgers as a premier entertainment option.

It soon became clear just how hand-in-glove Mulcahy's professionalized sports program was with the goals and aspirations of the Collegiate Licensing Company. A *Targum* story—"RU Acquires Marketing Savvy"—revealed the great strides made by Mulcahy and his associate athletic director for marketing, Kevin MacConnell, in creating brand recognition for Rutgers sports. The central showpiece was a children's book entitled *Hello, Scarlet Knight,* put out by a company that features sports mascots as story characters. "Children love mascots," the *Targum* quoted Aimee Aryal, one of the originators of the series, as saying. "They watch the game, but they're really there to see the mascot. The book makes the mascot come alive. It's just like characters in Mickey Mouse to kids. You can read about the mascot anytime." At the time she spoke to the *Targum* reporters, the Mascot series was being marketed at forty Div IA schools.

As it happened, I'd read a *Wall Street Journal* story, just before I came across this *Targum* piece, about advertising campaigns that were now being directed at children in the two-to-five-year-old age group. This was a revolution in advertising, which had previously always been directed at groups with disposable income. It seemed obvious why toddlers had so far been bypassed. Since most two-year-olds are more preoccupied with potty training than shopping at Wal-Mart, it wasn't immediately obvious what marketing advantage could be gained by spending advertising money on them. The *Wall Street Journal* story made it all clear. Research had shown that it's possible to "imprint" extremely young children with brand loyalty by bombarding them with logos and jingles and slogans so that, when they do grow up and have disposable income, they'll buy your products.

The *Wall Street Journal* story left me feeling very pessimistic. With the targeting of preschoolers, it seemed to me, we really had entered the age of cradle-to-grave consumerism. The soulless TV-and-advertising world portrayed in David Foster Wallace's *Infinite Jest* was seeming less and less like parodic exaggeration. This was exactly the marketing strategy reported in the *Targum* story about *Hello, Scarlet Knight.* The Rutgers Athletics Department, it turned out, had already purchased thirteen hundred copies to be distributed in New Jersey elementary schools. Marketing director Kevin MacConnell explained why. "In Nebraska," he told the *Targum,* "you just grow up thinking Nebraska football." Then he added, in a telling phrase, "You don't know any better." "It may be the same way in Michigan or Ohio," he went on. "But here it's not." The Rutgers marketing campaign, confided MacConnell, was even going after newborns. The Athletics Department was currently talking to hospitals about presenting the parents of newborn babies with a tiny Scarlet Knight T-shirt or bib. "We're trying to get everyone," he said, "from day one to 18."

Strangely enough, Mulcahy's marketing campaign helped me understand a paradox: why Rutgers 1000 at that point still had enlisted relatively few students. By now, the RU1000 Alumni Council had gained several hundred members. The RU1000 Faculty Council had added to its original thirty-seven members some two hundred more. But the student campaign, which had seen two undergraduate generations come and go, had enrolled fewer than 175 names. Although Rutgers 1000 explicitly opposed the commercialization of the university, it simply hadn't been possible to get across to Rutgers undergraduates that market ploys like mascot books were doing serious damage to the academic and intellectual values that Rutgers had represented for more than two centuries. The *Hello, Scarlet Knight* story explained why. The students now arriving on campus every September had grown up wholly inside a TV-and-advertising society. Their outlook had been determined by precisely the cradle-to-grave consumerism that outfits like the CLC were using universities to promote. The most recent generation of Rutgers students, to use Kevin MacConnell's telling phrase, "didn't know any better." That was why the *Targum* story about Rutgers athletics and mascot books had been so laudatory, its headline so impressed by Mulcahy and MacConnell's "marketing savvy." This is why the *Targum* reporters in the story about "Always Rutgers, Always Coca-Cola" could say—and believe—that the slogan-chanting communications professor embodied "the spirit of the university."

In a completely unforeseen way, however, it turned out to be precisely Mulcahy's obsession with marketing and promotion that would give a substantial boost to Rutgers 1000 student membership. In the spring of 2000, Coach Vivian Stringer's women's basketball team was making its way up the competitive ladder toward the Final Four of the NCAA's March tournament. As they advanced, *Targum* sportswriters wrote stories lamenting the lack of student support for Stringer's players. Finally, the sports editor himself, driven to extremes by the lukewarm response, wrote a column pleading with Rutgers undergraduates to hold rallies and go out to the airport to see Coach Stringer and her team off with pep bands, cheerleaders, chants— whatever mass frenzy it took to make Rutgers look good when they got on nationwide TV.

For years, the RU1000 students had been spotlighting the "March Madness" spectacle as an especially egregious example of what commercialized college sports were doing to universities. Having "student athletes" running back and forth on the TV screen between commercials, they argued, did no genuine honor to the institutions of higher learning whose names were on their jerseys. Any school that did this was simply letting its name be used to market the products of corporate advertising on TV: Pizza Hut, Pennzoil, Gillette, General Motors, Anheuser-Busch, Holiday Inn, Intel, Pepsi. The NCAA tournament was simply a more flagrant version of the Boise State University–Taco Bell deal. Now it was being promoted by network hype as a venerable college sports tradition. There was nothing Rutgers students could do to stop this. But, the question was, why should they celebrate seeing their university's name being used to increase sales at Pizza Hut?

So I was moved to write a *Targum* op-ed in response to the sports editor's plea for student support. I was careful to put my main point in purely hypothetical terms. *If* I were a Rutgers undergraduate, I wrote, I wouldn't be supporting Stringer's team because I wouldn't see her players as having any connection to me as a student. Given the current state of Div IA sports, it would be perfectly reasonable to view them as semiprofessional athletes brought to my university purely on the basis of physical skills. As a faculty member, I wrote, "I don't like it that Rutgers wastes $2.7 million a year on 'scholarships' that should be going to top New Jersey students." But I also made it clear that I saw none of this as the fault of the players themselves. "I don't hold any of this against the women," I ended by saying. "They're pawns in a game, a much bigger and sleazier game than basketball."

It was more than "Bob" Mulcahy could stand. He counterattacked in a *Targum* opinion column celebrating Stringer's players as "a group of students who have brought great distinction and honor to the university." He said that Rutgers deserved to be on the same level athletically as Duke, Virginia, and Stanford, "to name just a few." He said that Professor Dowling had no business making critical remarks about "his employer's basketball team." He strongly objected to my "tired rantings" and my characterization of the NCAA's March tournament as a TV-revenue-driven extravaganza. Rutgers, he triumphantly announced, more or less missing the whole point, "did not profit financially from the team's participation in the Final Four, and the NCAA underwrote all travel costs." He argued that Rutgers had, however, profited immensely "through the volume of positive exposure and excitement generated by the team's efforts."

I wasn't inclined to take Mulcahy's attack personally. We'd learned some time before in Rutgers 1000 that our real opponent was the abstract system of market relations that enmeshed universities in marketing extravaganzas like "March Madness." Vivian Stringer and her players weren't responsible for the TV-and-advertising exploitation of Rutgers's name. They simply didn't know any better. For all his intemperance, I really did think that Mulcahy was probably sincere in thinking that "March Madness" was a great thing for Rutgers, and that Stringer's players were just ordinary students who happened to have certain specialized athletic skills. In his own way, he, too, simply didn't know any better.

The Rutgers 1000 students disagreed. "Do you realize," one said to me, "that he used the 'What About Duke?' argument and the 'Everybody Knows

O. J.' argument against you? You'd think that after five years he'd realize that even the boosters don't take those seriously now." They wanted me to respond in another *Targum* op-ed. I tried to calm them down. I'd had my say, I told them, and Mulcahy had had his. It was obvious that we were talking past each other. Besides, I pointed out, the on-campus RU1000 campaign had fewer than 175 members. Mulcahy probably boarded a larger group than that onto every jet that flew the Rutgers football team to away games, if you counted the pep band, the cheerleaders, the coaches, and the administrators and faculty members who went along. Maybe when Rutgers 1000 got its own jet and went "first-class," I kidded them, Mulcahy would be more disposed to listen to their arguments.

The Mulcahy controversy wouldn't die, however. Not long after this, the new editor of the *Rutgers Review,* Josh Saltzman, showed up in my office. If I'd take the time to respond at length to a series of tough questions, Saltzman promised, he'd make RU1000's opposition to Mulcahy and the Big East the cover story in the next *Review.* After a bit of discussion, I agreed. Saltzman's questions were tough, as promised. He'd made a point of basing them on specific arguments Mulcahy had given in his *Targum* attack on me. For all my belief in my own detachment, I found myself getting more and more emotionally involved as the interview proceeded. I suspect this might have been Saltzman's intention all along. I did try to keep making the point that Rutgers 1000 saw Div IA sports simply as a visible symptom of the underlying disease of university commercialization. Still, it wasn't hard to glimpse my private belief that men like Lawrence and Mulcahy, whatever their conscious motives might be, were nonetheless complicit in the degradation of Rutgers as a university. Young Saltzman had come looking for provocative copy. Now he had it.

The *Rutgers Review* staff, sensing that demand for the number might be high, printed an extra-large run, depositing the copies in specially marked boxes on all the Rutgers residential campuses and other locations with a high volume of student traffic. Blazoned with a banner announcing an interview with "the professor who wants Rutgers out of the Big East," the issue hit the boxes on a day when I happened to be at home preparing classes. I'd asked an RU1000 student to pick me up a couple of copies. Later that morning I got a call from her. "They're all gone," she said rather breathlessly. "I've been to the student center and the bus stops and Murray Hall, and they're all gone." I told her not to worry. The *Review,* like the *Targum,* is occasionally late in arriving from the printers, and copies don't get put in the boxes until late in the afternoon. I said I'd pick up some copies myself when I came in to teach the following day. "No," she said. "You don't understand. The *Review* is out. You can see people walking around campus reading it. There're just no copies left."

If the *Rutgers Review* staff hadn't thought to save me a copy, I wouldn't have one today. (Because of the key part it turned out to play in the RU1000 struggle, the interview is printed as an appendix at the end of this book.) What was even more remarkable was the way the copies were being handed about on campus. Students were saving them to show to friends and room-mates. Some were sending copies home to their parents. In a walk through the student union, you could hear dozens of undergraduates, at different tables, debating the merits of Big East athletics. I received more than a hundred e-mail messages from students wanting to tell me that, having always before been casually opposed to Rutgers 1000, they'd now come over to its positions. Some told stories of recruiting episodes and academic fraud of which they said they had personal knowledge. They'd considered these iso-lated instances, but now they were seeing a pattern. A member of the *Review* business staff did a follow-up survey. This particular issue, he estimated, had been read by eighteen thousand undergraduates.

The effect on Rutgers 1000 membership was dramatic. Within a few weeks the campaign found itself with hundreds of new members, with names still coming in daily. By the following September, Rutgers 1000 would be as estab-lished a student organization as the Glee Club or the *Targum* or the College Avenue Players. Some of the core group would even find themselves grow-ing nostalgic for the days when they were a tiny band of students fighting a pitched battle against the Athletics Department and the Big East conference. I did my best to console them. I'd kept a copy of Fran Wood's *Star-Ledger* column about Mulcahy's lavish spending on athletics. In it, she'd quoted a Rutgers alumnus named Barry Evenchick who said that during his own undergraduate days he'd attended football games and watched Rutgers win and lose against teams like Lehigh and Princeton. When Rutgers entered the Big East, he told Wood, "that tradition ended, and it eliminated a part of the country's football culture that was special."

Evenchick was not unfamiliar with Div IA athletics. His daughter had attended the University of Michigan, and he'd had firsthand experience of big-time college football. It was just that he didn't think it was right for Rutgers. "I can't imagine Rutgers even getting to that point," he told Wood. "It hasn't been there. It's much more like the Ivy League, a good fall day at the stadium, and fun." I read this last part aloud to the students. Don't you realize, I asked them, that before the *Review* came out, only a handful of students on campus would have had a clue what this alumnus was talking about? Now, thanks to Mulcahy's *Targum* attack, there were thousands. But

Mulcahy hadn't done that on purpose, they protested. I had to agree. Still, somebody should be given credit. The facts were clear enough. They'd been a tiny group of students without a great deal of support on campus. Then, in the spring of 2000, Rutgers 1000 had seen an explosion in student membership. The person largely responsible was Robert E. Mulcahy III. It seemed to me that the campaign owed him a lot.

Sportswriters in Wonderland

Exhilarated by the explosive growth in student membership that followed the *Rutgers Review* interview, the RU1000 students were increasingly unhappy about the perfunctory coverage the *Targum* seemed to be giving their campaign. It wasn't as if the newspaper was covering bigger stories. A folder in the campaign's files contains a week's worth of typical *Targum* stories. Some samples: "Children Learn Organic Farming" ("Organic farming is better for humans and better for the land"); "Community Addresses Domestic Violence"; "RCPC Announces RutgersFest Lineup" (hip-hop artist "DJ Elephant Man" to be featured at student event); "Asian Heritage Month Spans April, Diverse Cultures"; "Groups Aim to End Diversity Stereotypes."

Those headlines reminded me of the funniest college newspaper parody I ever read. Every year, the *Lampoon,* Harvard's venerable humor magazine, pirates an edition of the *Crimson,* Harvard's student newspaper. One year the *Lampoon* editors were inspired to publish a *Crimson* in which absolutely nothing newsworthy happened: complete coverage of, so to speak, a no-news day on campus. The lead story, with a headline in the font size usually reserved for declarations of war, screamed, EXAMS TO BEGIN ON THURSDAY: STUDENTS TO BE TESTED ON COURSEWORK. The story then gave full details: the Harvard Coop revealed that examination blue books were selling steadily. Every department queried by the *Crimson* confirmed that it was giving examinations that semester. Students taking tests would be allowed to bring pens into the room. If they preferred, they could bring pencils. Some undergraduates interviewed by the *Crimson* confessed they felt "pretty confident." Others admitted they "still had some studying to do."

Given the relentless banality of *Targum* journalism, the Rutgers 1000 students were at first convinced that the paper's policy was a conspiracy of silence, broken only when one of its sportswriters wrote an occasional column attacking the campaign. I thought they were being oversensitive. But the more closely I looked at the *Targum,* the less it looked like a newspaper at all. The students were right that, outside of sports, the *Targum* almost never reported any real university news. There was no investigative reporting. Nothing about admissions policy or the politics involved in appointments to the board of governors. No mention of ongoing controversies about cheating and plagiarism, or the validity of teaching evaluations. Nothing about bitterly contested tenure and promotion cases. In a university that purported to be an intellectual community, there was little discussion of guest lecturers or books or ideas. Nor was there any detailed account of the millions Rutgers was pouring down the drain of Div IA athletics. For that, readers had to go to outside newspapers like the *Home News Tribune* or the *Newark Star-Ledger.* Was it purely coincidental, the students asked, that in recent years the inside track for becoming editor-in-chief had so often led through the *Targum*'s sports department?

Then there was the matter of the expensive advertisements bought by the Athletics Department, including a lavish special section each fall devoted to the football team. Just how much money the Athletics Department was paying to the *Targum,* however, was impossible to determine. When queried by Rutgers 1000 about Athletics Department advertising revenues, the *Targum* responded that the figures were "unavailable." It was an odd response, we thought, for a publication that was heavily supported by student fees. To discover the real extent of the Athletics Department subsidy of the paper, you'd need a good investigative reporter asking inconvenient questions. But even if the *Targum* had been disposed to take a critical look at its own operation, investigative journalism wasn't something its reporters knew how to do. It was during that period that I remembered a distinction once made by a distinguished Rutgers English professor, Paul Fussell. Real journalism, said Fussell, is what people don't want you to publish. Everything else is publicity.

At that point, however, Rutgers 1000 took the remark as a general principle. We couldn't have known how soon, and how exactly, Fussell's axiom would come to life at Rutgers. In the meantime, the RU1000 Web team was busily researching other college newspapers to try to provide a standard of comparison for the *Targum*. They were particularly struck by the contrast in two front-page stories. Both concerned recruiting. Both were published in the same week. From the *Yale Daily News*: "Yale Narrows Search for Southern History Professor." From the *Targum*: "RU Set to Ink 7-Footer." The *Yale Daily News* story concerned the visits to New Haven and the lectures given by the two leading candidates to replace C. Vann Woodward, the legendary scholar and teacher who had almost single-handedly created the field of postbellum southern history. Quoting from an interview with a Yale professor about the effect the appointment would have on the study of history at Yale, the story concluded with detailed accounts of the two historians' lectures and their most recent scholarly works.

The corresponding *Daily Targum* story—"RU Set to Ink 7-Footer"—was written by one of the sportswriters who would later go on to become editor-in-chief of the paper. The seven-footer in question was a high school basketball player named Joshua Moore. The story reported that Moore, just then completing his senior year at St. Thomas More Academy in Oakdale, Connecticut, was holding a press conference later in the day to announce that he had signed to play for Rutgers. In a room packed with sportswriters, photographers, and TV videocams, there was an elaborate charade in which Moore, solemnly feigning indecision, passed his hand back and forth over jerseys from all the schools trying to recruit him. Then, with a wide grin, he held up the Rutgers jersey. Flashbulbs popped. Videocams whirred. The next day, the *Targum* immortalized the moment in a huge full-color photograph on the front page.

Other Div IA student newspapers, the Web team discovered, were no better. Most gave detailed coverage of football and basketball games, featured interviews with star players, or carried stories about the hiring and firing of coaches. Much space was devoted to the signing of "blue-chip" recruits. There was a lot of what the RU1000 students called bulletin-board journalism—rewrites of press releases from the central administration and notices sent out by student organizations ("RCPC Announces RutgersFest Lineup"). Otherwise, they found almost no coverage of university affairs. It didn't take much Web surfing before you discovered why: there was a vicious circle at work. The student newspaper, aware that its readers have little interest in university or intellectual affairs, gives them no coverage. But then the student body, given no reporting on academic or intellectual matters, becomes even more ignorant about its own university. Into the vacuum—where university reporting ought to exist—flow comic strips and pizza ads and Div IA athletics. This is one reason why Div IA sports become, not just for players and coaches and boosters but for most undergraduates, indistinguishable from the university itself.

To see the difference this makes to undergraduates, look again at the *Yale Daily News* story about the two professors competing to replace C. Vann Woodward. To anyone outside Yale University, this may not be gripping stuff. Still, to get a sense of how real universities exist as intellectual communities, you need to see why it was important to the readers of the *Yale Daily News.* C. Vann Woodward was an internationally known historian, one of the luminaries of Yale's highly regarded faculty. To undergraduates, the question of whether Yale would be able to recruit a historian showing promise of the same distinction bore on the classroom experience Yale students could expect in coming years. Would the Yale History Department, through strong academic appointments, remain one of the best in the nation? Would Yale history majors be taking classes and seminars from the very best minds in their discipline, or would they have to settle for mediocre teaching from second-rate faculty? At a leading university, everyone from top administrators down to newly arrived freshmen has a vital interest in the answers to such questions.

The reason the *Targum* never ran stories like the one in the *Yale Daily News,* I came to suspect, is that the university as such was unreal to its editors. Rutgers has a faculty nearly as high-powered as Yale's, and in several important areas—most notably philosophy—considerably more high-powered. Yet most Rutgers students didn't know the names of even their most distinguished professors. Nor would students ever learn those names from the pages of the *Targum.* Instead of the continuous sense of institutional history implied by the *Yale Daily News* story—of pedagogical and scholarly traditions sustained or reinvented for a new generation—the *Targum*'s view of the university was fragmented and extremely short-term. In the *Targum*'s view, Rutgers's eighteenth-century founding and long history were unreal and irrelevant compared to the contentless cycle of Div I A sports, always the same, and "different" only in the changing roster of players and coaches: preseason recruiting, the season, the possibility of postseason play. To anyone glancing through the pages of the *Targum,* it wasn't long before Rutgers as an institution of higher learning would seem as flimsy and ephemeral as the pages themselves.

To the RU1000 students, however, the problem with the *Targum* was much more concrete. With its finances underwritten to an undisclosed degree by the Athletics Department and its student journalists disproportionately sympathetic to "big-time" sports, the newspaper now seemed to them to be wholly under the spell of Div I A reality. The problem wasn't simply that the paper operated as if it were staffed exclusively by sportswriters. The problem was the notorious journalistic failing of all sportswriters: with very few exceptions, they write as fans, not as reporters. Instead of maintaining journalistic independence and critical perspective, the *Targum* seemed to have bought into the fairy tale promoted by Div I A football and basketball. Beloved by the boosters, this was the enchanting and mendacious bedtime story about "student athletes" who really and truly were authentic college students, admitted, educated, and examined on exactly the same terms as other undergraduates.

In Div I A, boosters and sportswriters depend upon this self-serving fable to keep the unbearable truth at bay. For the grim possibility always looms that the complex collegiate machinery of deceit will fail—a professor will investigate, a tutor will talk, the "escort" assigned to a visiting recruit will complain—and the magic bubble of Div I A reality will suddenly burst. When it does, the "student athletes" will stand exposed as recruited semi-professional players chosen purely on the basis of physical skills, without any genuine connection to the university as an institution of higher learning. And the university that recruits such players on such terms will stand exposed as the agent of exclusively commercial interests—a betrayer of its own core of transcendental values and a traitor to its own vital purpose of treating persons as ends in themselves, not as means to the Big East championship or the "Final Four."

Within the magic bubble of Div I A reality, where sportswriters covering teams simply do not want to hear—any more than do the boosters of the Lobo Club or Scarlet R—that the recruited athletes on the football or basketball team are not in any real sense college students, it's essential that everyone both on and off the court or field cooperate seamlessly in the game of deceit. Keeping up the charade, as we've seen, is easy enough when it involves no more than the Scarlet Knight marketing gimmicks of Robert Mulcahy or the Collegiate Licensing Company. The difficulty comes whenever the essential functions of the university—inquiry, analysis, criticism, investigation—unexpectedly come into collision with the Div I A charade. This is what happened at Rutgers in the now-celebrated case of Fraidy Reiss, a student journalist naive enough to imagine that the campus newspaper at a Div I A school might have a place for real reporting.

I was away on research leave when the Fraidy Reiss story broke. My first awareness of it came from a newspaper clipping I found in my departmental mailbox when I returned. "American investigative journalism has a new heroine this week: Fraidy Reiss," wrote Matthew Engel in the *Financial Times*, "a student at Rutgers University in New Jersey who, as part of her journalism

"American investigative journalism has a new heroine this week." Fraidy Reiss at work.
Photo: RU1000 Archives.

course work, conducted a long investigation into the perks offered by Rutgers
to persuade star athletes to join the college. Reiss got an A+ from her teacher,
but the campus newspaper—the splendidly-named *Daily Targum*—refused
to run the article. Indeed, it refused to accept it even as a paid advert, and
the university then announced that henceforth journalism students would
be obliged to conduct their investigations off-campus." It turned out that
Fraidy Reiss's course in investigative journalism, which had been discontin-
ued several years earlier, had been reinstated by the Rutgers Department of
Journalism specifically at the request of the *Targum*. Taught by Guy Baehr, a
veteran *Star-Ledger* reporter now serving as a part-time lecturer, the course
required students to choose their own topics to investigate. The stories they
produced would be submitted for publication in the *Targum*.

As it happened, I'd met the new heroine of American investigative journalism at the end of the previous term, when Fraidy Reiss interviewed me for
this very story. A nontraditional student—a thirty-year-old mother of two
children who had returned to college to major in journalism—she'd conducted a very professional interview. We talked for forty-five minutes, and

I gave her some background materials from RU1000 files. As I later found out, the copy Reiss turned in for the course had not been sensationalistic. All she'd done was locate certain sections of several communications courses ("Fundamentals of Speaking and Listening," "Public Speaking") that catered to athletes. Funded by an endowment from a former Rutgers football player, these particular sections weren't listed in the university class schedules given out to regular students. They were, in effect, hidden classes. Nor were they known for extraordinary intellectual rigor. Reiss quoted Sean Axani, a former Rutgers basketball player, as saying they were known for being "easy." But there was no full-blown Lobo-style academic scandal involved. Reiss had simply established that Rutgers, like every other Div IA school in the country, had its own means of keeping intellectually rudimentary athletes eligible—a "hideaway" curriculum, where the only prerequisite was that enrollees be heavily recruited players of football or basketball.

Yet the Fraidy Reiss story had one interesting twist. It turned out that the move to suppress her story had come not when she actually turned in her copy but when several university administrators and Athletics Department employees she'd talked to suddenly realized exactly what she was investigating. The alarm bells seem to have gone off when Reiss put in a request, under New Jersey's Open Records law, for the grades given in the four "athletes only" sections of the two communications courses. She got the grades—without, of course, student names attached—but she also triggered the series of events that would briefly make her the heroine of college journalism. For the evidence suggests that these inconvenient questions, posed by a Rutgers journalism student about "academic support" for athletes, produced a high-level panic in the Rutgers Athletics Department. Who urgently called whom will probably never be known. Nonetheless, the public record tells a revealing story. After Reiss put in her Open Records request, her teacher, Guy Baehr, was summoned into the presence of John Pavlik, chair of the Journalism Department. Baehr was told that as of next semester, students in the investigative journalism course would no longer be permitted to focus on university affairs. Rutgers University students could investigate. They just couldn't investigate Rutgers University.

Public reaction was swift. "Rutgers University has banned students in its investigative reporting course from writing about on-campus issues for class, school officials said yesterday," reported Kelly Heyboer in the *Newark Star-Ledger*. One of the reasons given for the ban, noted Heyboer, was that student reporters—that is, Fraidy Reiss—had been "pressing the administration for information for their stories." "Though university officials said the ban of on-campus investigative stories was not due to the content of the pieces produced in the course last semester," reported Heyboer, "some students said Rutgers officials are trying to silence aggressive student reporters." Fraidy Reiss had just discovered for herself Paul Fussell's axiom: real journalism is what people don't want you to publish.

At the time the Journalism Department was ordered to keep its students away from university affairs, Fraidy Reiss still hadn't turned in her copy to the *Targum*. When she did, as you've heard, the *Targum* rejected it. Even though Reiss's story had earned an A+ from Guy Baehr in her investigative journalism course, the *Targum* decided that, all things considered, it fell short of the journalistic standards on view in "Job Fair Brings Employers, Students Together" and "Children Learn Organic Farming" ("Organic farming is better for humans and better for the land"). Members of Rutgers 1000 were puzzled. Other observers, certain that the story had been suppressed on orders from the administration, were openly derisive. Over the next few weeks, the Fraidy Reiss story would get picked up by every major media outlet in the country. There were radio spots, newspaper stories, editorials, and blog commentaries. As important, Reiss's appearance with Jon Stewart on *The Daily Show* guaranteed that the state of investigative journalism at Rutgers came to the attention of a huge audience of college-age viewers. The journalistic standards of the Rutgers student newspaper had become a subject of national discussion.

In the meantime, the administration and the Athletics Department had apparently concluded that its panic over Reiss's Open Records request had been more costly than they'd been able to foresee. There were, in any case, more meetings behind closed doors. There were more hasty consultations with the Journalism Department. Finally, journalism chair John Pavlik emerged to announce that next semester's journalism students would, on second thought, be allowed to look into university affairs. "It turned out to be a lesson in freedom of the press," wrote North Jersey Media Group reporter Patricia Alex in a story—"Rutgers Calls Off the Censors"—about this latest development, "for none other than the people who run Rutgers University's journalism department. The chairman of the department said Tuesday that he is reversing his edict that on-campus topics would be off-limits to students in the investigative reporting class. The change of heart came after a squall of media coverage and objections from faculty, including professors in his own department."

The saga of Fraidy Reiss shows how the alternative reality of Div IA athletics is able to penetrate to the heart of a university to subvert its most cherished values. Still, it was a minor episode. A more sensational episode, involving investigative journalism and a celebrated Rutgers sports personal-

ity, shows even more clearly the lengths to which partisans of big-time college sports will go to make their empire of lies prevail. That story involves
Jim Valvano, once a star basketball player and later a coach at Rutgers, who
achieved nationwide fame as head basketball coach of North Carolina State
University. Building NCSU into a basketball powerhouse, Valvano led the
team to a national championship in 1983. When his coaching career ended,
he became an enormously popular sports announcer for ESPN. Then he was
diagnosed with cancer, and just before his death he gave a courageous speech
at an ESPN banquet. A tape of this speech, aired annually during "March
Madness," is watched by millions of viewers.

Every year Rutgers students and alumni hear Valvano's speech, are moved
by it, and wonder aloud on sports boards why Rutgers pays so little attention
to "Jimmy V." For here is a courageous soul who mentions his alma mater
several times in the course of an inspirational speech that famously con-
cludes, "Don't give up. Don't ever give up." Yet the Rutgers Athletics Department was oddly reticent about any association with its most celebrated
alumnus. Watching a tape of Valvano's speech, I too was mystified about
Rutgers's strange resistance to using a celebrity alumnus, especially one so
strongly identified with Div IA glory, to promote its cause. After all, "Bob"
Mulcahy hadn't hesitated for a moment to go to James Gandolfini, star of
The Sopranos, for help in promoting Rutgers athletics. Gandolfini was only
very indirectly connected to sports. Valvano, a supremely successful coach
during his life, was still vividly associated in the public mind with sports
thanks to charitable events like the Jimmy V Celebrity Golf Classic and the
Jimmy V Men's Basketball Classic. I called an old friend who follows college
basketball closely to ask about the Valvano paradox. He laughed. "Get yourself a copy of *Personal Fouls,*" he told me. "By Peter Golenbock. Then you'll
understand why your A.D. doesn't want people associating Rutgers athletics
with Valvano."

The hardback edition of *Personal Fouls* was out of print. I managed to
locate the Signet paperback at a local bookstore. A quote from a *Washington
Post* review on its cover let me see why my friend had suggested the book.
"The story of Valvano and North Carolina State," the reviewer had written,
"is the story of big time college athletics, in which money and winning are
all and virtually everything else, from academic standards to the well-being
of 'student athletes,' are nothing." The *Post* called the book "devastating." I
found *Personal Fouls* absorbing. In its pages, every Div IA scandal I'd come
to know about—Ellenberger's forged transcripts at UNM, the outbreaks of
criminality at Miami and Virginia Tech, the sex-and-recruiting stories at
Colorado—seemed to have been distilled into a single prolonged episode in

which Valvano and a booster organization called the Wolfpack Club had managed to take over, more or less openly, a major Div IA university and then, when it became necessary, the legal machinery of a state government.

Though it gives an intimate view of Div IA sports corruption, the real fascination of Golenbock's narrative lies in its portrayal of a strange moral psychology. I'd often wondered, before reading *Personal Fouls*, how coaches in top-ranked programs recruit players. There are, one learns, a number of factors at work. The secret of recruiting success, of which Valvano had a greater mastery than any other Div IA coach at the time, involves techniques that use the high school star's awareness of his own status, and that of other highly ranked players, as a lure. A coach who already has one or two college stars in his program has a magnet. He's able to tell the high schooler that he, potentially as big a star as either of them, will give them a team certain to win the next national championship. A coach who has already signed one high school star can use that commitment as a magnet to draw others. A coach who has a commitment from two high school stars has an almost irresistible power of attraction: just these two are going to make us a Top 10 team, whether you come or not. With you, we'll be top in the country.

The weakness in the recruit's bargaining position, when besieged by offers from Div IA schools, is that he has to trust a coach's promises. Valvano's way of recruiting high school All-Americans was elegant in its simplicity. He would guarantee every recruit that he would start as soon as he joined the team, or, alternatively, that he would get a certain minimum amount of playing time as a freshman, then step right into the shoes of a departing senior as soon as he graduated. There was no reason to disbelieve this. A coach does have complete control over who plays, and how much. His recruits, moreover, are high-scoring stars, wholly ready to believe that no team could possibly win with them sitting on the bench. The problem was that Valvano saw no inconsistency in making identical promises to two or three high school seniors who played the same position. If all came to NCSU, the rules of both logic and basketball meant that several, despite everything Valvano had promised, would have to wind up sitting on the bench. When that happened, players who had listened to Valvano's promises began to suspect that they'd been deceived.

Then another dimension of Valvano's personality emerged. He had, he would tell the player, unaccountably forgotten his promise that the player would be starting, or playing at least twenty or twenty-five minutes a game. Now, he was ready to live up to that promise. Then, in the next game, the player would once again find himself sitting on the bench. A prime example in *Personal Fouls* is Teviin Binns, a junior college All-American recruited by 150 schools. Valvano had promised both Binns and his parents that the recruit would see at least twenty minutes of playing time in every NCSU contest. "He was dirty," Binns told Golenbock. "That's why I didn't respect him. He would just lie to you, in your face. My junior year my father came down plenty of times to talk to V, and V would tell him—Tev is going to play." At the beginning of Binns's senior year, *Personal Fouls* reports, "Valvano told him, 'You're going to start this year, Tev. . . . I want the seniors, you and Bennie, to start this year at forward, along with Shack, Lamb, and Drum.' Why Valvano kept making these promises, not even Teviin pretends to understand, but when the 1986–87 practice season began . . . Tev was back working out with the scrubs."

Valvano's recruiting techniques led to outstanding Div IA success. Valvano had been brought to NCSU by Bruce Poulton, chancellor of the university. Poulton was also a Rutgers alumnus. With Poulton backing him in the central administration, Valvano was able to consolidate his power within the university, arranging for his own appointment as athletic director, setting up elaborate machinery to bypass ordinary admissions procedures and then, subsequently, to keep his players academically eligible. The machinery was essential because Valvano's empire was built on the purely physical talents of his players. In several cases these young men were functionally illiterate, unable to read even a newspaper or the back of a cereal box. At a marginally higher level there were players like Charles Shackleford, a mainstay of the program who didn't have the reading and writing skills to pass freshman English and who never seemed to actually attend class. Still, none of the players doubted that Shackleford would retain his eligibility. "Shack was the Man," a teammate told Golenbock. "If Shack was off the team, we were going to lose. Valvano would do that with all his star players. They would be on the team no matter what."

The machinery that kept the players eligible was called the "official readmission process." Featuring an administrative body called the Academic Review Board, it was orchestrated by Chancellor Poulton. When a basketball player had flunked out of school, Valvano would reportedly testify before the board that Poulton had signed a contract permitting him to play during the coming semester provided that the player would (1) promise to attend classes, and (2) go to study hall. Then the player would make a personal appearance, to be asked questions like, "Are you capable of working toward a degree?" and "Are you willing to get academic assistance?" "All you have to say," one of the players told Golenbock, "is 'yeah, yeah, yeah,' and they let you back in." When the interview was over, this player left the room. The board discussed his case. Then the player went back to hear the decision:

"They said, 'We're going to let you back in because you have the capability to maintain a passing record.'"

Valvano's empire would collapse, suddenly and dramatically, when *Personal Fouls* was on the eve of publication. When it did, the hidden source of Valvano's and Poulton's power would be revealed as the Wolfpack Club, the NCSU booster organization. Peter Golenbock would learn about the power of the Wolfpack Club through a bizarre marketing accident. As the book was being printed at Simon & Schuster, dust jackets were sent by way of advance advertising to bookstores across the country, including several in North Carolina. The book jacket of *Personal Fouls* carried hints that Valvano's program was something less than a model of pure college amateurism. That was enough to set off alarm bells in the Wolfpack Club. Shortly thereafter, the CEO of Simon & Schuster, as well as its corporate counsel, John Bender, received a letter from Lacy H. Thornburg, attorney general of the state of North Carolina. "We are counsel for North Carolina State University," Thornburg's letter began, "and are writing in connection with your plan to distribute *Personal Fouls* by Peter Golenbock on January 23, 1989."

The story of NCSU's attempt to suppress *Personal Fouls* is told in Golenbock's epilogue to the Signet paperback edition. Lacy Thornburg's letter to Simon & Schuster is easily summarized. If the publisher went ahead with publication of *Personal Fouls,* the state of North Carolina was prepared to sue for $50 million in damages, that being the amount of athletics contributions the Wolfpack Club stood to lose through the inconvenient truths presumed to be contained in *Personal Fouls.* The letter contained, by way of substantiation, a series of accusations that would subsequently turn out to be wildly inventive—for instance, that Golenbock, who had done considerable research in the archives of North Carolina newspapers, had "pilfered" files—and calculated half-truths, such as that Golenbock "did not have any conversations" with Valvano, who had in fact refused to return his messages. "In our opinion," concluded Mr. Thornburg, "these facts form a nucleus of facts to establish a libel claim against Mr. Golenbock, Pocket Books, and Simon & Schuster."

What happened next will seem shameful to anyone who admires the muckraking and truth-telling tradition in American publishing represented by such works as Upton Sinclair's *The Jungle* and Ida Tarbell's *History of the Standard Oil Company.* Simon & Schuster, on the advice of its counsel John Bender, backed down. The publisher canceled Golenbock's contract and released a statement saying that *Personal Fouls* would not see print because it had not met Simon & Schuster's "professional standards" as a publisher. This was a period, as Golenbock says in his epilogue to the Signet edition, in which he felt like someone caught up in an episode of *The Twilight Zone*. He'd written a book that told the truth about one "big-time" basketball program. The booster subculture of NCSU had come at him with everything it had, including the gigantic machinery of state government and its legal system. His publisher had responded by folding at the first threatening gesture.

Nonetheless, *Personal Fouls* would in fact be published. Golenbock's unexpected reversal of fortune began with an almost comic episode in which a letter from Valvano's lawyer, Arthur Kaminsky, arrived at the offices of a small publisher named Carroll & Graff. "As you may know from reading the newspapers," it began, "we represent Jim Valvano, coach of the North Carolina State basketball team." The letter went on to recount the story to date: Simon & Schuster and Pocket Books had contracted with "one Peter Golenbock" for a book on NCSU basketball, advance notice made clear that it contained "a whole host of sensational allegations," vigorous protests had been lodged by Kaminsky on behalf of Valvano and Attorney General Thornburg on behalf of NCSU, and then, "presumably in response to facts raised by us in this regard, Simon & Schuster announced last week that it would not publish *Personal Fouls*." Kaminsky made it clear that Carroll & Graff, or any other publisher unwary enough to publish the book, would be faced with similarly dire consequences.

The Div IA empire of deceit had overreached itself. In the little world of North Carolina basketball, where figures like Valvano, Poulton, and Thornburg loomed very large indeed, it was assumed that the entire nation was gripped by the drama of their attempt to block the publication of *Personal Fouls*. In the New York offices of Carroll & Graff, on the other hand, nobody had ever heard of Jimmy V or the Wolfpack Club. But Carroll & Graff had been founded by two partners who'd begun their careers at Grove Press, publishers of such controversial authors as D. H. Lawrence, Henry Miller, and William Burroughs. Thus Carroll & Graff had some familiarity with censorship, and with government attempts to suppress publications entitled to First Amendment protection. They were intrigued. They contacted Golenbock and offered to read his manuscript themselves and have it examined by their own lawyers. If it proved to present reasonable claims to truth about NCSU basketball, they'd publish the book. Their lawyers, after careful scrutiny, found nothing libelous or scandalous in the manuscript. Carroll & Graff saw no bar to publication. *Personal Fouls* was published in 1989 and eventually sold more than a hundred thousand copies in hardback before being reissued as a paperback by Signet.

It would be too much to claim that *Personal Fouls* exploded the alternative reality of Div IA athletics at North Carolina State. But Golenbock's book did end the reign of James Valvano. In North Carolina itself, the first response was an outpouring of pure, blind, unreasoning hatred for Golenbock and all his works. Then, emboldened by the truth that had come to light in *Personal Fouls,* people at NCSU who had been frightened into silence when the university was completely in the power of Valvano and the Wolfpack Club began to step forward. Several professors testified publicly that they had witnessed grade and credit manipulation by colleagues in response to pressure from Valvano and Chancellor Bruce Poulton. Hugh Fuller, the head of the "academic support" program for NCSU's athletes, reported that he had been trying for years to put a stop to the widespread cheating and fraud taking place within the tutoring program. He'd hit a stone wall when his protests reached the office of either Valvano or Poulton. Finally, in a development unanticipated even by Golenbock, ABC News reported that four of the NCSU players in Valvano's program, all major characters in the story told in *Personal Fouls,* had been involved in point-shaving schemes for which they had received unknown amounts of money from professional gamblers.

At this point, the roof began to fall in on Valvano, Poulton, and others implicated in what was emerging as a program more corrupt than even its most severe critics had suspected. The first to back down was Lacy Thornburg, whose letter had set in motion the attempt to suppress *Personal Fouls.* An editorial in the *Greensboro News and Record* wryly reported that "Attorney General Lacy Thornburg said this week that after a careful reading of the controversial book *Personal Fouls,* he concluded that N.C. State has no grounds to sue the author for libel. He could have reached the same conclusion a lot quicker by reading the First Amendment." The second to go was Bruce Poulton, who resigned from office on August 21, 1989. "The coach and his allies are mistaken in blaming their woes on *Personal Fouls,*" observed an editorial in the *Raleigh News and Observer.* "Many of the problems cited in the book," said the editorial, might have been too minor "to bring down a chancellor or an athletic director and coach. But disregard for a university's academic mission—its very foundation—is reason aplenty, and in the last eight months that disregard has been reported and documented by the *News and Observer.* . . . Memorandums from the files of the university's tutoring program have confirmed flagrant academic abuses by the basketball program. . . . Now Chancellor Poulton has resigned. It is an example Mr. Valvano should follow."

The last to go was Valvano himself. In the initial heat of controversy, he agreed to give up his position as athletic director, perhaps hoping that throwing this bit of ballast overboard would save a sinking ship. As calls for his resignation as coach grew in volume and frequency, he refused to vacate a clause in his contract that promised him a $500,000 severance payout. Ironically, the person who represented North Carolina State in the negotiations was one Andrew Vanore Jr., a member of the same attorney general's office that had originally threatened Golenbock and Simon & Schuster with a $50 million lawsuit if *Personal Fouls* was published. As the Signet edition of *Personal Fouls* was going to press, Valvano was still negotiating with NCSU for his half-million dollar parachute, and still maintaining that he had done nothing wrong. He subsequently resigned, to resurface a short time later as a color commentator for ESPN, where he would, as we've seen, be enormously popular among the large audience that watches televised basketball games.

The *Personal Fouls* episode raises two important issues. First, there is the question why no North Carolina investigative reporter had thought to look into the NCSU basketball program during the years when Valvano was recruiting and winning with functionally illiterate players, when Chancellor Poulton's Academic Review Board was granting readmission to players who had flunked out of school, and when the players themselves were taking money from professional gamblers to shave points. Once *Personal Fouls* had torn down the blackout curtains and poured sunlight into the hidden world of Div IA athletics at NCSU, the *Raleigh News and Observer* did an admirable job of tracking down widespread academic fraud. But why had no sportswriter or reporter exposed Valvano's program to the light before that moment? Years before, at UNM, I'd asked myself the same question about Lobo basketball. Once the FBI wiretap brought to light the forgery of academic transcripts, the *Albuquerque Journal* reported the sordid details of Norm Ellenberger's reign. But where were the *Journal*'s reporters before that?

The answer, I'd come to understand, is that Div IA sports are covered not by reporters but by sportswriters, who constitute a distinct subculture in American journalism. The sportswriters who covered NCSU basketball, like the *Targum* sportswriters covering Rutgers football and basketball, were dwelling as much within the magic bubble of Div IA reality as the boosters who contributed millions to North Carolina State athletics. They did not want to hear, any more than did any member of the Wolfpack Club, that big-time athletics represent an alien and destructive presence in a university. Far less did they want to hear that Valvano's program had the power to hollow out and ultimately consume an entire institution of higher learning. In the same way, the *Targum* sportswriters regarded their truest constituency not as their fellow Rutgers undergraduates but as the boosters of Scarlet R. Until a Peter Golenbock or Fraidy Reiss comes along to puncture the alternative reality of "big-time" professionalized sports, the vast majority of Div IA sportswriters are happy to do their part in sustaining the NCAA's fable of college amateurism. To recall Paul Fussell's axiom, it's writers like Golenbock and Reiss who produce journalism. Sportswriters provide publicity.

The other problem raised by the *Personal Fouls* episode concerns Jim Valvano's posthumous canonization as a saint of Div IA basketball. For Golenbock's book had no permanent impact on Div IA athletics. Today, the Wolfpack Club is back raising millions of dollars for NCSU sports—most recently, more than $45 million for a twenty-thousand-seat basketball arena—and offering million-dollar salaries to football and basketball coaches. Every March, ESPN airs Valvano's "Don't give up" speech to millions of viewers. No sportswriter or sportscaster feels compelled, by inward scruple or sense of journalistic responsibility, to mention that his was a coaching career based on rank moral cynicism and academic corruption. In the world of big-time college basketball, the magic bubble retains its improbable magic. So it is that, every March, Rutgers student sports fans are once again mystified about why their Athletics Department seems to want to forget one of its most famous alumni. "It is an insult to me as a Rutgers student," one undergraduate angrily wrote about Valvano on a booster board, "that his jersey is not hanging in the rafters of the RAC. I want to honor this great man. It's about time Rutgers does something good and honorable."

Sympathy for the Devil

The Wolfpack Club's attempt to block publication of Peter Golenbock's *Personal Fouls* brought North Carolina State into the national spotlight as an extreme case of sports booster domination. Not only were principles and procedures within the university itself debased to satisfy the boosters' demand for a winning basketball team, but North Carolina sports fans were eager to mobilize the machinery of state government to try to shield Jim Valvano's program from legitimate criticism. More commonly, however, booster influence on state universities is less visible. It's precisely in these more commonplace cases that the deeper damage done by booster dominance can be glimpsed. Consider the University of Tennessee. There, a scandal arose in the UT football program when a professor asked too many questions, and then talked to a TV journalist when she failed to get any satisfactory answers.

The professor was Linda Bensel-Meyers. As the newly appointed director of UT's writing program, she'd been reviewing course records. She found some puzzling. In freshman composition alone, for instance, she noted more than a hundred grade changes within a relatively short period. In one case, a grade had mysteriously been raised all the way from F to A. Bensel-Meyers also learned that whenever composition teachers had turned in evidence that a paper hadn't been written by the student who'd submitted it, their reports were routinely filed away without administrative action. When

Professor Bensel-Meyers correlated the names of students receiving these upward grade changes with names of players on the UT football roster, a pattern emerged. Someone or something, it seemed obvious, had been running interference for the UT players against any threat of academic ineligibility.

The Tennessee administration ignored Bensel-Meyers's repeated attempts to call attention to the irregularities. Faced with its stonewalling, she turned to Tom Farrey, a well-known ESPN investigative reporter. Bensel-Meyers had been an undergraduate at the University of Chicago. In telling the story of widespread grade changes for football players, she assumed—naively, as it turned out—that an aroused public opinion might exert a bit of moral pressure upon an unresponsive university hierarchy. In fact, it did bring about an aroused public response, but not in the way she'd expected. For Tom Farrey's ESPN story turned into a furious *cause célèbre* in the state of Tennessee. Instead of shining a light into the dark corners of sports corruption at the university, Bensel-Meyers found herself standing in the harsh glare of public criticism. Worse, she found herself standing there isolated and alone. As she told me later, she'd gotten almost no support from her fellow UT professors during her ordeal. A few were honest enough to admit privately that they were simply too frightened of Tennessee's booster subculture to speak out.

To fully grasp the grim reality of Bensel-Meyers's situation at UT, you need to listen to the voices of the boosters who attacked her. Like Peter Golenbock when he wrote about Valvano's program at North Carolina State, she received death threats and threats of personal injury. In a way, though, it's the less violent and more typical messages she got from UT boosters that seem most depressing. Professor Bensel-Meyers sent me a substantial file of these communications. "Who gives a flying fuck what these football players are doing?" asked one booster. "It fucking happens on every college campus throughout the world. What makes your fucking horse so much higher than everyone else's? Screwing our school over financially for a couple of years just to put those evil bad tutors in their place. Like I said, who gives a flying fuck?" Other boosters had theories about why a faculty member would object to academic fraud in the athletics program. "You grew up resenting atheletes," one hypothesized, "always beleiving they were treated better than you. Your first crush was probably on an athelete who would not give you the time of day." (Here, as elsewhere, I reproduce the original spelling and punctuation in booster communications.)

Other boosters pointed out that in Tennessee many more people saw the university as being about sports than about learning or education. "Why don't you just shutup about the illegal tutoring there at the University," one wrote. "You're forgetting that a lot of people go to UT because of their athletic program, and this (their tuition) pays you're salary. I would've fired you by now." "Give it a rest!" exhorted another. "The taxpayers of Tennessee like winning teams. The players pay your salary. Go to Harvard or Yale or some private college and teach if you want a perfect institution." Intemperate as they were, such communications display a certain shrewdness. The last correspondent was right, for instance, to remind Bensel-Meyers that Tennessee draws a certain type of student, in overwhelming numbers, because of its athletics program. An episode that occurred in connection with the ESPN story proves his point.

The night after the ESPN story was aired, Tennessee students painted a large boulder on campus with the words "ESPN SUCKS." The next day's student newspaper carried a picture of the boulder on its front page. When a national news commentator remarked that "ESPN SUCKS" was something one might expect from "trailer trash," not from college students, a new furor broke out. On one UT sports board, a student responded angrily to a Tennessee alumnus who'd said he thought the commentator was right. "Im sick of people like you guys," this student wrote, "because you let someone go on national radio and call us trailer trash and then you have the nerve to kiss thier ass thinking that will convince them were not trash. They don't care. We will always be trash to them. So screw em."

In the same way, the correspondent who told Linda Bensel-Meyers to go teach at Harvard or Yale was on to an important truth. At schools like the University of Tennessee, that's precisely what the best faculty do, as soon as they can get away. The same is true, as I'd already found at UNM, at other state universities with major sports programs. It's true that only a tiny percentage make their way to Harvard or Yale. But almost everyone who does original scholarship and is capable of teaching bright students will sooner or later have the chance to escape a sports factory for a better school. That's why faculties at schools like Tennessee so often consist, except for a few recently arrived assistant professors, of professors no other institution wants to take. Most of those who are left behind have talents and abilities far beyond anything demanded of them at the university where they're stranded. But most, too, have long since come to terms with the hard truth that this will be their last stop. That's why there is so often an atmosphere of silent desperation on Div IA faculties.

I was painfully reminded of my UNM experience when I got a call recently from a friend who teaches at Ohio State. He's a well-known scholar, someone who got a senior appointment at OSU when he was quite young and was regarded as one of the rising stars in his discipline. He's now been at Ohio State for more than twenty years. When I talked to him, he was close to despair. He'd called to ask whether I knew of any college or university with better students who might be looking for someone in his area.

"I don't," I said. "Everybody's trying to hire assistant professors because they're cheaper."

"I know, I know." There was a terrible weariness in his voice.

"Look," I said. "At Rutgers, getting great students is easy. All you have to do is teach demanding material and give lots of essays and test and grade rigorously. It acts like a filter. You get the most intellectually serious students on campus. They tell their friends about you. Have you thought of just trying to raise the level of your teaching?"

"It wouldn't work at Ohio State."

"Why not?" I asked.

"Because the administration cancels any class that doesn't enroll twenty-five students. If you tried to teach at college level out here, you'd wind up drawing about four students. They'd cancel the class. So everybody tries to make their courses easier and easier, to draw enough students to let them at least teach literature. It's a race to the bottom."

In recent years, as the job situation in academe has become tighter, and as the Div IA booster subculture has become more powerful, the choice confronting faculty at sports-dominated public universities is stark: either keep silent, as did Bensel-Meyers's colleagues at Tennessee, or speak out and face the threats and vicious abuse encountered by Bensel-Meyers herself. (Fortunately, Bensel-Meyers was later able to move to a better position at a private university.) A few of the trapped faculty who opt for silence at Div IA schools attempt to disappear into their research. Many others seek refuge in outside interests—in sailing, perhaps, or real estate, or restoring old cars. For the occasional professor willing to speak out, the only reward is likely to be abuse.

That's why, for instance, the UT booster insisted on reminding Linda Bensel-Meyers that the taxpayers of Tennessee like winning teams. Mounted on her "fucking horse," Professor Bensel-Meyers needed to be brought down to earth. Distasteful as his viewpoint may seem, this booster was entirely correct. For taxpayers do elect the politicians who provide funding for state universities like Tennessee and North Carolina State. And, increasingly, the only connection to the state university felt by many taxpayers is through their Div IA sports teams. Professors who try to reassert academic or intellectual values in a way that might weaken the football or basketball program are, as this booster perfectly well sees, attacking the ultimate source of their own livelihood. In this context, the booster who told Bensel-Meyers that the Tennessee football players "pay you're salary" was also correct.

I want to take a moment to look more closely at one distinctive note in such booster diatribes: their obscenity. Given the widespread influence of such contemporary forms as gangsta rap and prison chic, obscenity has become common in day-to-day American life. Still, it's crucial to recognize that the obscenity used by Tennessee boosters against Professor Bensel-Meyers represents something else. It's a deliberate cultural assault, meant to warn a female college professor that in interfering with U T football she's intruded on a world dominated by men who spend much of their time drinking beer and arguing about the point spread in the Super Bowl. Nor does it count against such boosters that they speak substandard English—"you grew up resenting athletes"—and can't spell—"you have the nerve to kiss thier ass"—or punctuate very well. For in this context, erratic spelling and punctuation constitute part of the threat. The point is to remind college professors who meddle with Div I A sports that it's the boosters, in their guise as "taxpayers," who run the university. And the "taxpayers" want winning teams.

Today, the voices of the boosters who attacked Linda Bensel-Meyers at Tennessee can be heard on college sports boards scattered across the Web. Anyone who doubts that Bensel-Meyers and others who attempt to do something about Div I A sports corruption are up against a violently crude and defiantly anti-intellectual booster subculture should take half an hour to visit one of these boards. But be warned: it makes for a profoundly depressing experience. Here, for instance, is an exchange of insults, chosen at random from innumerable similar exchanges, between a University of Miami booster and a Virginia Tech booster. I'll call the Miami booster "Cane"—a shorter version of his board name—and the Virginia Tech booster "Hokie" on the same principle. Hokie was visiting the Miami board to boast about a recent Virginia Tech victory in football. Cane was displeased at his presumption:

CANE: Keep cumming all over yourselves about this "stellar" 10–3 season. We went
   9–3 and we're calling for serious changes. Going 10–3 and beating Miami by 6
   isn't a huge deal. Except maybe for Hokie fans.
HOKIE: I didnt cum on myself it was in ur moms mouth
CANE (to his fellow boosters): Just try and ignore Hokie. He has a problem with wetting the bed. Just bare with him, the more he posts, the better it is for him.
HOKIE: why dont you go jerk off to the thought of a kid wetting his bed
CANE: 3rd grade must be a real bitch for you hunny! . . . 1st of all, when's the last time
   you crotch sniffin' ass leaches ever won a fuckin' title at anything? Why the
   fuck is your loser lil time Popkie ass here anyway?! Do ya actually think suckin'
   our cane nutzz and ridin' our coat tails into the "A"ll "C"anes "C"onference
   will get you some kinda clout?! . . . Naaaa, your still our lil drunk toothless

Friday night $2-dolla back aley @#/%$! Shoulda stayed in the Big East hunny!!
. . . Your last Heisman hopeful/wonder child still can't take a stroll in the park
without shittin' her britches from her last ass rapin' at the OB. . . . So, what
makes you inbreds think this time's gonna be any different?!

Several years ago, when *Sports Illustrated* celebrated its fiftieth anni-
versary, a writer named Geoffrey Norman talked in the *Wall Street Journal* about the ways the magazine had changed sportswriting in the United
States. *SI*'s greatest contribution, said Norman, had been to publish material
that was "resolutely not intended for the sad, stats-drenched sports yahoo
who can play the trivia games but has no inner life and cannot imagine one
in anyone else." Norman is alluding to Jonathan Swift's great satiric portrait
of the Yahoos in *Gulliver's Travels,* a race of creatures that Gulliver doesn't
at first recognize to be human beings like himself: "I beheld several animals
in a field, and one or two of the same kind sitting in trees. . . . A herd came
flocking about me from the next field, howling and making odious faces; but
I ran to the body of a tree, and leaning my back against it, kept them off. . . .
Several of this cursed brood getting hold of the branches behind leaped up
into the tree, from whence they began to discharge their excrements on my
head: however, I escaped pretty well, by sticking close to the stem of a tree,
but was almost stifled by the filth, which fell about me on every side."

When I teach *Gulliver's Travels* in my eighteenth-century literature classes,
I make the point that in such scenes Swift is not satirizing humanity as such.
Instead, his point is that in ordinary human society being a Yahoo is a matter
of moral choice. That is, there's a Yahoo inside every one of us—Swift was
an Anglican clergyman, and the theological doctrine of original sin looms
in the immediate background here—and the forms of self-degradation are
limitless. One kind, as old as human civilization, is the brute sensuality associated with alcohol or drug addiction or mechanical and impersonal sex. On
a higher level, however, a simple refusal of the gift of rational consciousness
is enough to make one a Yahoo. In a society in which everyone has access
to education—a world of books and ideas miraculously available to even
the poorest citizen—just turning one's back on its possibilities is enough to
create a Yahoo where a thoughtful human being might have existed instead.
In American higher education, Cane and Hokie are the voices of Swift's
Yahoos. The portal through which they enter public universities is Div IA
athletics.

There's another point to be made about booster obscenity. Listen again to
the Tennessee booster who objected when another booster agreed with the
radio commentator that "ESPN SUCKS" wasn't public language worthy of

college students. "Im sick of people like you guys because you let someone go on national radio and call us trailer trash and then you have the nerve to kiss thier ass thinking that will convince them were not trash. They don't care. We will always be trash to them. So screw em." This Tennessee student went on to say, "Your the idiots that keep us from getting the respect we deserve," and finished up with "WE STILL WENT 13-0. they can't take that away!" For all its semiliteracy, his post clearly expresses what Friedrich Nietzsche called *ressentiment:* an inferiority complex that is compelled to seek revenge in symbolic terms. Those who harbor *ressentiment,* Nietzsche said, are denied any real outlet in action because of the perceived power or social superiority of their opponent. That's why they're driven to compensate for their weakness with an imaginary revenge.

In the case of booster *ressentiment,* that revenge is an attempt to exert symbolic ownership of the university through Div IA sports. This is one major reason why boosters are so eager to commercialize universities through professionalized athletics. The more the campus is plastered with logos saying "Always Rutgers, Always Coke!" the less it will seem like an alien citadel of ideas and higher culture. The more often a university faculty member can be persuaded to lead fans in chanting advertising slogans, the less one has to feel intellectually inferior to professors as a remote and cerebral caste. The sooner the university resembles a shopping mall—with "customers" instead of students and "consumer preferences" instead of course requirements and a coherent curriculum—the more rapidly the boosters' ever-present fear that someone, somewhere, is trying to live life on a higher level than that of Monday Night Football and satellite pornography can be assuaged.

So far at Rutgers, I'm glad to report, there are only a few boosters like Cane and Hokie posting on its sports boards. Nor does the Rutgers student body include a lot of students with an "ESPN SUCKS" mentality—though as we'll see in the next chapter, this has begun to change. But the silent, continuous damage done by boosters can already be felt on the Rutgers campus. For even an emergent booster subculture is already relentlessly hostile to ideas and intellectual values. I've already described how an emphasis on professionalized sports at UNM appeared to me to be working to drive the brightest New Mexico students out of the state. But I want to say a few words here about what happens to those students who remain at a university that has begun to come under domination by its athletics boosters.

Imagine, as a sort of thought experiment, two nearly identical college students. I'll call the first one "Cole Bryan." Cole's had an undistinguished high school career. He doesn't have much going for him intellectually. Thanks to runaway grade inflation in high school, he is able to apply to college with a decent grade point average. But he's never read any books. He has few outside interests beyond video games and watching TV. His combined SAT verbal and math score is 960, which puts him in the bottom 37 percent nationally. If Cole were attending a university like Columbia or the University of Chicago, he'd be hopelessly over his head academically. The students around him would have combined SAT scores three or four hundred points above his own—stratospherically out of his intellectual range—and the coursework and reading assigned by his professors would be determined by that higher level of expectation.

Suppose, though, that we're close friends with Cole Bryan's parents. We want to help the boy get into college, and we happen to know powerful people at the schools he's applying to. We call Yale and Chicago on his behalf. We freely admit to admissions officers that Cole isn't very good at mathematics. Granted, his reading comprehension is little better than rudimentary. But he's a pleasant young man, and his parents are fine people. Then we present our knockdown argument: Cole Bryan is just one student. At a university enrolling thousands, it takes much more than an occasional substandard undergraduate to degrade the level of teaching and learning at the institution as a whole. Even supposing that the university were Yale or Chicago, how could fifty Cole Bryans with their sub-1,000 SAT scores affect the thousands of bright students who set the tone of the university in both the classroom and outside?

In itself, this argument is correct. It's not the percentage of Cole Bryans enrolled by a university that alters the character of the school, driving good students and faculty away and poisoning its intellectual atmosphere for those who remain. It's the public emphasis the institution puts on the presence of such intellectually substandard students. If a selective university were to admit one hundred or two hundred Cole Bryans, but kept their presence entirely secret from high school applicants, the general public, and the regular student body, damage would be minimal. The harm would only come if the university itself, without specifically meaning to do so but compelled by forces beyond its control, suddenly found that tiny minority of substandard students in the spotlight. This is the point at which bright students cease to apply and talented faculty begin to look for jobs elsewhere.

To understand how this process works, let's turn to our second college student, whom we'll call "Brian Toal." Unlike Cole Bryan, Brian Toal isn't a fictional character. He was an actual high school football star being heavily recruited by Rutgers coach Greg Schiano. According to recruiting bulletins, Brian Toal had, like the imaginary Cole Bryan, an SAT score of 960. He'd agreed to make a campus visit to Rutgers, which was alone enough to cause intense excitement among members of Scarlet R and the Touchdown Club, Scarlet R's more specialized organization for football boosters. The plan was to take Toal to a game in the RAC, the school's basketball arena, to let him personally witness the immense enthusiasm for sports that he could expect if he enrolled as a Rutgers athlete.

To see how Div IA professionalized athletics transmits powerful signals about a university, you need only look at the messages that began appearing on Rutgers booster boards. Here's a sample. Booster #1 thinks that the winning plan is to fill the intervals of the basketball game with chants pleading with Toal to come: "Can you guys PLEASE organize some WE WANT TOAL chants at the game?" Booster #2 thinks chants aren't enough: "I think the key is signs. A lot of times a chant will start and you will have no idea of what they are saying. . . . But if you have a few signs it helps people to figure out that 'EE AAA OH' = 'WE WANT TOAL.'" Booster #3, a current Rutgers student, improves on this idea: "How about some students get FOUR big signs, spelling out Toal's name, and do a 'Give me a T . . . Give me an O . . .' etc." After the visit, a sportswriter for the *Newark Star-Ledger* reported that Toal "was given the clear impression that he was the school's top recruit . . . from the game-long chants of 'We Want Toal' . . . to the smattering of Rutgers jerseys with No. 1 on the front and Toal's name on the back."

It's easy enough to see from such episodes how boosters transmit a signal to the state's brightest students that they ought to go elsewhere. But, as I've said, New Jersey has an applicant pool so rich in talent that even with 70 percent of the state's top students leaving for out-of-state schools Rutgers still draws outstanding students. Reading through the "We Want Toal" posts, though, I remembered one of my own students, a physics major who had done superb work for me in literature classes. In physics, his work was so advanced that even some of his own professors had difficulty understanding his senior project. "If Rutgers produces a Nobel Prize winner in physics," one of them told me, "he'll be the one." This student was accepted at every top graduate program in the country. He chose Harvard. Yet at Rutgers—to borrow a metaphor from physics—he'd passed through the institution like one of those mysterious massless particles called neutrinos, isolated and unperceived. In physics he was worth a dozen Brian Toals in football. But nobody knew he was there. While the university should have been giving him the intellectual recognition his talent deserved, Rutgers as an institution was sitting in the RAC chanting, "We Want Toal."

Still, the case of one brilliant student doesn't show the full harm of booster domination at public universities. To grasp that, you'd need to comprehend the effect of booster subculture on the much larger but mostly invisible segment of college applicants I call "America's missing million." These are the more average students, the steady workers in classes and seminars who don't particularly stand out. They were never going to go on to Harvard. Nonetheless, at a university that remains true to genuine teaching and learning, such students find themselves engaged by ideas, undergoing a process of real personal and intellectual growth. At Rutgers, where Div IA athletics hasn't yet had a chance to wreak its full damage, I've been lucky enough to teach many such students. Sometimes you become aware of what college meant to them only years after graduation, when they write to tell you what a difference a course or a conversation made in their lives.

The crucial point is that students like this are as much influenced by the atmosphere of an institution as the brilliant ones. When the general attitude toward intellectual life and academic achievement is undermined by professionalized college sports, these students feel the change as well. They're also the least able to resist it. As the worldview of Cane and Hokie begins to dominate at a university—or even more significantly, as the university itself is seen to be promoting the change—real education becomes more difficult, and finally impossible. Sensitive to the atmosphere on campus, these more ordinary students adjust their expectations downward to try to fit in, painting their faces for football games and joining their more boorish classmates in screaming obscenities at basketball games. The process is invisible. The loss, both to the students themselves and to the society they will soon enter as citizens, workers, and parents, is immense.

Given what I knew about booster subculture at other Div IA schools, I didn't expect my relations with Scarlet R boosters to be smooth. So at the beginning of the Rutgers 1000 campaign I wasn't surprised when I got anonymous hate mail like that Linda Bensel-Meyers received at Tennessee. Like hers, a lot of mine was violent and obscene. Some Rutgers booster boards even posted the times and locations of my classes and office hours, urging loyal fans to show up and confront me personally the next time I stepped on campus. All this was predictable enough, and it didn't bother me unduly. The Scarlet R boosters, feeling threatened by Rutgers 1000, needed someone to demonize. It might as well be me.

What I didn't expect was that I'd find athletics boosters among the Rutgers faculty. After all, hundreds of Rutgers professors had already signed the Rutgers 1000 memorial. Even those who hadn't joined, I assumed, were painfully aware that booster subculture is deeply antagonistic to the intellectual ideals professors tend to associate with universities. I found out otherwise only when I gave an interview to a *Sports Illustrated* writer doing a feature on

"By the mid-1990s, I had become for most Rutgers boosters the Devil personified."
WCD talking to a reporter at the Drake Conference on College Sports Corruption.
Photo: RU1000 Archives.

Rutgers football. Describing the damage done to Div IA universities by their booster subculture, I told the *SI* writer that neither President Lawrence nor the Scarlet R contingent on the board of governors had the least notion that their sports fixation was driving New Jersey's brightest students away from Rutgers. These people didn't understand, I said, that when the remaining cohort of very bright students had vanished, the most distinguished scholars at Rutgers would begin to leave as well. The real problem, I said, was that boosters who chanted "We Want Toal" were sending out unmistakable signals that they cared far less about students who were brilliant at Greek or physics or philosophy than about some low-SAT moron being recruited for the football team.

The magic word was "moron." *Sports Illustrated* had barely hit the newsstands before New Jersey sportswriters fanned out, pencils poised, to ask RU football players what they thought about the Rutgers professor who'd called them morons. There were angry diatribes on radio talk shows, and a new flood of obscene letters in my departmental mailbox. With a sense that the exercise was probably pointless, I did my best to explain that I'd been talking specifically about the way Div IA boosters invariably go crazy over low-SAT recruits in football or basketball while caring nothing about bright students stranded at their university. My example when talking to the *SI* reporter had been Chris Washburn, a basketball player with a combined SAT score of 470 recruited by Jim Valvano at NCSU. If it were a choice between a student brilliant at Greek or physics and Chris Washburn, I'd been saying to the *SI* writer, the boosters would go for Chris Washburn every time.

I expected New Jersey sportswriters to try to whip up a controversy about my *Sports Illustrated* interview. But there was one response I never expected. It came from fourteen Rutgers faculty members who turned out to constitute something called the "Academic Oversight Committee for Intercollegiate Athletics." In all my years in Rutgers 1000, I'd never heard of this body. I learned of its existence when its members wrote a letter to the *Daily Targum* professing themselves to be "horrified and embarrassed" that a Rutgers professor had called football players morons. Such generalizations, they wrote, were "unseemly and degrading," and had no place in their community. That was how I found out that the Rutgers faculty harbored its own Scarlet R contingent.

The committee's attack on me was reprinted in other New Jersey newspapers. Since I'd never heard of the Academic Oversight Committee for Intercollegiate Athletics, I tried to learn more about them before writing a response. As far as I could discover, the committee bore a certain resemblance to the "Academic Review Board" run by Chancellor Poulton and Jim Valvano at North Carolina State, except that the Rutgers group operated at entry level. Instead of examining athletes with failing grades for readmission, they interviewed recruits during their campus visits, ostensibly to ensure that they could meet the university's high academic standards.

In purely abstract terms, such a process might do something to weed out academically and intellectually substandard athletes before they were exposed to the pitiless glare of the public spotlight. The trouble was, it was hard to find a recruit the Rutgers committee had ever turned down.

Even though I'd begun to suspect that the Academic Oversight Committee might be a rubber stamp for the Athletics Department, part of the public relations machinery used to promote the NCAA's myth of the "student athlete," I couldn't be sure. So I put off writing my response, wanting to think things over. Then, providentially, I was saved by an unexpected development. Just before the season opened, the Rutgers football team signed a top-ranked defensive lineman named Nate Robinson. The Scarlet R boosters went wild with jubilation. The New Jersey sportswriters declared that Rutgers football had at last turned the corner. The Tostitos Bowl was in sight. Nearly lost in the excitement was the news that Nate Robinson's combined SAT score was 800. Completely lost in the excitement was the fact that Nate Robinson had been pronounced competent to do college-level work by the Rutgers Academic Oversight Committee.

An 800 combined SAT puts a student in the bottom 14 percent of the nation's students academically. Still, under the NCAA's latest formula, an 800 is enough, in combination with stipulated course grades, to make a player eligible for a Div IA athletic scholarship. Earlier, Nate Robinson had signed with the University of Miami, ranked no. 2 in football the preceding year. But now Miami, with its pick of the nation's top high school players, was seemingly trying to do something to repair its reputation as a program built with criminals and outcasts by requiring a slightly higher SAT score—820—than the NCAA minimum. Only after he failed to meet this marginally higher standard—reportedly after intensive tutoring and multiple test-takings—did Nate Robinson announce that he'd abandoned Miami and was going to Rutgers instead. And only because he happened to get caught in the narrow range between two rock-bottom SAT scores—the NCAA's 800 and Miami's 820—did Robinson's own score ever become publicly known.

Poor Nate Robinson's academic difficulties, however, helped bring to light the real nature of the Rutgers Academic Oversight Committee. For given its validation of his admission, there seemed to be only two choices. Either Rutgers was a university where an 800-SAT student could honestly do the work—in which case Rutgers was little more than a glorified high school—or the entire "academic support" system keeping such athletes academically eligible was fraudulent. "Could we be serious for a second?" I asked in my response in the *Targum*. "A student with an 800 SAT score might be able to do the work at Rutgers if he spent every available moment of his time on his courses. It would be difficult even if he spent 60 hours a week studying, but maybe, just maybe, it could be done."

It was brutally dishonest, though, for anyone—and for faculty members, most of all—to pretend it could be done by an academically unprepared freshman compelled to put in forty to fifty hours a week developing various physical skills, as well as to go on frequent weekend trips away from campus. I had been aware, I said, that at sports factory schools like Ohio State and Tennessee there were faculty who were happy to cooperate with the Athletics Department in exchange for a few privileges and a little stroking.

But I hadn't thought they existed at Rutgers. "It seems to me," I finished by saying, "that any member of the Rutgers faculty who steps eagerly forward to parade an 'outraged' sanctimoniousness when someone says a word against commercialized athletics at their university . . . lacks any sense of personal shame, and any idea at all of what an institution of higher learning ought to be." I haven't heard from the committee since.

It would be pleasant to report that Rutgers 1000 finally opened the eyes of the boosters on the Rutgers faculty and in Scarlet R to the damage done by professionalized Div IA sports to public universities. But it isn't so. Still, there did come a moment when a few more thoughtful boosters glimpsed what Rutgers 1000 had been fighting for and were honest enough to say so. The moment came about unexpectedly. All during the period immediately following Rutgers's entry into the Big East, it had been Rutgers's great good fortune (as we in Rutgers 1000 considered it) to have a series of losing seasons. With RU1000 monitoring illegitimate recruiting and retention practices, there could be no quick and dirty athletic rebuilding programs. With Scarlet R lacking the immense financial resources of the Wolfpack Club in North Carolina, there could be no hope of bypassing legislative funding to establish a sports franchise. The result was a grace period. So long as the Rutgers teams were losing, the television networks weren't interested. And so long as the networks weren't interested, the university was preserved from the worst effects of commercialized Div IA sports.

Then commercialized Div IA sports, tired of Rutgers's losing teams and lackluster TV ratings, decided to throw Rutgers overboard. In 2003, the Big East athletic conference collapsed. I'll tell the story of that collapse in detail in Chapter 10. At this point all that's needed is a quick summary. Moved by promises of higher revenues and greater TV exposure, its two most successful programs, Miami and Virginia Tech—quickly followed by Boston College—deserted the Big East for the commercially more successful Atlantic Coast Conference. For more than a decade Rutgers 1000 had been trying to warn students and alumni about the moral contagion spread by commercialized college sports. Now, for the first time, I began to get mail from boosters saying that after all these years, they had begun to see what Rutgers 1000 had been talking about. Some apologized for having sent abusive messages, or having attacked me on sports boards. Among them, one stands out in my mind as marking a turning point in the struggle to save Rutgers from commercialized Div IA athletics. Entitled "Sympathy for the Devil," it was written by Michael Fasano, a Rutgers alumnus who hosts a Rutgers sports board. This is what he posted on June 29, 2003, on Mike & Big Dog's Rutgers Fan Site:

Sympathy for the Devil

By Mike Fasano

Few people are demonized more by Rutgers sports fans than William C. Dowling, Professor of English at Rutgers University.

There's a reason for this. Dowling wants to end Division I sports at Rutgers. He thinks that Division I athletics is corrupting the noble role of education in America. In an article he wrote:

> The naming of post-season bowl games after products or corporations—The FedEx Orange Bowl, the Equitable Liberty Bowl, the Toyota Gator Bowl, the Chick Fil-A Peach Bowl, the Southwestern Bell Cotton Bowl—has been taken as a symptom of the takeover of American consciousness by commercial culture.
>
> This is correct, but what it misses, when big-time sports is the issue, is the sense in which commercial culture also represents a symbolic form of "ownership," a powerful and reassuring sign that one's university—especially one's state university—is not an outpost or citadel controlled by an alien "higher" culture of ideas or knowledge.
>
> The fans who view the Tostitos Fiesta Bowl on television, in short, are watching not only a football game but a demonstration that the same culture that generated *The Jerry Springer Show* and cable-TV wrestling has been able to penetrate, and to hollow out from within, the university as an institution.

Strip those paragraphs of the pedantry and the message is simple: *Big time college athletics has become so commercialized that it is damaging the colleges that promote it.*

You know what?

He has a point.

The recent spectacle of the raid on the Big East by the ACC should be Dowling's Exhibit A.

Let's think about it.

The word "collegial" comes from the Latin word "collegialis," meaning "of colleagues." Well, it doesn't take much thought to ascertain what types of values should thrive in a "collegial" setting. And it doesn't take much reflection to determine what values you would like to see in your colleagues. These would be the values of honesty, loyalty, fair dealing, integrity, and harmonious respect for the well-being of all, just to name a few. Most everyone would agree that those are the values a good university would promote. Colleges and universities, most would say, should be "honorable," and should instill a sense of honor in their students.

Do our colleges behave in "collegial" fashion? Are they honorable institutions? Are they promoting the values consistent with a sound education? If you gauge your answer by the behavior of many schools on the east coast over the last few months, it's not even a close call. That behavior has been so dishonorable it is embarrassing to recount.

Quislings and Fools

Virginia Tech started out the spring as a solid member of the Big East. They didn't know at the time that they were about to face a character test, but they were.

They faced it. They failed it miserably.

When it became apparent that an ACC raid of the Big East was on, Virginia Tech was asked where it would stand when the chips were down.

Tech said it was with the Big East all the way.

VT joined Rutgers, Pittsburgh, West Virginia and Connecticut in a lawsuit against the ACC. Tech made bold statements about its resolve to save the Big East. As for the Big East, Virginia Tech athletic director Jim Weaver announced, "Our commitment is unwavering." As for a possible offer from the ACC, Virginia Tech President Charles Steger proclaimed, "If an offer came today, we would not accept it."

Tech's loyalty to the league wouldn't last long. In fact, despite its vows of eternal fealty, Tech's loyalty lasted only a couple of weeks. That's when the Hokies got a surprise invitation to "Tobacco Road." What followed was an almost blinding display of hypocrisy. The day after they received an ACC invitation, Tech removed themselves from the lawsuit against the ACC. They hurriedly scheduled "site visits" with ACC officials and made a formal announcement that they would accept admission to the very conference they had been suing up until that very same morning.

Think about that. Just think about it. If you or I behaved like that, can you imagine what words people would use to describe us?

Hypocrite. Phoney. Double dealer. Scoundrel.

That's what people would call us. And you know something? The epithets would fit.

Truth be told, few of us would behave in such a fashion. We'd be too embarrassed to show our faces in public afterwards. But that indeed is the behavior we've seen from one of the major universities in the nation.

And let's not just pick on Virginia Tech.

What about Boston College? . . . [Here Mr. Fasano detailed the hypocrisy and double-dealing of BC, which was eager to sell itself to the Atlantic Coast Conference when ACC expansion was initially announced. BC seemed temporarily to have been left behind but was ultimately successful, after numerous twists and turns, in gaining admission. So now Miami, Virginia Tech, and Boston College had all abandoned

Rutgers's Big East Conference for the ACC. As Mr. Fasano points out, the maneuverings involved were much more like a corporate merger than anything to do with college athletics.]

The Power Brokers

The ACC needed 12 teams and access to northeast media markets. If they could "take" those markets, they would. Economic needs drove these decisions and no one cared if others got hurt. . . .

The bottom line?

Weren't we talking about educational institutions here?

That avarice such as this had little to do with the great humanistic tradition of the west seemed lost on those who were cutting the deals. That such conduct had been treated as evil or dishonorable in great literature for untold ages was a point missed by the participants. That such deeds made a mockery of the collegial, democratic notions of education in this country was an issue discussed occasionally by the commentators but only rarely by the deal makers.

A handful objected. Duke, North Carolina, a coach here, a faculty committee there spoke out. Most went along regardless of the price in moral terms.

This wasn't academia. This was business.

And that brings us back to William C. Dowling.

A Sort of Homecoming

In an essay critical of "big time" athletics Dowling recounts this anecdote about a college athlete:

> When he left Creighton, Mr. Ross had the overall language skills of a fourth grader and the reading skills of a seventh grader. Consequently, Mr. Ross enrolled, at Creighton's expense, for a year of remedial education at the Westside Preparatory School in Chicago. At Westside, Mr. Ross attended classes with grade school children. . . . In July, 1987, Mr. Ross suffered what he terms a "major depressive episode," during which he barricaded himself in a Chicago motel room and threw furniture out the window. To Mr. Ross, this furniture "symbolized" Creighton employees who had wronged him.

Many Rutgers fans think of William Dowling as the devil, but give the devil his due. The exploitation of young people in pursuit of an institution's athletic dreams is truly despicable. Dowling's activities have pointed out a dark side to college athletics often ignored in the glitz and glamour of the spectacle of college sports. To the extent that he opposes the exploitation of youth, I stand wholly with him.

But Dowling goes farther. He believes that the commercialization of college sports has become a cancer on the soul of academia in America. That cancer, he says, must be excised in its entirety.

Has Dowling made his case?

In the past few months I haven't heard a peep from him.

Of course, he didn't have to speak a word. Virginia Tech athletics was speaking volumes about loyalty, Boston College fans about integrity, Miami about humility, and so on.

Why, with such able advocates for his cause, should William Dowling even open his mouth?

I would think that he would remain silent and watch the spectacle with a knowing smile. The sharks of unbridled greed were devouring one another and thus, in the process, devouring themselves. William Dowling didn't need to lift a finger.

Still, the question is there.

Has Dowling made his case?

I don't know, but if the truth be told he may never have to.

If what we have seen says anything about the future of big time sports, college athletics seems intent on making it for him.

A dozen people sent me copies of Mike Fasano's column. A while ago I wrote him to say that I'd like to use it in *Confessions of a Spoilsport*. We've written back and forth. Though he remains committed to Rutgers's participation in Div I A, he's no longer as steadfast as he once was. I think the notion that alumni had more fun going out on an autumn afternoon to watch Rutgers play Princeton as they ever did attending Virginia Tech or Miami games no longer seems as strange to him as it did a few years ago. I've tried to persuade him that, with real students out there on the field wearing your school's name on their jerseys, the odor of corruption that fills the air in places like Miami and Blacksburg, Virginia, is blissfully far away. Win or lose, you know that you went to a real university, and you know that the young people coming out of your school are real college graduates. We've made a deal, Mike Fasano and I, that if Rutgers is ever rescued from Div I A, I'll take him to lunch before our first Patriot League home game. Then we'll go to the game together. If it happens in our lifetimes, it's an afternoon I'm looking forward to.

"I Am an Alumni!"

In recent years, analysts of educational policy have begun to deal in a gingerly way with the explosive subject of college selectivity. What makes universities like Harvard and Yale, or liberal arts colleges like Swarthmore and Amherst, schools that any very bright high school senior in the country would be eager to attend? What permits Berkeley, as a public institution, to draw the top students in California year after year? How does a small public liberal arts college like William and Mary, competing with the University of Virginia for top students in its own state, draw so high-caliber a student body? In New Jersey, what permitted an obscure local institution like Trenton State to transform itself over two decades into The College of New Jersey, one of the leading public liberal arts colleges in the United States? Conversely, why did Rutgers University in New Brunswick, only twenty-five miles away, undergo a severe drop in student selectivity during the same period?

The answer lies in the theory of peer effects. Bright and intellectually engaged students understand intuitively that education is a mutual enterprise. "Students educate students," explains Gordon C. Winston, a Williams College economist who pioneered the study of peer effects, "and some do it better than others. Students will learn more, think more carefully, and perform better by associating with academically strong fellow students." Winston also makes the point that the principle of high-level intellectual performance extends far beyond the classroom. "Defending one's position in a late-night dorm discussion is simply more educational," he observes, "if the debate is rigorous than if it is sloppy—even if the argument is about what went wrong on a date or whether God exists." "At a college with intellectually engaged students," he adds—he's thinking of American residential colleges, but in my experience the same holds true at nonresidential European institutions like the Sorbonne—"education goes on all the time."

I've said that commercialized Div IA sports steer bright students away from a university, sending out signals that the institution is under the control of a booster subculture antagonistic to academic or intellectual values. In more specialized writings about Div IA athletics I've called this the "symbolic ownership" of a university by its boosters—the signals transmitted by the Wolfpack Club, for instance, when it raises $20 million in a fiscal year for athletic facilities, when it provides a red Cadillac to be driven around campus by Chancellor Poulton, or when it establishes, through administrators like Poulton, machinery like the Academic Review Board to keep Jim Valvano's basketball players eligible for Div IA competition. Students with high intellectual motivation take in such signals subliminally when they're choosing a college.

The theory of peer effects helps explain why Div IA athletics have put down their deepest roots at lower-tier or nonselective universities, which offer the least resistance to booster subculture. I've just taken from my files a copy of the final top twenty-five NCAA football rankings for 2003. In the same folder I have a list of the top twenty-five academically ranked schools in the U.S. News rankings for that year. To a casual observer, the most striking fact is likely to be that there is virtually no overlap. The twenty-five top-ranked football schools are what U.S. News designates as second- and third-tier institutions such as Ohio State and Kansas State and Washington State and Oklahoma State and Nebraska and Tennessee and LSU. Some, like Boise State in Idaho—the school, you will recall, that renamed its basketball pavilion the Taco Bell Arena in return for a corporate contribution—failed even to make the U.S. News rankings of the top 248 institutions—162 public, 86 private—in the United States.

The U.S. News list of twenty-five top-ranked academic institutions for the same year includes the names you'd expect: Harvard, Yale, Princeton, Dartmouth, MIT, Columbia, Cornell, Penn, Johns Hopkins, Brown, Emory, Washington University in St. Louis, and similar institutions. No simple list of schools can explain why academic distinction should be connected to amateur or collegiate-level sports. Still, it does seem worth noting that most schools in the top twenty-five U.S. News academic rankings play football either at the Div III nonathletic-scholarship level, like Emory and Washington University, or at the Div IAA nonathletic-scholarship level, like Harvard, Yale, Princeton, and the other Ivies. The only university to show up on both lists is the University of Michigan, which squeaked in as no. 25 in the NCAA football rankings. Otherwise, the lists designate two quite separate spheres in American higher education.

Even the solitary presence of the University of Michigan on both lists, though, might seem to leave one anomaly unexplained. It's easy to see why a bright student wanting to join a vibrant intellectual community would feel a powerful attraction to Harvard or Amherst or the University of Chicago. It's also easy to understand why such a student would be likely to feel lonely or isolated at a school like Nebraska or Boise State. What's not so obvious is why a student in search of intellectual community shouldn't be happy to attend Michigan, where some 15 percent of entering freshmen have SAT verbal scores over 700, and an even larger number—around 25 percent—score over 700 on the mathematics section. Given three to four thousand students on campus who share one's own intellectual fascination with Latin poetry or medieval history or Gödel's theorem, it's not clear why Michigan's top-twenty-five football team should be an obstacle to intellectual community.

The answer is that intellectual community involves group dynamics. Even at a school like Michigan, Div IA football and basketball work relentlessly to marginalize bright students. Nor is this surprising. When a hundred thousand spectators pack the university's stadium to watch a tiny handful of low-SAT athletes—Michigan football players average around 850 on the SAT—an unmistakable message is being sent to students who, at Yale or the University of Chicago, would feel themselves to be at the center of institutional life. At universities with higher SAT averages, such as Duke, a highly visible Div IA sports program filters out intellectually serious applicants, leaving the admissions office with a pool of shallow or mindlessly hedonistic candidates—for reasons that will become clear, I'll call these "party animal" students—out of which to form an entering class. The explanation is that intellectual community demands, in addition to mere cognitive ability, a sense of intellectual engagement. This is something you won't find, as a rule, among undergraduates who see themselves as future Div IA boosters.

Consider Duke. Many people became aware of Duke's party animal culture only in 2006, when a scandal involving Duke lacrosse players and other athletes, "exotic dancers" from nearby Raleigh, and off-campus drunkenness made their way into the national press. Somewhat earlier, an ESPN story suggesting that Duke basketball players were being kept eligible by what Murray Sperber and other critics call a "hideaway curriculum" drew some attention. So did news accounts of wealthy Duke boosters alleged to have given parents of heavily recruited Duke players high-paying public relations jobs. To people inside higher education, however, the story of Duke's failure to attract intellectually engaged applicants had long been an open secret. The television-viewing public is normally aware of Duke during "March Madness." Inside academe, people are far more likely to think first about Duke's party animal problem.

Duke has tried hard to solve the problem. Consider, for instance, the Duke program that awards full tuition scholarships, plus a summer of study at Oxford, to the top fifteen students in its entering class. The program is sometimes dismissed as a crass attempt to buy a group of Ivy League students for its entering class, giving Duke some claim to be able to compete with Harvard and Yale and the other Ivies for the nation's best applicants. That seems to me unduly harsh. For all but a few wealthy families, financial considerations do have to enter into college choice. If an older daughter given only a partial scholarship at Harvard is given a full subsidy at Duke—a package worth $100,000 to $200,000 when the Oxford summer is counted in—the family has to think about the money this frees up for the education of younger brothers and sisters. Plus which, Duke is not Boise State. Even with a high-visibility Div IA basketball team, it has a student body, as measured by SAT scores, nearly in the Ivy League range. The academic sacrifice seems minimal. The financial gain is huge. The inducement is understandable.

Still, the parents are looking at Duke from an outside perspective. The daughter who goes there, on the other hand, ends up inside Duke's party animal culture. It's then that she's likely to discover that the intellectual community she'd been looking forward to, and which she realizes she would have found at Harvard or Yale or Amherst, isn't something that can be measured in dollars. In 1993, a story in the *Chronicle of Higher Education* reported, the Duke administration, deeply concerned about anti-intellectualism among its students, gave Dean William H. Willimon the task of investigating and preparing a report on the problem. Meeting with freshmen and sophomores who had been given these full tuition scholarships, Dean Willimon was astonished to learn that more than half had already put in transfer applications to other universities. Worse, they were only a percentage of newly arrived Duke undergraduates who had done so.

At Harvard alone, the *Chronicle* reporter was able to track down four students who had transferred from Duke in the previous two years. The story of one, Lauren Feldman, may be taken as a virtual parable of the fate of bright students at any Div IA school, even at Duke's higher-SAT level. Like most intellectually serious students, Ms. Feldman was a reader. She always carried in her backpack a book she was reading in her spare time. Other Duke students, seeing the book, occasionally asked what course it was assigned for. When they heard she wasn't reading it for a class, reported Ms. Feldman, they invariably responded with disbelief. At Duke, this bordered on irrational behavior. So why didn't Ms. Feldman, realizing that she was an oddball at Duke, just settle down and go with the flow? She tried it, she said. "I didn't enjoy walking into a frat house with six inches of beer on the floor," she told the *Chronicle* writer, "and having some guy suck on the back of my neck and say 'Hey, baby, have a brew.'" So, understandably enough, she transferred to Harvard.

Still, why should Duke's party animal student culture have anything to do with Div IA athletics? If Duke were to withdraw from the Atlantic Coast Conference tomorrow, abolishing athletic scholarships and moving to Div III, doing away with Duke's high-visibility basketball program and severing ties with its booster subculture, what's the evidence that Duke would begin to attract students more nearly resembling those at Harvard or Columbia or Amherst, or, at a minimum, those who attend such highly regarded Div III institutions as Tufts or Emory or Washington University in St. Louis? The answer can be seen in the role acted out on campus by the so-called Cameron Crazies, a group of Duke students who paint themselves blue and—reportedly after a good deal of pregame drinking—sit in the stands and scream slogans and insults at players on the opposing team. They take their name from the Cameron Indoor Stadium where Duke basketball games are played.

The Cameron Crazies obviously symbolize an important aspect of Duke's student culture. What's less obvious is that they also symbolize the relation between every Duke undergraduate and Div IA athletics, whether or not that student goes to basketball games. In Tom Wolfe's satiric novel *I Am Charlotte Simmons,* whose fictional Dupont University is widely assumed to be based on Duke, the thoughts that pass through the mind of an athletics tutor talking to Dupont's basketball coach capture the structure of this relationship. "Why on earth," the tutor thinks to himself—these are the thoughts he doesn't dare express to the coach—"do Dupont University students with average SATs of fourteen-ninety get excited, scream their hearts out over 'their' basketball team . . . who live a life completely apart from the real students, who feel infinitely superior to them, . . . who have tutors to do their schoolwork for them, who say *you ain't, he don't,* and *nome saying?,* who look upon friendly student fans as either sluts or suck-ups—why are they *fans* of such people?"

The answer exposes the dark underside of the theory of peer effects. It's that Div IA athletics attract students who, though they're not strong enough to resist the social pressure that pushes them toward college, share the deep antagonism of booster subculture to intellectual pursuits. "Despite its PR into which the administration pours millions to glamorize it as 'the Harvard of the South,'" wrote one recent Duke graduate on an Internet board discussing Wolfe's novel, "it is no such thing. 'Dupont' (Duke) is in fact a ruthlessly anti-intellectual environment of half-bred slouches in baseball caps, who are educated on textbooks, dislike thinking or reading, and live only to carouse and make fools of themselves." The sentiment is echoed by Duke faculty. "The thing that holds us back by the minute at Duke," English professor Reynolds Price said in a widely reported speech, "is the prevailing cloud of indifference, of frequent hostility, to a thoughtful life." At a really good university, Price told his listeners, "students find themselves invited into a more or less constant discussion of serious ideas." At Duke, they find themselves invited to basketball games.

In recent years the public has become aware of the connection between Div IA athletics and drunken or violent behavior among students, which is what the Duke alumna quoted above means by a disposition to carouse and make fools of themselves. At Duke, such behavior has gone well beyond the slogans and insults yelled out by the Cameron Crazies. In 1991 and 1992, for instance, drunken Duke students celebrated winning basketball seasons with "bench burnings," building huge bonfires with the wooden benches set outside their dormitories. In 1998 Duke public safety officials tried to avoid a repetition of this behavior by stationing campus police at strategic points around campus. It didn't work. Students stayed drunk and defiant, building bonfires in hard-to-reach locations and chanting obscenities directed at Duke president Nannerl Keohane. "At the bonfires," the campus police chief told *Duke Magazine*, "students were physically preventing officers and fire fighters from putting out the fires." The students were also, the chief reported, using accelerants: "several full gallons of gasoline were confiscated" from undergraduates heading toward the flames.

At Div IA schools, such scenes have become common in the era of commercialized college sports. In 2002, hundreds of students at West Virginia University—a member of the same Big East conference to which Rutgers belongs—tore up street signs and started fires in the downtown area after a victory over Virginia Tech. The game, as it happened, had been played in Blacksburg, Virginia, more than a hundred miles away. In Ohio students started fires and overturned cars in downtown Columbus after Ohio State defeated Michigan. At the University of Connecticut—also a member of the Big East—students went on a rampage when police tried to put out a bonfire that was threatening to burn down a nearby residence. To celebrate a basketball victory, students started fires, overturned automobiles, and spray-painted graffiti on cars and buildings. Pictures posted on the Internet by the UConn campus police showed students vomiting, cheering for classmates who were upending parked automobiles, and passing out dead drunk within inches of bonfires built with smashed furniture.

The campus police, doing their best to make sense of such behavior as some new type of student activism, were mystified. "There's not a cause," said UConn police chief Robert Hudd somewhat plaintively. "There's not a stand, there's not a message, there's not a theme." His confusion is understandable. To anyone thinking of the civil rights and antiwar activism of the 1960s, such student behavior seems wholly unmotivated. Yet to anyone who remembered that this behavior began when UConn—like Rutgers at about the same time—had only recently entered the world of commercialized Div I A sports, or who had heard about the Cameron Crazies and bench burning at Duke, the theme or message was perfectly obvious. When thousands of adolescents deeply hostile to learning or education are herded together in an institution ostensibly committed to what Duke's Reynolds Price calls the discussion of serious ideas, antagonism to their environment builds relentlessly. The rioting is a release for a pent-up sense of collective frustration.

That's why the real stakes in the struggle against Div I A sports involve the notion of the university as an enclave in a society where consumerist ideology—that ceaseless barrage of logos and brand names meant to empty out human consciousness until only consumer preferences remain—is the great antagonist of serious thought. At the obvious level, consumerism scores its victories when the revenues produced by its advertising machinery—the $6 billion paid by CBS for rights to "March Madness," for instance—persuade universities to put themselves on display between commercial breaks in the Tostitos Bowl or the Final Four. At a less obvious level, it does so when a university like Boise State agrees to name a sports facility for a fast-food franchise like Taco Bell. At the point when Div I A athletics has wholly taken over a university, it does so by handing over institutional control to booster organizations like the Wolfpack Club. This is the stage when, like a body with a weakened immune system, the campus itself passes into the control—to give the Duke example a wider application—of its bench burners and Cameron Crazies.

At Rutgers, RU1000's opposition to Div I A athletics and the school's relative lack of success in football and basketball combined, through the 1990s, to preserve the university from a takeover by party animal students. While UConn students were setting fires and overturning cars and passing out drunk in public, Rutgers preserved, at least on the surface, the appearance of an older and better university. As we've seen, there was a slow attrition of top New Jersey students, but even in the mid-1990s there were still one to two thousand undergraduates on campus who, in terms of SAT scores and all-around intellectual achievement, might have been at any Ivy League university. The way the Div IA sports buildup affected them was less to make them feel like a tiny besieged minority in the midst of a vast population of party animals—the sort of sensation that Lauren Feldman must have experienced many times at Duke before transferring to Harvard—than to give them a sense that they were being inexorably marginalized in relation to a wholly new kind of Rutgers undergraduate.

I got my first intimation of what was going on when one of my honors freshmen came into my office looking distraught. This is normal enough. Freshman year is a strain on most students. Her wan appearance might have had any number of explanations: a missed assignment, an uncle who'd had a heart attack, a mother who was upset at having her child away at college.

"Do you want to talk about it, Emily?" I asked.

She started to cry a little, and it all came out. The previous evening, in the common room of Brett Hall, our honors dorm, there had been an orientation meeting for freshman. It was about the usual topics—how to get advanced placement credit, how to get into the honors seminar you wanted, how to deal with deans and professors—but the upperclassman who was to run the meeting turned out to be about twenty minutes late.

"Everybody spent the whole time," Emily said, "asking each other where they'd *really* wanted to go to school."

"Instead of Rutgers?" I asked.

"Instead of Rutgers," she confirmed, dabbing at her eyes with a Kleenex. "But that wasn't the bad part."

"The bad part was?"

"When the girl who was running the meeting finally showed up. She walked in, took off her coat, introduced herself, and said, 'Welcome to the Hall of Broken Dreams.'"

It would be easy to see Emily's distress as simple misery at not being at an Ivy League school. The New Jersey applicant pool is so rich in intellectual talent that every Rutgers honors student has high school friends at the nation's top colleges. In the age of e-mail, our best students stay in touch with friends at places like Yale and Amherst and Swarthmore. You might imagine that, comparing teachers and classes, they'd begin to find the contrast with Rutgers unbearable. But, for a number of reasons, that explanation seems wrong to me. I'd watched the "hall of broken dreams" syndrome emerge, and then become more and more acute, under the presidency of Francis

Lawrence. It became still more pronounced after the university's entry into the Big East and the rise of The College of New Jersey as an alternative to Rutgers. What Emily was upset about was a growing perception of Rutgers as what she and her friends call a school of last resort.

As with Lauren Feldman's unhappiness at Duke, what Emily was missing was the sense of intellectual community she associated with schools like Harvard and Columbia. Prior to Rutgers's entry into the Big East, our best students had found this sense of community in the Rutgers College honors program, which offered small seminars taught by senior faculty, most of them renowned scholars in their fields. Some of my own richest teaching experiences at Rutgers came in these seminars. I think particularly of one called "The Face of Battle"—a title borrowed from a book by John Keegan, the great military historian—which dealt with the primordial terror of the battle experience as represented in literature (Shakespeare, Hemingway), history (Thucydides, Keegan, Alvin Kernan), and film (*Saving Private Ryan*, Branagh's version of Shakespeare's *Henry the Fifth*). It was, given the subject, a course in moral philosophy and psychology as much as in literature and history. For both faculty and undergraduates, such seminars were a vital center of intellectual community, with benefits that reached far beyond the individual classroom.

Part of the secret lay in the admission process. Preliminary screening was based on SAT scores. Then, to apply specifically to the program, students wrote essays on an assigned topic. These were read and graded, on a volunteer basis, by faculty who taught honors seminars. The first time I participated in the process, I remember thinking that Rutgers honors might conceivably have the most high-powered admissions committee in the nation. All around me, heads bent over the essays they were reading, were colleagues whose names were known throughout the academic world—Pulitzer Prize winners, recipients of the National Book Award, past Guggenheim fellows, prizewinning scientists and mathematicians—giving painstaking attention to work written by New Jersey's brightest high school seniors.

I've said that the best Rutgers undergraduates during this period might have been at any Ivy League university. I found this out when one of my brightest students came in one day to say, with some embarrassment, that her parents were extremely upset. They'd asked her to come and talk to me. "It's my sister," she said. "She got turned down by the honors program." Well, I said, it happens. The admissions process is very selective. It's nothing to get upset about. "But my sister has been accepted at Brown and Columbia," my student said. "My parents just don't see how Rutgers can be harder." I could understand their puzzlement. The next morning, I went to the honors office and asked for the sister's folder. The answer, it turned out, was her essay. Her SAT scores were very high, but she'd written a banal and perfunctory essay for the honors program. Both faculty readers had agreed that its writer would be unlikely to make a lively intellectual contribution to a Rutgers honors seminar. After reading through the essay, I had to agree. My student's sister went to Brown.

Then, in the mid-1990s, the honors program was eviscerated. Rutgers was facing a severe budget shortfall, we were told, and could no longer afford a system of small seminars for its most talented students. In Rutgers 1000, this struck us as a case of misplaced priorities. Just the amount spent on flying the football team to a recent game in California, one of our economics faculty estimated, could have kept the honors program operating for two years. Still, there was little we could do. We couldn't alter the university's budget allocations. Then we learned that the same dean who had presided over the dismantling of the honors program was a major figure on the Athletics Department's committee for interviewing and admitting low-SAT football players. This dean, it also turned out, made a habit of traveling on the plane with the football team to away games. His football jaunts seemed to explain why, when the honors program was being all but eliminated in the name of budgetary stringency, he'd never seen fit to object to the $30 million a year being thrown away on Big East athletics.

As Rutgers's years in the Big East went by, more and more of our brightest students began to transfer to other schools. For me, one of the most melancholy times in spring semester began to come when I'd find a line of students, all with very high SAT scores and grade point averages, waiting to ask me for letters of recommendation to better universities. The special sadness was that, if Rutgers had still been the school at which I'd arrived in the late 1980s, none of them would have been transferring. Their presence at Rutgers, even in the Big East era, had been enriching the college experience of the more average classmates they were leaving behind. Here's part of a letter I wrote for a student who transferred to Columbia.

I'm personally sorry to hear that Steven Rubel is thinking about transferring to Columbia, but I understand his reasons for wanting to transfer. Steven was a student of mine in English 219, Introduction to Literary Study. I'm known as a "hard" teacher, so I tend to have a highly self-selected constituency of students.

In that very fast company, Steve was one of the best students in the class. He writes well, thinks clearly, and is intellectually fast on his feet. He's articulate and a pleasure to hear when making contributions to class discussion. His was a group that took almost no teaching, in the sense that once a discussion was focused—219 as I teach it is a course devoted entirely to the "close reading" of earlier English poetry—the students did the rest.

Steve almost counted as one of the teachers of the class, despite the fact that two other students were much more take-charge and outgoing. Steve, quieter and less given to self-assertion, would almost always top the others in the incisiveness of his comments and readings at crucial points. A delight to have in the classroom, as you might guess. . . .

I'll look forward to hearing that Steven has been accepted at Columbia, and I look forward to hearing from him about his adventures there. It's the right choice for him, and he's the right sort of student for Columbia. He'll make a real contribution to undergraduate life, in the classroom and out of it.

These days, I write ten to fifteen letters for students like Steven every year. Not all go to Ivy League schools. Several have gone to N Y U, several others to the University of Chicago. In the period before Rutgers entered the Big East, I'd written two or three such letters, at most, each spring semester. As it happens, I got a letter from Steve several weeks ago. He's entering his senior year at Columbia, and he's still bubbling over with excitement about his classes. Columbia's core curriculum, based on a sequence of writers extending from Homer, Sophocles, and Plato in ancient Greece, to Augustine and Dante in the Middle Ages, to Cervantes in the Renaissance, has meant a great deal to him. It's given him a framework, he says, for everything he's learning in his elective courses. (Rutgers offers nothing like this to provide its students with a common body of core knowledge.) Reading his letter, I was happy for Steve, but sad for my own university.

Toward the end of the 1990s, a quiet panic set in among Rutgers administrators. They'd finally begun to understand that New Jersey's brightest students were shunning the university in large numbers, and that others were leaving almost as soon as they'd arrived. In the years immediately after 2000, plans for wholesale reorganization of the university began to take shape, partly in the hope of reversing the downward trend. Task forces were formed. Study groups began to meet. Teams of faculty and administrators were sent out to interview the dwindling number of very bright students who had come to Rutgers and who, for whatever reasons, had decided to stay rather than transfer out. The interviewers, so far as one can tell, didn't have a clue that Div I A athletics, in removing Rutgers from its ancient association with institutions like Colgate and Princeton and associating it instead with places like Miami and Virginia Tech, might be at the root of the problem.

I had a long talk with a student who met with members of a reorganization task force. I still have my notes from our conversation. I'd asked her about her experiences in Brett Hall, the honors dorm. "We compared rejections like war wounds," she told me. "Nearly everyone had a story to tell about how they were shoo-ins for such-and-such an Ivy, but were stuck attending Rutgers instead. I can think of at least three people who were valedictorians or salutatorians of their high schools, and certainly hadn't wanted to go to Rutgers. It seems wrong, somehow, that we began our careers at Rutgers talking about where we would rather have been." The story of this student's freshman year in Brett had a certain poignancy. She told me about students who taped their Ivy rejection letters to their dorm walls, as though to remind themselves that they were stuck in an educational purgatory.

I winced, overwhelmed by a sense of bitter paradox. My student looked puzzled. I tried to explain to her why, though she couldn't be aware of it, she'd been demonstrating how good a university Rutgers had been in the pre–Big East era. Though the number of top students was now dwindling rapidly, the very existence of those Ivy rejection letters said something important. My students at the University of New Mexico had no Ivy rejection letters to tape to their walls. The Ivy League was so far beyond their academic reach that it would have been delusional to apply. In the schools in the NCAA's top-twenty-five football poll—the Oklahoma States and Kansas States and Boise States—students decorated their walls with football posters, not Ivy rejections. In Rutgers's own Big East conference, undergraduates at schools like West Virginia and Virginia Tech weren't papering their walls with rejections from Brown and Columbia and Dartmouth. The story she'd just told me, I said, was really about the last traces of an older and better Rutgers. She looked thoughtful. She hadn't, she admitted, ever looked at things in exactly that light.

She'd arrived at Rutgers after the evisceration of the honors program. The old admissions process had been abolished. A few token seminars, taken on an elective basis, were all that survived. As a small gesture of protest, I'd declined to teach in the new program so long as the dean who traveled with the football team remained in office. I asked her what students thought of the revised program. "Most of us," she told me, "consider the honors program a sham—a mere title used to make students feel special. Getting into honors doesn't require anything but decent SAT scores and a respectable class rank in high school. There's no application process, no essays, nothing of the sort. And once the student is in the program, it's ridiculously easy to stay there—all you need is a cumulative GPA of 3.5. In Rutgers College, students have the *opportunity* to take seminars, but no obligation to do it. It's perfectly possible to be a so-called honors student and drift through Rutgers without ever challenging yourself intellectually. Let's face it, a 3.5 GPA really isn't very hard to maintain."

Still, even as bright students were being increasingly marginalized, Rutgers wasn't yet dominated by its own equivalent of Duke's bench burners and Cameron Crazies. If top students like Emily were frustrated by the lack of any sense of intellectual community, the higher proportion of substandard students we were now accepting were just as frustrated by the lack of opportunities to get drunk and build bonfires. Significantly enough, such students took to venting their sense of frustration on Rutgers sports boards, as though they recognized in the university's booster subculture a mirror of their own mentality. Over the years, the RU1000 Web team kept a separate folder of undergraduate posts on booster boards. It's entitled "Party Animals," the RU1000 shorthand I've borrowed in this book.

The posts in the "Party Animal" folder are dated by day, month, and year. It's easy to trace the rise of a student subculture resembling West Virginia and UConn virtually from the moment of Rutgers's entry into the Big East. During the first years, there are very few posts. Then the voice of a new type of undergraduate begins to be heard more frequently, usually expressing deep frustration at the absence of the Cameron Crazies type at Rutgers. Very often, there is rage directed at Rutgers 1000 for its opposition to Div IA athletics. Here is a typical post, from a student writing under the name "Paisano." As before, I've left spelling and punctuation intact:

Im a freshman and I live on Livingston. Almost every obstacle has been placed in my way to enjoy myself here. My room is next the RAC, the 4 other guys on the floor, do nothing but sit around on Thur/Fri/Sat nights, they are against parties and are antagonanostic to people who enjoy them.

This is a microcosm of what is wrong with the RU community. Here at Rutgers we have a group (a vocal one at that) that want to impose their will on the rest of the student body, these are the same groups that are protesting outside of Brower everday.

They say (the people I live with) that these parties are nothing more than LOUD music (no I don't live in a nursing home) drinking, "slutty" girls and people acting stupid and immature. DAMN RIGHT AND WHATS WRONG WITH THAT????

I have tried hard to meet people who like me (they do exist and feel just like I do) like parties, booze, and chicks. I go to frat parties almost every week, I went to almost every home B-ball game and football game. But these people make it hard.

Now these same groups are the ones hurting RU athletics. Groups like the Rutgers 1000 are snobs who thumb there nose at athletic achievement. I was angered by the comment made in the Targum by some RU 1000 dork, Dorothy Wu, who said after seeing the workout video that the Big East was a mistake and "the players are paying for it with their lives." Obviously she has never participated in any sporting competition and cant appreciate the hardwork that athletes undertake. I guess she only values the hardwork of studying for some calc exam. There are other things in life ya know.

We need a stronger and more vocal student body that will fight just as hard as the RU 1000 in favor of RU sports and "less culturally valuable and wholesome activities." RU has to be a place where were safe to have parties whenever we want.

Paisano needn't have worried. By the end of the 1990s, Div IA athletics were making students like him feel at home. Not being an undergraduate, I can't report on the party scene—what Paisano plaintively refers to as the "parties, booze, and chicks" ethos he so ardently desires at Rutgers—but I can report that, especially at basketball games, the university was producing its own Cameron Crazies. In the student section of the RAC, pregame drinking had gotten serious enough that undergraduates were throwing up and passing out. The slogans and insults yelled at opposing players grew more and more obscene. At a game against Seton Hall, student behavior got so gross that even Robert Mulcahy, who as athletic director had been hosting some Trenton politicians at the game, was embarrassed. In the *Targum,* he went so far as to publish a letter mildly suggesting that students, while laudably filled with school spirit, might want to damp down a bit on the obscenities.

The golden opportunity for Rutgers's own Cameron Crazies came in 2000, when the basketball team finally won enough games to go to the National Invitational Tournament in Madison Square Garden. In recent years, as the billions of dollars poured into the NCAA's "March Madness" spectacle has given it greater national visibility, the NIT has become a consolation event for teams that didn't qualify. Still, it was a tournament. Rutgers hadn't had much to celebrate in sports for quite a while. There was another reason for celebration. Madison Square Garden, in midtown Manhattan, is a short train ride away for Rutgers students and fans. As it turned out, the Rutgers team made the NIT finals against the University of Michigan. The RAC student section, like migratory birds answering some mysterious call, moved en masse toward Madison Square Garden.

My own sense of what went on at the NIT finals is based on booster board postings. In the student section, there was a great deal of drunkenness. There were obscenities hurled at players on the opposing team. And in Madison Square Garden, where fans from the two teams were mixed together in the same sections, Rutgers students were proud of having physically intimidated Michigan supporters. "There was a brawl behind me between two drunk RU students," one undergraduate reported. "The Mich egghead fans were very scared all night. They were literally afraid to cheer. The atmosphere definitely had an edge to it. We have great fans and last night was awesome." I didn't quite understand why these students—undergraduates, after all, at my own university—seemed so filled with pride about ugly or violent behavior. But there seemed to be no question that they were proud. "No fights around where I sat," one reported, "but before the start of the game, there were many, many chants on 'Michigan sucks' on the way up to our seats." Another student was pleased by the atmosphere of intimidation he and his classmates had produced. "I saw several RU younger fans giving the middle finger to the face of the middle-aged Michigan fans in the area," he proudly told the boosters. "Michigan fans just walked away."

When the game was over, New Jersey commuters got a firsthand view of the new Rutgers that was emerging in the Big East era. There were numerous fights on the New Jersey Transit trains taking undergraduates back to New Brunswick. "The poor people in that train did not know what hit them," one student boasted happily. "We filled that train with scarlet and RU chants were started on the train. One passenger who I was standing next to commented that he hopes RU doesn't get too good, because it would make their lives a living hell!! I thought that was great. I said, 'you better learn to love it. You better learn to love it'." The resemblance of these students to the bench burners at Duke, or the Ohio State students who set fires in downtown Columbus, needs no comment. Still, Mr. Mulcahy and the Scarlet R boosters seemed to see nothing wrong. Nor did the *Daily Targum*, which filled its next day's issue with celebratory stories about "Scarlet Pride." Nor did the sportswriters at the *Home News Tribune*, one of whom quoted a Rutgers freshman as saying that, sitting there in the stands at the NIT, he had felt for the first time that he was "at a real university."

By the time Rutgers played in the NIT, Francis Lawrence had been in the presidency for a decade. The university had been in the Big East for six years. In my teaching at Rutgers, I'd begun increasingly to feel as though I existed inside a magic bubble—like some space station or undersea ecosphere with its own purified atmosphere—that was isolating me from the new population of Paisanos and Madison Square Garden rowdies. If I hadn't been active in Rutgers 1000, with a Web team continuously providing evidence of the shift taking place in the student population, I doubt I would have given the matter any thought. For the friend who had called me from Ohio State to ask about jobs elsewhere, Div IA athletics was giving him a type of student no teacher wants to deal with. For me at Rutgers, that type of student was still something I'd never seen in person.

In the *Chronicle of Higher Education,* it's true, I'd been reading more and more frequently about a new kind of ugly classroom behavior, the sort of thing associated with urban high schools in the era of *The Blackboard Jungle.* "It was the class from hell," one *Chronicle* story arrestingly began. "Some students slept, others chatted. They showed up late and left early. The few who tried to pay attention were distracted by the majority who didn't." "I got to the point where I hated going into the classroom," the professor teaching this class told the *Chronicle* reporter, describing himself as frustrated and depressed. The same story recounted the experience of another professor who'd ventured to remonstrate with a student who had been fast asleep during her lecture. "She informed him that sleeping in class was equal to an absence," the *Chronicle* reported. "The sleepy student's response: 'F— you.'"

Still, I didn't think of this as a Rutgers problem. In an era of open admissions, as I'd discovered years before at the University of New Mexico, a great many universities are filled with students who don't belong in a college classroom. It was only a matter of time before such institutions became the blackboard jungle of our own era. The only experience I'd ever had with this sort of behavior at Rutgers had come when I was giving a guest lecture in a "Sports in American Culture" course taught by my American Studies colleague Michael Rockland. In that class, an extremely tall young man—I found out he was a star player on the Rutgers basketball team—had slouched into class thirty-five minutes late, distributed himself in segments over a long row of front seats, and promptly fallen asleep, snoring loudly. But that, as I later found out, had been a class filled with athletes picking up eligibility credits. If Rockland saw nothing objectionable about such behavior, it wasn't my place to object.

So it was that my own encounter with the Paisano type came, right at the end of the Lawrence presidency, in a course entitled "Worlds of Autobiography." A bit of background is in order. Every two or three years, to give non-English majors some exposure to literary analysis before they graduate, I try to schedule what I call an outreach course—that is, one firmly centered on analysis of theme and literary structure, but not needing previous English courses as a prerequisite. In "Worlds of Autobiography," the central concept has to do with what we mean when we speak of "the world of medicine," "the world of sports," "the world of war," etc.—a self-contained sphere of rules, rituals, tribal beliefs, taboos, and perceptions giving it status as a separate reality. The autobiographical structure studied in the course is one in which an "I" or ordinary consciousness enters into such a world, passes through it as a *rite de passage,* and emerges as a newly constituted being.

This literary structure is perfect for an outreach course, one that premeds and philosophy majors and mathematicians might find compelling when a course on Renaissance poetry or Augustan satire would seem daunting. The books I assigned for the class included Hemingway's *A Moveable Feast,* James Watson's *The Double Helix,* Melvin Konner's *Becoming a Doctor,* Scott Turow's *One L,* Jim Bouton's *Ball Four,* Stanislaw Ulam's *Adventures of a Mathematician,* and Colin McGinn's *The Making of a Philosopher.* The course began well. The students were enchanted with *A Moveable Feast,* Hemingway's memoir of his days as a young writer in expatriate Paris just after World War I. Even those who had no intention of going to law school found *One L,* Turow's radically ambivalent account of his first year at Harvard Law, a gripping autobiographical narrative. The letdown came when, having moved on to *Ball Four,* I discovered that this class contained my own personal Paisano.

I teach courses like this one in Murray 210, a midsized lecture room that holds about a hundred students. Already, when lecturing on Hemingway, I'd noticed that one student far in the back was behaving oddly. He always wore a gigantic cap made of white leather. He kept it on in the room. In the next few classes, he wandered randomly in and out. I lecture on each book for two days and then, on the third day, throw the class open to discussion—problems or puzzles that cropped up in the reading but that I hadn't addressed in my lectures. On our third day on *Ball Four,* I looked out over the class to discover that the student in the white leather cap had put his head down and was slumbering heavily. I was, I admit, a bit nonplussed. I'd never seen anything like this at Rutgers. Then an inspiration came to me. I *had* seen this behavior before, in Michael Rockland's class. Since we were reading a sports book, I told, as a kind of self-deprecating joke, the story of the snoring basketball player in "Sports in American Culture." Nobody, I observed, ever seemed to fall asleep when I was talking about Hemingway. It must be something about sports.

The students laughed. Some of them had been looking over at him surreptitiously. Now everybody turned around to see what they'd been looking at. As the laughter grew, the student stirred in his sleep, blinked, looked up, and gazed around him in bewilderment. I asked him to speak to me after class. The exchange wasn't pleasant. I could tell, I said mildly, that he was used to a different standard of classroom civility from my other students. I asked him to drop the class.

"I can't," he mumbled. "I need the credits."

Well, I said, there were ways around this. In extraordinary cases, the dean's office and the registrar would authorize a transfer to another class. I'd helped one of my students to do this several years before, when a personal crisis at home made it impossible for her to make the class she was enrolled in with me.

"Hey, what's the problem?" he wanted to know. "Everybody sleeps in my other classes."

I don't know to this day whether this was a bit of bravado on his part or the simple truth. But I was curious. "What year are you?" I asked.

"Fourth year."

"And you've sat through four years of classes at Rutgers and in them all you've seen people putting their heads down on their desks and snoring and no one has said a word?"

"Most of them."

"Do you mind explaining why you do this?"

"I learn better when I'm sleeping."

Well, I told myself, it was better than "F— you."

My own personal Paisano stayed in the autobiography course. His written work was execrable—looking over some work of his that I kept, I see that he was given to spelling words like "restaurant" as *resteraunt* and "holiday" as *holliday*—and the assigned readings seemed to be beyond his comprehension. He kept on wearing his hat in the classroom. But after our exchange, he stopped wandering in and out of the room. His way of getting through class was to bring along a CD player and earphones. As soon as the lecture had begun, he'd put his feet up on the back of the chair in front of him, lean back in his seat, put in his earphones, and spend the class rocking back and forth and drumming his fingers to the music. Having flunked the majority of the quizzes I give at the beginning of each class—his quiz average was nearly fifty points below that of the next-lowest student—he finally dropped the course. It is still a mystery to me why he stayed as long as he did.

It's not a mystery, though, why Div IA sports draw students like this to a university. If you read carefully through Paisano's post as given earlier, you'll see that there is a seething mass of resentment simmering just beneath his talk about parties, chicks, and booze. As I've said before, it's a version of what Nietzsche called *ressentiment,* the inarticulate antagonism of those who are unable to do anything directly about forces they feel to be oppressing them, and so have to take revenge in symbolic form. At Div IA universities, the oppression is felt to be the university itself, with its ancient associations with a "higher" culture of knowledge and ideas, and, on the individual level, its demands for reading and analytic thinking. The symbolic revenge is what occurs around the bonfires at Duke or Ohio State, or, in Rutgers's case, the drunken brawls in Madison Square Garden.

It's not an accident, I would come to realize, that the Rutgers students who drank and started fights and asserted a swaggering dominance over the commuters on New Jersey Transit rushed, as soon as they got home, to report their doings on Rutgers booster boards. The *ressentiment* that drives the Paisanos and Cameron Crazies on campus bears a strong resemblance to that of the Wolfpack Club or the Lobo Club or Scarlet R as they assert symbolic ownership of a Div I A university, transforming it from an institution of higher learning into a semiprofessional sports franchise controlled by boosters who, as we heard Geoffrey Norman say, have no inner life and cannot imagine one in anyone else. Booster *ressentiment* has always been the dark secret of Div I A sports. It's not surprising to see it spread to the Paisanos of American higher education.

You've already read the original Paisano's contribution to the athletics debate at Rutgers. You may be interested to know that he made it through to graduation. Four years after he'd attacked Rutgers 1000 as a freshman, he posted a message on the same sports board. He'd just received his degree. He invited the boosters to congratulate him. The subject line was "I am an alumni!" That seemed to me to say it all.

The Hour of Victory

If you count an undergraduate generation as lasting four years, two generations of RU1000 students had come and gone by the year 2000. The original group of organizers had departed into the wide world. The day they'd come to my office to say that the UNM nightmare of professionalized athletics had materialized at Rutgers seemed to belong to the distant past. The founding students, together with the next generation, had set in motion the events leading to the formation of the RU1000 Alumni Council, the publication of the Friedman statement, and Rutgers 1000's landmark victory in the *Rutgers Magazine* case. They'd established and developed the remarkable RU1000 Web site that led to national awareness of the campaign. By the end of its run the Web site recorded more than two hundred thousand hits. As I looked back on those early glory days, though, Rutgers 1000 seemed to me to have reached an impasse. Despite the campaign's best efforts to mobilize public opinion against the ruinous promotion of "big-time" sports at the university, Francis Lawrence still remained in office, and Rutgers continued in the Big East.

"How is he *doing* it?" I remember one reporter from a Gannett newspaper asking me about Lawrence. How had a president known mainly for his lack of leadership and his public relations blunders been able to stay in office in the face of steadily growing opposition? By now, a large part of the Rutgers faculty had mobilized against him. It wasn't surprising, perhaps, that FAR, the Faculty Alliance for Rutgers—a group organized specifically to oppose the university's decline under Lawrence—should have become a strong voice within the university senate. But recently an entirely different body, the Rutgers University Faculty Association, had commissioned a study from the American Arbitration Association, a nonprofit public service organization, asking for a numerical rating of President Lawrence in nineteen crucial areas of university governance. When the responses were tallied, the results were devastating. On a ten-point scale with ten as the highest rating and zero as the lowest, Lawrence came in below five in eighteen of the nineteen categories. His lowest rating came on athletics policy. When asked to measure the effect of his Big East athletics program on the university's core academic values, the faculty gave Lawrence a 2.3.

In Rutgers 1000, we'd spent most of a decade asking ourselves the question the Gannett reporter asked me: "How is he *doing* it?" Only gradually had we come to suspect that there must be a hidden structure of power relations sustaining the president. We'd been assuming that Rutgers, with a complex governance system deriving from its colonial heritage, had a decisive advantage over other public universities. At most state schools, booster subculture comes to exert control over an institution through straightforwardly political means. When the Wolfpack Club called upon state attorney general Lacy Thornburg to suppress Peter Golenbock's *Personal Fouls,* for instance, the deep roots of NCSU boosterism in North Carolina politics were evident to anyone looking on. Nor was it surprising when a Nebraska state legislator sponsored a bill to pay salaries to University of Nebraska football players out of state funds, for Nebraska's football program had long since become a professional franchise in everything but name. To most Nebraskans, the legislator's claim that the NCAA's "student athlete" pretense was depriving hard-working semiprofessional athletes of their just rewards would seem perfectly logical.

As the North Carolina and Nebraska examples suggest, control by the state government leads at most state universities almost inevitably to control by a politically active booster subculture. In North Carolina, members of university governing boards are chosen directly by the state legislature, which is in no position to resist the power of a booster organization like the Wolfpack Club. In New Jersey, by contrast, the state university is governed by a system designed to insulate Rutgers from state politics. According to the 1956 legislation that made Rutgers the official state university of New Jersey, the policymaking body overseeing the university—the board of governors, at Rutgers always called the BOG (pronounced Bee-Oh-Gee)—was to be made up of six members appointed by the governor of New Jersey and five members elected by and from the eighty-odd member board of trustees. The six "public governors" were meant to provide oversight on behalf of New Jersey taxpayers who were now underwriting the costs of the university. The five "trustee governors" were meant to represent the interests of the alumni and the traditions of a historically private institution whose charter predated the American Revolution.

In the mid-1950s, it was a reasonable system. What designers of the 1956 legislation couldn't have foreseen was that an emergent local boosterism, incited by televised spectacles like "March Madness" and the FedEx Orange Bowl, would grow strong enough to overcome the careful balancing of public and private interests. What allowed it to do so was an accident of geography. As most successful Rutgers alumni—those who went on to become federal judges, medical school professors, scientists, or high-level corporate executives—scattered across the United States, the board of trustees would pass into the control of a small group of local alumni who lived within driving distance of New Brunswick. Living nearby, and fond of socializing with each other, they took to scheduling frequent meetings, effectively excluding out-of-state alumni from the board. The percentage of Scarlet R boosters among them was high.

There was another unforeseen development. Although the 1956 legislation had been intended to balance public and private interests, it had made no provision for keeping the two categories of BOG members separate. Once a trustee governor had completed his or her term, he or she could be immediately reappointed as a public governor. By 2002, nine of the eleven seats on the BOG would be occupied by members who had come up through the board of trustees. By the same token, the chairmanship of the BOG by 2002 would have been held for twenty-three years by trustee governors. Again, there was a high percentage of Scarlet R boosters among them. In effect, the larger public perspective supposed to be represented on the BOG by the public trustees had, in the prevailing climate of local cronyism, given way to the viewpoint of a small group of local alumni overwhelmingly devoted to big-time sports.

At first, Rutgers 1000 took little interest in what seemed mere procedural details. It's true we'd heard that Lawrence had been brought to Rutgers in a search process manipulated by a prominent member of the Scarlet R boosters club. We had also taken notice when one pro-Lawrence chair of the BOG subsequently moved over to the executive committee of Scarlet R. But we didn't really wake up to the workings of booster cronyism until 2001, when yet another chair of the board of trustees was promoted to the BOG. Reading the press release about his appointment, I was dismayed to see that he'd previously been chair of the Scarlet R Foundation for a full decade and had long been a large contributor to the athletics program. Once appointed to the BOG, he was immediately made chair of its Athletics Committee. Within a short time, he would also become vice chair of the BOG. Suddenly it looked as if Rutgers 1000 had been aiming at the wrong target all along. We thought we'd been opposing Francis Lawrence and "Bob" Mulcahy. Now it seemed clear we'd really been up against something both more entrenched and more dangerous: Rutgers's own version of the Wolfpack Club.

The Rutgers 1000 Alumni Council, largely made up of alumni living outside New Jersey, was the first to become aware of the problem. Still, when I suggested to the RU1000 students that the real problem might derive from a silent booster takeover of the BOG, they were unperturbed. Even if the board of governors was completely controlled by Scarlet R, they argued, its athletics ambitions would end with Lawrence's resignation. At this point, the BOG was totally identified with Lawrence, supporting him against criticism that now bordered on general public contempt. By now it was clear to everyone in New Jersey that his BOG support was based entirely on Lawrence's allegiance to Div IA sports. Two BOG members had publicly declared, after all, that Lawrence's "national stature" was proved by his having been chosen Big East conference chairman. Getting rid of Lawrence, the students argued, would automatically mean getting Rutgers out of the Big East. That was the part I was no longer sure about. But the students were confident. All that was needed was one last big push to win the battle against Div IA athletics. Their predecessors in Rutgers 1000 had pushed the Lawrence presidency to the edge of the cliff. They only needed to nudge it over.

If anyone could do it, it would be this newest generation of RU1000 students. The steering committee now consisted of students like Brendan Prawdzic, who would later win a Rotary graduate fellowship to St. Andrews in Scotland, Huck Finne, who would go into the U.S. Navy's officer training program for nuclear submarines, and Anna Lewis, a Rhodes scholar finalist who would take her *maîtrise* at the Sorbonne before returning to enter the English Ph.D. program at Yale. Others included Kevin Felix, Laurie Agnese, Dorothy Wu, Naomi Silverman, Ben Remsen, and Deborah Sands. They were writers, musicians, artists, and athletes. They were endlessly resourceful. Prawdzic and Finne, for instance, instantly saw that the machinery of student government, usually meaningless at large public universities, could be turned to the purposes of serious student activism. I still have copies of flyers listing slates of RU1000 candidates for RCGA, the undergraduate senate. Along with flyers, they handed out campaign buttons ("The Big East is a BIG mistake!"). Many from the RU1000 slate were elected, and many were the *Targum* stories about speeches from the floor warning against the degradation of Rutgers by commercialized Div IA sports.

This new crop of RU1000 students favored unannounced actions they called symbolic interventions. The most memorable took place at "Pep Nite," a much-publicized rally to introduce Greg Schiano, the newly hired football coach, to a large crowd of cheering undergraduates. After the pom-poms and marching songs, Coach Schiano was slated to give an inspirational speech about Rutgers football. Then would come a question-and-answer period. Scattering themselves among the crowd, the RU1000 students had come prepared with questions that neither "Bob" Mulcahy nor Coach Schiano had been expecting. The result was a near riot. I still have a photo of Anna Lewis holding up a hand-lettered sign, asking why nearly $3 million a year was being wasted on athletic scholarships when top New Jersey students were deserting Rutgers in droves. Another shows Brendan Prawdzic, standing straight and calm amid an angry crowd of student football fans, asking why a university that had played schools like Colgate and Princeton for a hundred years should now be trying to model itself on Virginia Tech and the University of Miami. Yet another shows Deborah Sands, small and indomitable, facing down a glowering mob of huge male students, their fists clenched and their faces twisted in rage.

Among the Pep Nite boosters that evening was the student you met in the last chapter as "Paisano." The next day, Paisano gave his own version of Pep Nite on a booster board. "I was at the Schiano speech," he told the boosters. "I saw those punks get up I booed the hell out of them, and yelled a few 'cusses' to let them know what they can do. I didnt know it at the time, but I was sitting in the back surrounded by RU1000 members. They told me to 'respect the protestors right to speak.' Yeah f-ckin right! Later when that bitch got up to ask GS an obnoxious question (she was sitting right behind me) that was obviously meant to try and embarrass him, I turned around and told her to SHUT THE F-CK UP and sit down." Paisano was talking about Anna Lewis, the Rhodes scholar finalist. RU1000's Pep Nite intervention will always stay in my mind as the symbolic confrontation of an older Rutgers with a new Rutgers coming into existence in the Big East era: an encounter between a Rutgers alumna who would take her *maîtrise* at the Sorbonne before entering the English Ph.D. program at Yale and a soon-to-be-self-described Rutgers "alumni" about whose subsequent career history has remained silent.

Actions like the Pep Nite intervention couldn't, by themselves, bring down the Lawrence presidency. Still, they were having a visible impact. As

"I saw those punks get up and I booed the hell out of them." Pep Nite crowd watches as RU1000 student rises to ask football coach Greg Schiano an unanticipated question. Photo: RU1000 Archives.

Paisano's furious outburst shows, RU1000's steady opposition was blocking the smooth transition to "big-time" sports power that Lawrence, Mulcahy, and the Scarlet R faction on the BOG had been counting on to solve—or at least paper over—the problem of Rutgers's academic decline. Given enough "school spirit" of the sort seen at UConn basketball rallies or Miami football games, they clearly believed, nobody would care about things like the accelerating flight of top New Jersey students or decaying classrooms or the massive hemorrhaging of money on Div IA sports. But that "school spirit" wasn't emerging. Even worse, from the Scarlet R point of view, was that people were increasingly objecting to the grand project of transforming Rutgers into Virginia Tech or UConn, where students like Paisano ruled the institution. At Rutgers—perversely, as it must have seemed to Mulcahy and the boosters—the Paisanos did not yet predominate.

Then, suddenly, the Lawrence presidency fell. It was as if a house of cards had collapsed. The moment of Lawrence's downfall came on an Amtrak train speeding from New York to Washington. Riding the train was New Jersey's newly elected Democratic governor, going to the nation's capital to testify about state funding needs. Back in Trenton, his transition team was holding a meeting to discuss the future of New Jersey higher education. In the same Amtrak car was Benjamin Barber, an eminent political scientist and author of the best-selling *Jihad vs. McWorld*. For years, Barber had been one of Francis Lawrence's most outspoken critics. Now, after having taught at Rutgers for thirty-two years, he had decided to leave for another university. As news of Barber's departure spread, many on the New Brunswick campus had been nervously asking themselves if this marked the beginning of the long-dreaded flight of prominent faculty.

When the governor saw Barber sitting a few rows ahead, he moved up to a vacant seat beside him. Talk turned to Rutgers and Francis Lawrence. Barber, looking back on his decades of teaching at an older and better university, gave full vent to his accumulated feelings about the Lawrence presidency. Without a word, the governor took out his cell phone and dialed the conference room where his transition team was meeting. Pausing to ask someone to turn on the speaker phone in the room, he handed the receiver to Barber. "Tell them what you just told me," the governor said. Accounts of what happened next vary in their details, but everyone agrees that it was as though Barber, given a sudden opportunity to say what thousands of people in New Jersey had been thinking for years, achieved a moment of inspired eloquence. By the time the phone call ended, everyone present knew the Lawrence presidency was over.

Francis Lawrence would linger on for another two months, finally handing in his resignation in early February 2002. When he did, there was general rejoicing on campus. In the flurry of news stories that followed, commentators noted the role Lawrence's devotion to Div IA athletics had played in finally bringing him down. "Dr. Lawrence was a major proponent of the sports program," wrote the *New York Times*, "which has been under fire for much of the last decade from a vocal chorus on campus that questioned the wisdom of spending millions of dollars on sports teams." His departure, the paper observed, "raises questions about the future of major athletics at the university." Former New Jersey governor Thomas Kean was a good deal blunter. Kean, who'd become a university president himself after leaving office, was the leading member of the transition team on higher education that Benjamin Barber had so unexpectedly addressed. When interviewed about Lawrence's resignation by the *Chronicle of Higher Education*, Kean responded—perhaps with Barber's angry eloquence still echoing in his ears—that what Rutgers needed was "somebody, frankly, who cares more about having the best English department in the country than about having the best football team."

"FAR celebrated its victory amid the clink of champagne glasses." (*Left to right*): John Gillis and Peter Lindenfeld, founders of the Faculty Alliance for Rutgers, with WCD on the evening of the Lawrence resignation. Photo: RU1000 Archives.

The groups who had spent more than a decade opposing Lawrence's presidency began to disband. A few days after Lawrence's resignation, FAR, the Faculty Alliance for Rutgers, celebrated its victory amid the clink of champagne glasses. The next week, three members of the RU1000 student steering committee arrived at my office, proposing that Rutgers 1000 also vote to dissolve itself, now that the struggle was at an end. Pleased as I was about the president's departure, I counseled waiting. FAR, I reminded them, had been organized specifically to oppose the university's academic decline under Lawrence. Rutgers 1000, on the other hand, had been organized to get Rutgers out of the Big East and into a nonathletic-scholarship conference. Though it was immensely encouraging, Lawrence's resignation didn't mean that Rutgers would be withdrawing from the Big East, at least not immediately. After all, the next president of Rutgers would be chosen by the same BOG that had kept Lawrence in office for twelve years. And that BOG was still dominated by Scarlet R boosters.

As the search for a new president got under way, others began to share my sense that celebration might be premature. The BOG put together a twenty-six-member search committee composed, as far as one could tell, entirely of people who either favored Big East membership or who had remained neutral on the issue. No one from Rutgers's "loyal opposition"—most notably, from FAR or Rutgers 1000—was named to the group. Then the BOG announced that it had chosen the executive headhunting firm A. T. Kearney Executive Search to conduct the presidential quest. The faculty, acutely aware that university presidents chosen from the rolodex of firms like Kearney were almost always colorless bureaucrats, began to murmur. There was another reason to be worried. As education writer Brian Kladko pointed out in the *Bergen County Record* ("Super Personality Sought to Polish the Face of Rutgers"), many Rutgers faculty mistrusted A. T. Kearney specifically "because it's the same firm that Rutgers used to find Lawrence in 1990." After interviewing students, faculty, administrators, and legislators, Kladko concluded that what everyone wanted for Rutgers was a president who was as nearly as possible the opposite of Francis Lawrence.

The board of governors conducting this search, Kladko reminded readers, was "the same board that stood by Lawrence for years." Unhappy with the BOG's selection of A. T. Kearney and mistrustful of the BOG's ability to choose the right candidate, the faculty began lobbying for the selection of a candidate who would preside over a revival of academic and intellectual values at Rutgers. Their candidate was Richard Foley, dean of arts and sciences at New York University. Foley had previously served as a highly regarded dean of arts and sciences at Rutgers. As chair of the Philosophy Department, he had played a major role in building the top-ranked department in the country. By no means extroverted, Foley was, if anything, introspective, soft-spoken, almost ruminative. Yet he communicated a sense of self-confidence and moral integrity that reminded many of Mason Gross. As one of my colleagues said, anyone who knew Foley knew he would get Rutgers back on track.

Meanwhile, the Rutgers 1000 Alumni Council was mobilizing on behalf of a different candidate. This was Richard L. McCormick, then president of the University of Washington. He'd begun as a professor at Rutgers, joining the History Department in 1976. Like Foley, he had become chair of his department and then dean of arts and sciences. He'd left when invited to become provost of the University of North Carolina. In outward terms, McCormick was something like Foley's opposite. He was energetic, voluble, and outer-directed. A profile of McCormick in *Seattle* magazine that circulated widely at Rutgers described him as a bundle of energy, briskly moving from faculty meetings to board rooms to social gatherings, staying late at the office, universally admired by regents, business leaders, state legislators, and ordinary taxpayers in the state of Washington.

The Rutgers 1000 alumni were impressed by McCormick's energy, but they rallied to McCormick for a stronger reason. They saw him as the personification of a living Rutgers tradition. Many remembered McCormick's father, Richard P. McCormick, as a beloved former Rutgers history professor. Others knew his father as the official university historian, author of the bicentennial history of Rutgers published in 1974 as part of the school's two-hundredth birthday celebration. Widely known as "Mr. Rutgers," McCormick Sr. had arrived at Rutgers as an undergraduate in 1932. He'd spent his life in the service of the university. He had been close to Mason Gross during the years of Gross's distinguished presidency. The inner circle of RU1000 alumni were aware, as well, that McCormick Sr. had been a longtime supporter of Rutgers 1000. He'd at one point published a much-discussed letter to the *Targum* in favor of participatory athletics. His son had literally grown up on the Rutgers campus.

As a faculty member, I felt torn. Either McCormick or Foley would, I thought, be an excellent choice for president. As a member of Rutgers 1000, though, I found my mind returning again and again to one important point. McCormick Jr. had attended Amherst as an undergraduate and gone to Yale for his PH.D. Neither school permits athletic scholarships. McCormick, I thought, would be absolutely certain to understand the importance of participatory athletics. In discussing the presidential search with members of the RU1000 Alumni Council, I found that their one reservation concerned his strength of personality. Could McCormick stand up to a board of governors dominated by members of Scarlet R? On this point, I felt I could reassure them. A decade earlier, my own department had come under tremendous political pressure to hire Amiri Baraka, the African American poet later discredited for anti-Semitic poems blaming the destruction of the World Trade Center on a Jewish conspiracy. After much debate and heated discussion, the English Department had declined to hire Baraka. McCormick, as dean of arts and sciences, had the power to reverse their decision. But amid an atmosphere of TV cameras and demonstrations and angry speeches delivered over bullhorns, he hadn't yielded an inch.

When the news got out in Seattle that President McCormick of UW was at the top of the Rutgers presidential list, a reporter from *Seattle Post-Intelligencer* contacted members of every group playing a role in the search. Richard Seclow of the RU1000 Alumni Council frankly admitted his preference for McCormick. "His name comes up on the dream list all the time," he told the *Post-Intelligencer*. A Rutgers faculty leader, Rudolph Bell, said the same. "The first two names that occur to 90 percent of the faculty who have been here 10 years or more are those of Richard Foley and Richard McCor-

mick." Still, presented with these strong demonstrations of interest, McCormick himself categorically denied any interest in the Rutgers position. U W
presidents, he told the *Post-Intelligencer,* had a long and honorable tradition
of longevity in office. He was not about to break with it. "That's all there is to
it," he said. "I am very happy in my position at the University of Washington." If this wasn't enough to discourage his supporters in New Jersey, there
was also the fact that McCormick's wife of nearly twenty years, women's
historian Suzanne Lebsock, was a tenured member of U W's History Department. They were said to be a close family, with two children at school in the
Seattle area.

By this point I'd had several conversations with Seattle reporters. One of
them, an education writer for the *Post-Intelligencer,* knew a good deal about
the Rutgers 1000 campaign. Why on earth, he wanted to know, were our
alumni backing McCormick? "Don't they know he's got a couple of huge
athletics scandals brewing out here?" he asked me. I was taken aback. What
athletics scandals at Washington? I did know that U W's football coach, Rick
Neuheisel, was under investigation for serious recruiting violations. But
those had taken place earlier, at the University of Colorado, before Washington had lured him away with a huge salary. "What about McCormick's investigation by the ethics committee for the Rose Bowl junket?" this reporter
asked. We don't know anything about that either, I had to admit, feeling a
bit embarrassed. We'd been so focused on the Rutgers search that we hadn't
asked about McCormick's relation to U W athletics.

A bit shaken by the reporter's questions, I undertook some research. On
the face of it, the reporter seemed to have a point. There were numerous
stories about McCormick's vocal support of Div I A athletics at U W. From
the outside, he did look like someone who'd been eager to do the bidding
of U W's booster subculture. And Washington boosters did seem to bear a
strong resemblance to those at Miami and North Carolina. But all that, I
found myself telling this reporter, was the way any president had to behave at
a school where the boosters ran the institution. After all, Nannerl Keohane at
Duke and Gordon Gee at Ohio State had faced the same situation. Both had
been estimable presidents, doing their best to hold the boosters at bay while
trying to strengthen the institution academically. At Rutgers, McCormick
would have a far weaker booster subculture to deal with, and very strong
support from alumni and students opposing Div I A athletics.

A few weeks later, the Rutgers search committee announced the selection
of Richard McCormick. As expected, the B O G offered him the presidency.
But, true to what he'd told the *Seattle Post-Intelligencer,* McCormick turned
the offer down. He'd felt compelled to talk to the Rutgers search committee,

he explained to the *Daily*, the University of Washington's student newspaper, simply because Rutgers was his old school. It would have been discourteous to do otherwise. But when the offer of the Rutgers presidency actually came through, he hadn't felt the slightest temptation to accept it. He had, McCormick told the UW student reporter, unconditionally withdrawn his name. "I am no longer under consideration. I am very happy in my position at the University of Washington." McCormick told other newspapers the same thing. "In the case of Rutgers, because it was my home university," he said to the *Seattle Times*, "I felt I really had to talk to them." But this had been merely a gesture of courtesy.

Back in New Jersey, the BOG was stunned. They'd made it clear to him that money was no object. McCormick could name his own salary. His wife would be hired by the History Department. She'd also get a high salary, plus a drastically reduced teaching schedule to free her up for presidential social functions. But nothing had worked. As the BOG withdrew into closed conference, apparently paralyzed by its unexpected setback, pressure began mounting from faculty and alumni to make an immediate offer to Richard Foley. Foley was known to be second on the search committee's list. Several of his close friends on the Rutgers faculty told committee members he was prepared to accept the appointment. Rutgers 1000, too, threw its weight behind Foley's candidacy. Though he lacked the depth of McCormick's institutional ties to Rutgers, we believed Foley had more than enough strength to stand up to the board of governors and the boosters on the athletics issue. Reportedly, the BOG was only twenty-four hours away from making an offer to Foley.

Then, abruptly, Richard McCormick changed his mind. Ever since saying no, he told the BOG, he'd spent sleepless nights, his mind crowded with thoughts of his Rutgers childhood, his happy years on the faculty, his fond memories of his stint as dean of arts and sciences, and his strong ties to aging parents who still lived at the edge of the Rutgers campus. All the purely practical considerations that had prompted him to decline their offer now seemed insignificant. He had decided to listen to his heart. "I look forward to coming home," McCormick told the editors of a Rutgers newsletter. "I'm a loyal New Jersey son who grew up along the Banks. . . . I love Rutgers, and I am honored that my family and I have been a part of its long and distinguished tradition of excellence." Several months later, giving a rousing speech amid all the pomp and circumstance of his official inauguration, Richard L. McCormick would be formally inducted as the nineteenth president of Rutgers University.

The RU1000 students paid another visit to my office. Hadn't the moment arrived *now*, they asked, to dissolve Rutgers 1000's on-campus campaign? Wouldn't McCormick need a certain amount of time to withdraw Rutgers from the Big East? Wouldn't our continuing opposition at this point only stir up the BOG and tie the new president's hands? We'd been talking in Rutgers 1000 for more than a decade about the "invisible university"—the ideal institution that would emerge only under a president who knew what intellectual community was. We'd even come to call that invisible university the "Rutgers model," convinced that if only one major public university were to throw off the yoke of Div IA professionalized sports, others would soon follow, realizing how comparatively easy academic and intellectual distinction was to achieve when the school cut its ties to a retrograde booster subculture.

This time, I was happy to agree. Against all odds, Rutgers had come out of the Lawrence era as a public university where the ideal of democratic education might yet flourish. Crass commercialism and boosterism had not yet penetrated to its heart. Among all the Rutgers constituencies—faculty, students, alumni—there were people who understood what a genuine university could be. If the "Rutgers model" were to prosper anywhere, it had to begin at Rutgers. President McCormick deserved his inaugural honeymoon. The best gift we could give him would be the room he needed to maneuver against the anti-intellectual forces seeking to dominate the university. On the first of December, 2002, the student steering committee voted itself out of existence. Absurdly jubilant, they and I were convinced that it was the hour of victory. The struggle had been long and difficult, but Rutgers 1000 had won in the end.

Requiem for Rutgers 1000

The new president of Rutgers had hardly arrived when Rutgers 1000 realized it had made a tragic mistake. Shortly after the board of governors announced Richard McCormick's appointment, I'd given an interview to the *Home News Tribune*. "It's important to remember that Dick McCormick literally grew up on the Rutgers campus," I told the *Home News* reporter. "He was 14 years old when Rutgers had the most memorable year in its football history, going undefeated, ranking 15th in the nation, and producing a first-team All-American. He will remember that the schedule that year was made up entirely of the traditional rivals that Rutgers had been playing for nearly a century, including such institutions as Columbia, Princeton, Colgate and Lafayette." I didn't mention that our new president's father, Richard McCormick Sr., had supported Rutgers 1000 from the beginning. Our new president had repeatedly mentioned his family's long Rutgers tradition as a major reason for changing his mind about leaving the University of Washington. His father was the living symbol of that tradition.

Then, some months after his arrival, President McCormick began granting interviews to New Jersey sportswriters. It was as though he was conducting a deliberate public relations campaign to distance himself from Rutgers 1000. The interviews had a common theme: McCormick's devotion to Div 1A athletics and the Big East was every bit as strong as that of his predecessor, Francis Lawrence. "McCormick has made it abundantly clear that none of Rutgers 1000's recommendations will come to pass during his tenure," reported a *Home News* sportswriter. McCormick repeated Lawrence's argument that "academics and big-time athletics can go hand in hand." "A successful athletic program can help draw the community to campus," McCormick told this reporter, "and raise the university's profile in the public eye." He also went out of his way to endorse Rutgers's membership in the Big East. "The Big East is the pre-eminent athletic conference in the Northeast," he declared. Belonging to it was "consistent with the university's overall goal of excellence."

I immediately began to get anxious calls from RU1000 alumni and old members of the student campaign. How, they wanted to know, could we have been so wrong? What about President McCormick's relationship with his father? Hadn't we been assured that he listened respectfully to his father's counsel? Hadn't McCormick himself talked about his loyalty to older Rutgers traditions when he changed his mind about leaving the University of Washington? Hadn't I, during the presidential search, testified to his courage when asked if he'd be strong enough to stand up to the Scarlet R boosters on the BOG? Why was he calling in sportswriters to give interviews declaring allegiance to the Big East? I had to tell them that I was just as stunned as they were. I had no answers. None at all.

I made some phone calls to reporters with sources in the central administration. An amazing story began to emerge. If true, it seemed to explain why McCormick was publicly endorsing big-time athletics. There had been, I was told, an apocalyptic meeting with the board of governors. McCormick, exactly as Rutgers 1000 had hoped, had brought to the BOG proposals for phasing out Div IA athletics. The BOG had been lying in wait for just this moment. For the next hour, the room was said to have been filled with angry voices and red faces and denunciations of anyone who would consider writing off the university's $100 million investment in Big East athletics. There was reportedly much marshaling of statistics, and talk about how New Jersey, as much as Nebraska or Tennessee, deserved winning teams. During the diatribes, McCormick reportedly sat silent, his eyes sinking lower and lower as one BOG member after another spoke. When he was at last permitted to say something, he is reported to have raised his head, looked around the table, and said, "I will never bring up this subject again."

In its barest outline, the story didn't seem wholly implausible. A newly appointed president, aware that Rutgers has a long-established tradition of participatory athletics, arrives on campus persuaded that the university is in a favorable position to eliminate Div IA sports. The board of governors who appointed him, on the other hand, is acutely aware that the widely known resistance to Div IA athletics at Rutgers might have put precisely this idea into the president's head. At the first mention of athletics policy, they are prepared to show that the BOG, dominated by a core group of Scarlet R boosters, considers this a make-or-break issue. The argument about athletics is secondary. The essential point is that their newly appointed president serves at the pleasure of the BOG. The president, listening to an hour-long lecture about the importance of big-time athletics, sees what he's up against. At the end of the hour, he raises a flag of unconditional surrender. In phone conversations with our alumni, I apologized shamefacedly for having ever told them that McCormick would have the personal strength to stand up to the BOG.

Then, suddenly, an unexpected development changed everything. I'd been told that President McCormick surrendered to the BOG on, specifically, the issue of Big East membership. Now the Big East was beginning to disintegrate. The stronger football schools in the conference, news reports said, were going to desert to the Atlantic Coast Conference. In mid-May 2003, details began to trickle in. John Swofford, commissioner of the ACC, had his eye on the money that would come in if the conference expanded to twelve teams. In football alone this would permit a playoff game generating a television payout of $10 to $12 million. The new president of the University of Miami was Donna Shalala, who as a Clinton cabinet member had played a prominent role in defending Bill Clinton's innocence in the Monica Lewinsky affair. She was reportedly very receptive to Swofford's overtures. Paul Dee, Miami's athletic director, was even more enthusiastic. Swofford had promised, said reports, to permit Miami to name two other Big East schools who would be invited to join the ACC. News stories mentioned various possibilities, with Syracuse and Boston College leading the list.

At Rutgers, nobody took much interest. Whoever Miami took with it out of the Big East, Rutgers would be left behind. Among veterans of Rutgers 1000, there was a certain grim satisfaction in the story of betrayals and double-dealing that now began to unfold. The Big East had always been a made-for-television conference. What commercialism had joined together, it had turned out, commercialism could put asunder. Among the obvious Big East left-behinds, there was a desperate attempt to save the day by offering Miami a larger share of conference revenues. President McCormick, asked about his role in the negotiations, told reporters that he'd been on the phone personally pleading with Donna Shalala not to leave Rutgers in the lurch.

The man of the hour, though, was Robert Mulcahy, whose history of political deal-making at the Meadowlands now seemed to offer hope. As President

McCormick faded into the background, Mulcahy hopped a plane to Ponte Vedra, Florida. There he would attend an emergency meeting of Big East athletic directors, including the University of Miami's rotund and genial Paul Dee. On the ground at Ponte Vedra, Mulcahy immediately set about countering the general impression that Miami had already struck a private deal with Swofford and the ACC. "I think it's important people understand that Miami committed to being totally open about the process," he told reporters. "I think Paul was very straightforward and very honest and I'm optimistic. I don't see people running around to break up the conference. What we're trying to do is strengthen the conference."

During the Ponte Vedra meeting, newspapers reported that Mulcahy, so renowned in New Jersey for his political skills, had taken the lead in trying to stave off the ACC's raid. "Sure, I have hope," he told an Associated Press sportswriter. "I think the one thing that was made perfectly clear was that Miami came in here with a totally open mind and they have not closed it." "At a certain point," he told the *Roanoke Times*, "you have to take people at their word and face value. If they say they're not out the door, then you've got to believe they're not out the door." Other observers, more cynical in their estimate of Shalala and Dee, took Dee's posture at Ponte Vedra as a polite charade. The point, they said, was simply to deflect charges that Miami, motivated by what might otherwise seem rapacious commercialism, had never had the slightest intention of remaining in the Big East.

Over the next few months the twists and turns of the Big East melodrama dominated news in the world of big-time college sports. Rutgers 1000 veterans, young and old, paid little attention. We'd been trying for years to warn our own university that the monster of commercialized Div IA athletics always ends by devouring its children. This was simply a dramatic example of what we'd been talking about. When reporters called to ask about RU1000's response to the spectacle, I had to tell them that there was no response. The RU1000 Faculty Council had dissolved itself when Francis Lawrence resigned. We'd assumed that the BOG, through Lawrence's downfall, had learned its lesson about big-time athletics. The student steering committee had dissolved itself on December 1, 2002, the day McCormick took office, certain that their new president would complete the task they'd begun. The RU1000 Alumni Council was still active but had turned its attention to university governance.

Shortly thereafter, Miami announced that it was leaving for the ACC. Asked by a North Carolina newspaper to comment on the Big East meltdown, I wrote an op-ed—"From Rutgers: Champagne and Goodbye"—saying that hundreds of Rutgers alumni, students, and faculty had rejoiced to hear the news. For a decade, I wrote, Rutgers 1000 had been using two schools, Virginia Tech and Miami, as examples of how commercialized sports dishonor higher education. "We have argued, for instance, that Rutgers has been disgraced by its association with Virginia Tech, a program that in one recent year had 19 football players facing criminal charges including rape and assault and battery." Miami, I said, with its own history of criminality, its cash payments by boosters to football players, its mysteriously "lost" drug test results, and its illegal steering to athletes of nearly $700,000 in federal Pell Grant money, was arguably even more corrupt. That was why, I told readers in North Carolina, "you can hear the popping of champagne corks up here in faraway New Jersey."

Then came the most amazing twist of all. Virginia Tech, which had been assuming that it would be among the Big East left-behinds, got a wholly unexpected invitation to join the ACC. There were protests from some of the more respectable ACC schools. At the University of North Carolina, I was told, my op-ed had been read aloud on the floor of the faculty senate. In interviews on North Carolina radio stations I made it clear that many at Rutgers were taking this as the best news to have reached us since the board of governors took our university into the Big East. If getting rid of our association with Miami had been a moral victory for those opposing Div I A athletics, getting rid of Virginia Tech at the same time was an outright moral triumph.

The good news kept coming. After a bit of complicated maneuvering, the ACC announced that Boston College would be joining the conference as its twelfth team. This would permit the conference playoff that would generate an extra $10 million in TV revenues. With its three strongest football members gone, the Big East was now a burnt-out shell. A tiny group of stunned survivors—West Virginia, UConn, Pittsburgh, Syracuse, Rutgers—had been left stumbling about among the smoking ruins. My phone began ringing with calls from alumni and old Rutgers 1000 students. The campaign, having made its mistake about President McCormick, had dissolved itself prematurely. Couldn't it be resurrected now on a short-term emergency basis? Though our numbers had never been large—counting alumni, faculty, and students, we'd ended the campaign with something under fourteen hundred members—we might still be able to make a difference.

For the first time since Rutgers's entry into the Big East, RU1000 and the Scarlet R boosters seemed to have a common interest. The boosters had seen Rutgers humiliated by the obvious eagerness of Div I A football powers like Miami and Virginia Tech to get out of its company. They'd been left stranded among the ruins of a shattered and now minor conference. Even for those who had dreams of seeing Rutgers become a Tennessee or Nebraska, there were no options left. They'd surely see the logic of trying to save the university's honor by getting out of Div IA and writing off the whole Big East experiment as a short-lived institutional nightmare. Rutgers 1000 had spent years laying the groundwork for the university's return to participatory athletics. Now was the time when its expertise and contacts could be supremely useful.

There was another argument. President McCormick had reportedly thrown in the towel when the Scarlet R members of the board of governors challenged him on Div IA athletics. But now these same members were as demoralized as everyone else. Even Robert Mulcahy, in their eyes arguably a far a more considerable figure than McCormick, had recently been surprisingly frank, for the first time, about Div IA corruption. In a radio interview, he'd acknowledged that Virginia Tech had built a winning football program by, as he put it, "bringing in a bunch of thugs." It's true that McCormick had reportedly told the BOG that he'd never bring up the athletics issue again. But it was also true that events beyond anyone's control had raised the issue in a way that couldn't be ignored. For both Rutgers 1000 and the BOG, now was the time for President McCormick to ride forth as a white knight coming to the rescue of an imperiled university.

By phone and e-mail we put the old RU1000 network back together. There were consultations about strategy. I was given the task of getting in touch with our Patriot League contacts to see if the league, consisting largely of the schools that had been Rutgers's athletics rivals for nearly a century, would admit Rutgers as a Div IAA nonathletic-scholarship university. The great obstacle, we thought, would be admissions policy. When I arrived, in the late 1980s, Rutgers College, our most selective undergraduate unit, had admitted about 38 percent of its applicants. During the academic decline of the Lawrence years and the shift to an "enrollment goals" policy, more than 60 percent of applicants were being admitted, and an entire echelon of very bright students had been lost. Would selective schools like Colgate, Lafayette, Lehigh, and Bucknell admit a Rutgers that had fallen so far in academic reputation?

My most notable conversation was with William D. Adams, president of Colby College in Waterville, Maine. Earlier, as the president of Bucknell University, Adams had been one of the moving spirits of the Patriot League. He knew its history intimately. He was very encouraging about Rutgers's chances of being admitted. He pointed out aspects of the current conference realignments that I'd never thought about. Army and Navy, for instance, were members of the Patriot League in every sport except football. Both military academies had once been considered "honorary" members of the

Ivy League. Like Rutgers, both had been enticed into the world of commercialized Div IA football only recently, with similarly dismal results. Should they now decide to play Patriot League football, the league would instantly assume a place alongside the Ivies as a national symbol of an old and honorable tradition in college athletics.

I spoke with President Adams about the disparity in size between Rutgers and such smaller schools as Colgate and Lafayette. His intuition was that size didn't matter when sports were played by real students at the school. In checking out the landscape of major university Div III athletics, I found that this was precisely the case. In the preceding year, for instance, both the University of Chicago (4,000 undergraduates) and Emory (6,000 undergraduates) had beaten NYU (20,000 undergraduates, 58,000 students total) in basketball. For Rutgers, the example of NYU, a very good private university that in recent years had risen spectacularly in academic distinction, seemed an ideal model. If NYU could pursue sports successfully at the Div III nonathletic-scholarship level, Rutgers could certainly do the same in the Div IAA nonathletic-scholarship Patriot League.

In the midst of the Big East breakup, the *Home News Tribune* asked me to write an op-ed column on its implications for Rutgers. In my column— "Turning Point for Rutgers"—I recounted my conversation with President Adams. I noted especially his observation that in the wake of the Big East– ACC realignment there was a general climate of conference instability, in which the Patriot League was itself looking at expansion. "Adding Rutgers, along with Army and Navy, as football members," I wrote, summarizing Adams's remarks to me, "would amount to a powerful statement in favor of genuinely collegiate competition in athletics." At the end of our talk, I told *Home News* readers, I'd asked whether Adams thought the Patriot League would accept an application from Rutgers. "My guess," he'd said after a pause, "is that right now the Patriot League would be very interested in a conversation with Rutgers."

Spontaneous faculty support was developing for getting Rutgers out of Div IA. The RU1000 Faculty Council had more than two hundred members. Now hundreds more, including many who had thought Rutgers 1000 too radical, were rallying round. "Every penny we dedicate to trying to win football or basketball games is twice lost," the chair of the French Department said in a *Home News* story. "It's a penny that won't go into our academic activities, and it's a penny that legitimizes an anti-intellectual culture that has always threatened those who care about thinking." "I think the faculty would overwhelmingly applaud McCormick and the Board of Governors for making a decision that says 'Let's have no more Div IA football,'" said a senior history professor who was an old friend of Richard McCormick. "I think there would be massive support for it."

It wasn't just the Rutgers faculty. Since the publication of my column on Rutgers and the Patriot League, I'd been getting calls and letters from people across New Jersey, people who had earlier stayed on the sidelines but now wanted to throw in their lot with Rutgers 1000. On the board of governors, a kind of paralysis seemed to have set in. Mr. Mulcahy, no doubt feeling the ground crumbling beneath his feet, was reportedly working his political contacts to try to strengthen the resolve of BOG members who had begun to waver. In June 2003, the legislature passed a resolution—Resolution No. 319, 210th Legislature—urging "Rutgers, the State University of New Jersey, to continue to participate in National Collegiate Athletic Association, Div I-A football." Copies were to be sent, the clerk was instructed, "to Rutgers University President Dr. Richard L. McCormick and every member of the Rutgers University Board of Governors."

Still, nothing was heard from Dr. Richard L. McCormick. Beside the copy of Resolution No. 319 on my bulletin board, I posted a sentence from Bernard of Cluny: "The hour is very late, and the choice of good and evil knocks at the door." After a decade of struggle, Rutgers 1000 had dissolved itself in the conviction that Richard McCormick would complete the work that hundreds of students, alumni, and faculty had begun. The Big East had disintegrated. The crass commercialism that had eaten the heart out of so many Div IA institutions had been exposed. The Scarlet R boosters were disheartened and demoralized. The Patriot League beckoned. President McCormick, obviously aware of the groundswell of support for returning Rutgers to its older and nobler traditions, had only to say the word. Yet from Old Queen's came only a brooding silence. Why?

The answer, when it came, was a bombshell. Out of the blue, a story published in the *Seattle Times* broke the news that the University of Washington regents, when they heard that McCormick had received an offer from Rutgers, had ordered him to leave. McCormick had been carrying on an extramarital affair with a woman in the University of Washington administration. There were widespread charges that the woman had benefited considerably from presidential favoritism. Questioned by UW's board of regents, McCormick denied that any such relationship existed. During the same period, a number of major sports scandals had been brewing at the University of Washington, where McCormick had played a highly visible role as a cheerleader for UW football and basketball. Though the news of his marital infidelity was more recent, the regents were said to have been dissatisfied with his performance on numerous other grounds. He had no future, they told him, as president of the University of Washington.

When the *Seattle Times* story broke at Rutgers, it was as though a spotlight had been thrown into a number of murky corners, shedding sudden illumination on matters that had remained puzzling or mysterious. In Rutgers 1000, we'd believed McCormick's story about his sudden change of mind. We loved and were loyal to Rutgers. It seemed natural that he should feel the same way. Still, we'd always wondered why it had taken him two entire weeks to feel the strength of old school ties. Now the chronology seemed clear. It must have taken some days for the UW regents to hear that McCormick had turned down Rutgers. It would take another week to check out McCormick's marital infidelity and the widespread perception of favoritism to which it had given rise. Then they'd have to assemble the board for a meeting to agree that their president should be told to leave for Rutgers. Only then would McCormick have been able to dash out of a meeting with Gerald Grinstein, head of UW's board of regents, to telephone BOG chair Eugene O'Hara at Rutgers with the urgent news that he'd had a sudden change of heart.

The *Seattle Times* story also seemed to explain McCormick's surrender on athletics policy. It would turn out that the *Times* had been calling McCormick constantly since he arrived at Rutgers, asking if he wanted to go on denying his extramarital affair. Did he also want to keep denying that he had been pressured by the regents to leave the University of Washington? McCormick held firm. There had been no marital infidelity. The UW regents had never told him to leave. He had been drawn back to Rutgers, as he had said many times, because his personal ties to the university were stronger than he'd at first realized. Yet the calls had continued. The *Times* made it clear that it would soon have enough independent evidence to go with the story whether or not McCormick went on issuing denials. The McCormick who had walked into a BOG meeting to raise the issue of Div IA athletics, in short, could be understood as a haunted soul tremulously aware that the bubble of his triumphant return as Rutgers's favorite son might burst at any moment.

Among Rutgers 1000 members, the most significant part of the controversy that followed the *Seattle Times* story was the mention of athletics scandals. I put in a call to a Seattle reporter I'd talked to a number of times during the Rutgers presidential search. "That's what I was trying to tell you," he said with just a hint of exasperation in his voice. "The regents knew that athletics scandals were going to blow the lid off this place. They knew that McCormick was tight with the boosters and the A.D. He made a huge deal out of being a Husky supporter in football and basketball. They wanted him off the premises before things blew up. That way they could tell the NCAA that they'd already started to clean house." My mind went back to the interviews McCormick had given to New Jersey sportswriters, saying that he knew Div I A athletics and academic values could coexist. He'd seen it happen, he told reporters, at the University of Washington. I apologized to the Seattle reporter for having been so obtuse.

The U W athletics scandals had by now become public. The basketball team had been put on probation for serious recruiting violations. Football coach Rick Neuheisel, already notorious for shady recruiting practices at Colorado, was under investigation for his recruiting at Washington. While that investigation was going on, Neuheisel was fired for having gambled on NCAA athletics. A U W team doctor was revealed to have been supplying athletes with illegal drugs. The regents had refused to renew the contract of the athletic director. Yet what seemed to us more disturbing were McCormick's relations with Washington boosters. He had eagerly taken part personally, we learned, in recruiting football and basketball players, having them brought to the president's office for a U W sales pitch. He had once gone down on the field to bark like a Husky—the U W mascot—after a football victory. He had been investigated by a state ethics commission for flying friends and family, at state expense, to a football game. He had gone to extraordinary lengths to justify Neuheisel's $1.1 million salary. "To get the very best," he told the Seattle press, "you have to play in the market." He had assured citizens of Washington that "in Rick Neuheisel, we have the very best."

At Rutgers, McCormick's solidarity with key BOG members on Div I A sports was about to pay huge dividends. Already under a cloud in New Jersey for what many took to have been a drunk driving episode earlier in the year, the president now had to call BOG chair Eugene O'Hara to warn him that the *Seattle Times* was about to disclose his marital infidelity. The *Times* would also be reporting that U W's regents had unloaded McCormick on Rutgers. O'Hara assured the newly appointed president that he would have the board's support. At a press conference, McCormick, with his wife, Suzanne Lebsock, standing grimly beside him at the podium, said he was personally sorry for the pain his actions had caused. Eugene O'Hara issued a ringing statement of support. McCormick, he declared, had energized the university. He saw eye to eye with the BOG on every issue they considered important. "President McCormick," said O'Hara, "has provided exactly the kind of leadership we expected. We intend to work with President McCormick on the challenges that lie ahead."

"McCormick said he was personally sorry for the pain his actions had caused." Richard L. McCormick with his wife, Suzanne Lebsock, press conference, Winants Hall, Rutgers University, November 2, 2003. Photo courtesy of the *Home News Tribune.*

In its positive enthusiasm for McCormick's presidency, O'Hara's statement needn't necessarily have been disingenuous. In the age of Bill Clinton and Monica Lewinsky, after all, one might view McCormick's marital infidelity as simply one of the sexual peccadilloes to which prominently placed males now seemed prone. His having an affair with a woman in his own administration doubtless showed bad judgment, but McCormick had shown contrition. The news that the UW regents had unloaded him on Rutgers was more worrisome—similar circumstances said to have surrounded Francis Lawrence's arrival were, some felt, giving Rutgers a reputation as a dumping ground for administrators not wanted elsewhere—but that could perhaps be rationalized in terms of a difference of institutional culture. The BOG had supported Francis Lawrence for twelve long years of institutional decline. The new note of confidence in O'Hara's statement could be taken as a sign that they honestly felt themselves, this time, to be backing a winner.

Then came the news that the McCormick-O'Hara press conference had been entirely scripted by a New York crisis-management firm, Rubenstein Associates. It numbered among its clients such dubious public personalities as Leona Helmsley and George Steinbrenner. In a feature in the *Newark Star-Ledger,* education writer Kelly Heyboer interviewed a number of public relations experts to get a sense of how well Rubenstein Associates had managed the case. One told Heyboer that the script obeyed the first rule of crisis management, "to have the central figure in the scandal show he or she is sorry and prepared to do penance and move on." McCormick had done this. "It seems to me," said this expert, "that Rutgers has handled the situation well at the moment." Another expert, head of his own public relations firm, stressed the importance of getting the story out fast, as McCormick and the BOG had done. "It's called the 'golden hour,'" he told Heyboer. "Get it done in the first hour and it goes away much faster." Eugene O'Hara, at any rate, seemed highly pleased with the work of Rubenstein Associates. "I am overwhelmed with the amount of support coming in," he told Heyboer.

Among alumni and old RU1000 student members, there was total disenchantment. We'd had to take in stride what the students were calling McCormick's athletics betrayal. We'd misjudged the new president, and we were responsible. This was different. In a *Targum* op-ed, recent graduate David Portilla spoke for many younger alumni in saying that, among his own wide circle of friends, support for McCormick was a great deal less than overwhelming. "It is insulting to learn that McCormick and his administrators believe our University can be 'spun' in just the way that politicians so often try to put the spin on stories going out to a distracted and ill-informed public." The BOG's panicky hiring of Rubenstein Associates, Portilla said, was an insult to the very notion of the university as a deliberative community. He quoted Rutgers's former president, Mason Gross, on attempts to manipulate the minds of those capable of independent thinking. "The free spirit will never be taken in," Gross had written, "by appeals to thwart our natural energies and cripple our instinctive strength." For having attempted such manipulation, Portilla observed, as much as for McCormick's behavior since coming to Rutgers, "he should be ashamed and we should be outraged."

Shortly after President McCormick's press conference, RU1000 alumnus Rudolph Rasin wrote a *Home News* op-ed—"McCormickgate: The Real Scandal"—focusing on the culture of cronyism and inside control that many now saw as Rutgers's deepest problem. "As with their previous support of a badly compromised Francis Lawrence," Mr. Rasin wrote, "the BOG has now circled its wagons and taken McCormick into its protective fold. He is in no position to exercise the kind of independent judgment and principled leadership needed to initiate a process of meaningful change. Instead, he finds himself deeply in debt to those with very little grasp either of the issues involved in this latest scandal or, more importantly, of the academic and intellectual values that ought to be at the center of Rutgers as an institution." The real problem was the BOG. "Should Richard McCormick resign tomorrow," Mr. Rasin pointed out, "it is this same BOG who would choose the next president. That, it seems to me, is an alarming prospect."

The project of getting Rutgers out of Div IA, it was clear, would be getting no help from Richard McCormick. Nor were the Scarlet R members of the BOG more than temporarily demoralized by the Big East breakup. With their spirits rallied by legislative Resolution No. 319, they gave Robert Mulcahy leave to scour the country for schools to fill the slots left vacant by Miami, Virginia Tech, and Boston College. Inside the university, there was great consternation that the list of candidates most frequently mentioned—East Carolina State, Central Florida University, Louisville, Cincinnati, the University of South Florida—contained names that were obscure even to those who had spent their lives in academe. But football, and not academic distinction, was the criterion. Eventually, Cincinnati, Louisville, and the University of South Florida were added to the conference. However ignominiously, the Big East had risen from the ashes.

On the board of governors, the McCormick scandal seemed to have given a new sense of vitality to the core group of Scarlet R members who had stood by their new president during his personal crisis. They had now been joined on the BOG by George R. Zoffinger, head of the same New Jersey Sports and Exposition Authority—the Meadowlands—that had been Mulcahy's bailiwick before he arrived at Rutgers. Eugene O'Hara had yielded his place as chair to Albert Gamper, reportedly a keen supporter of Div IA athletics, but continued to sit on the board. Ronald Giaconia, who had served as chair of the Scarlet R Foundation for a decade before joining the BOG, remained as head of its Athletics Committee. Soon, New Jersey politicians and other major athletics boosters were receiving invitations to join McCormick and members of the BOG in the presidential skybox at Rutgers home football games.

A member of the RU1000 Web team called me to say that they wanted to put up a page on the Rutgers 1000 site. "What's the point?" I asked. Like everyone else who'd joined in the last great push during the Big East meltdown, I was dispirited. We'd come so close, it seemed, only to see victory snatched away at the last moment by McCormickgate. "The point," he said firmly, "is that we shouldn't just fade away into the night without leaving a sign that we ever existed. There were hundreds and hundreds of people in this struggle. We owe them a goodbye." It was fine with me, I said, but the Web team would have to work fast. The AOL account that hosted the RU1000 site had been terminated. The site would be shut down in about three weeks, when the last monthly payment ran out. That was okay, he told me. They'd get something up in the next few days.

Their farewell page was a requiem not simply for Rutgers 1000 but for the university that vanished when the board of governors took Rutgers down the path of big-time athletics. At the top was an old New England grave-stone bearing the inscription RUTGERS 1000—R.I.P. Then came a list of the schools Rutgers had played in its undefeated 1961 football season, giving their current *U.S. News* academic rankings. So, for instance, Princeton (no. 1) was currently designated a Tier 1 school, as were Penn (no. 5), Columbia (no. 11), Colgate, Bucknell, Lafayette, and Lehigh. Two others, Delaware and Connecticut, were Tier 2. The average academic rank of Rutgers's opponents in that bygone pre–Big East era was, in today's terms, twenty-nine, well up within Tier 1. Then came a list of the schools associated with Rutgers in the new Big East, led by Louisville (no. 193, fourth and bottom tier), and followed by South Florida (no. 165, third tier), and Cincinnati, (no. 150, third tier). The average academic rank of the new Big East schools was 169, putting them far down in the depths of Tier 3. The rankings stared out like a grinning skull, a bleak emblem of what Div IA athletics had done to an old and once proud university.

A letter to the office of alumni relations seemed to me another grave marker for that lost and better Rutgers. It was written by RU1000 alumnus Howard Sands. A copy arrived in my mailbox a few days after the Web team put up its memorial page. Even now, I read it with a sense of something very like personal sadness. "I have been working for the better part of seven years," wrote Mr. Sands, "to move the University away from its current path toward big time sports and abandoning academic distinction." He was writing now to ask the office of alumni relations to remove his name from the member-ship roll of the Rutgers Alumni Association, the *Rutgers Magazine* mailing list, and its list of donors to the Rutgers Foundation. The academic decline of the university in the era of its Big East involvement, said Mr. Sands, "has, I fear, left me no other choice than to totally divorce myself from all associa-tion with Rutgers."

As I read Mr. Sands's letter, my mind went back to the scene of his daugh-ter Deborah, tiny, fiery, and indomitable, facing down an angry crowd of huge glowering male students at Pep Nite, the event at which RU1000 mem-bers confronted Robert Mulcahy and football coach Greg Schiano. Those had been good days. Now, Mr. Sands told the vice president for alumni rela-tions, Rutgers was recruiting football players with a combined SAT average of 800, a clear admission that academic values had become a mockery at his alma mater. "I am writing this," he told the vice president, "on Yom Kippur, when it is traditional to ask for the forgiveness of those whom one may have intentionally or unintentionally injured by one's actions. I feel that at this time it would entirely appropriate for the University to ask forgiveness from the students, alumni, and people of New Jersey," and "not least from the academically unqualified athletes whose lives and bodies they are using for cynical and indefensible purposes."

At the bottom of the farewell page was a line from Shakespeare's *Henry the Fifth:* "Shame, shame, nothing but shame." In the play, this is cried out by the Constable of France when his large, well-mounted army is vanquished by a small, ragtag band of English yeomen fighting on foot. In the wars over commercialized athletics at Rutgers, the small ragtag band had been Rutgers 1000. Their opponents had won. Still, it does not seem to me that there was any shame in their having lost in the end to a powerful booster subculture and the billions of TV dollars that drive Div IA athletics. They had been, to rephrase what Henry V says to his soldiers before the Battle of Agincourt, enough to do their university honor. As Rutgers began play in the new Big East, a post appeared on a Rutgers football board, sent by a Rutgers booster now living in New Mexico. Given my own awakening to Div IA sports corruption at UNM twenty years earlier, it seemed to me to project a sublimely unconscious irony. "Rutgers," he exclaimed, "is where New Mexico was in 2001—which is a very good thing! The Lobos will be going to a bowl game for the second consecutive year. The Governor and State Legislature have so much confidence that the Lobos have turned the corner that they recently pumped $5 million into stadium renovations. Progress is being made in the right way in New Brunswick, just like I've seen it in Albuquerque. Good things are on RU's horizon, my friends!"

Epilogue: A View from the Banks

In the midst of writing an early chapter of *Confessions of a Spoilsport,* I broke off to go to a Rutgers athletics event. Our lightweight crew was rowing that day against Princeton and Cornell for the Platt Cup. The event takes place at Lake Carnegie, about a mile from where we live. I almost always make it out to the Platt Cup race, but since I had two students in the lightweight varsity boat that semester—three, actually, but one of them, Jacob Goodman, was at Oxford this year on study abroad, where he rowed for Oxford in the annual race against Cambridge at Henley—getting out to cheer them on seemed especially important.

I expected the worst. I knew we had a good boat that spring, but Princeton and Cornell were both ranked well ahead of Rutgers in the latest collegiate rowing poll, and both are perennially strong programs.

You have your choice about watching the Platt Cup race at Lake Carnegie. You can either go down to one of the bridges by the Princeton boathouse and watch the start, following the boats with your binoculars toward the finish line about a mile away. Or you can park by the finish, on a wide sandy stretch by the water that has a small set of spectator stands and a loudspeaker for an announcer in the race boat, who calls the early part of the race.

The little park by the finish line was crowded, mostly with family and friends of the rowers. There were kids and dogs and older people sitting in lawn chairs with their binoculars at the ready. Most of the spectators wore some sign of their school affiliation. It's always a small matter of embarrassment to me that Rutgers, with more than twenty thousand students just twelve miles away, is usually heavily outnumbered by spectators from the other schools.

I'm a special fan of the lightweight crew because it's one of the only purely amateur athletics programs at Rutgers. The heavyweight crew coach is allowed to give some scholarships and half-scholarships, meaning that at least some of his rowers are at Rutgers on just the same terms as Greg Schiano's football players or Vivian Stringer's basketball players. They've been scouted, recruited, and rewarded with scholarship money.

The lightweights, on the other hand, are kids who have gone out for crew in the same spirit as their friends go out for theater or orchestra or the *Rutgers Review*. They put in a huge number of hours practicing and getting in shape for competition, they balance athletics with genuine intellectual interests—the crew members who take my classes always seem to major in subjects like philosophy, political science, literature, or math and science—and they stay totally outside the miasma of commercialism that surrounds sports like basketball and football. I admire them tremendously.

Thinking about all this out at Lake Carnegie, I was reminded of something that I forget from time to time, one of the most underdiscussed topics in the area of college sports. When I was an undergraduate at Dartmouth, we had two undefeated football seasons and three Ivy League championships in my four years. I went to a lot of games—Dartmouth was all male then, and football weekends were an occasion to date girls from women's colleges like Wellesley and Smith—and I supported the team as staunchly as anyone else in the student body.

But here's the thing. When you were watching an Ivy football game in the 1960s, there was always what I now think of as an organic relation between the players down on the field and the students in the stands. They were us, so to speak—a bit bigger and more coordinated, maybe, and possessing certain physical skills we didn't have, but other than that just kids who lived down the hall from us in the dorm, or who sat next to us in a history seminar, or who you'd run into in the library stacks when you had a paper due for the same class.

It's true that those teams didn't play very good football. I remember that, during one of the two seasons when Dartmouth went undefeated, we got a little cocky about how well the team was doing. That season had come down to a final game against Princeton, also undefeated that year, and Princeton had been featured on the cover of *Sports Illustrated*. Their captain made the fatal mistake of looking past Dartmouth to football immortality. Unforgivably, he remarked to the SI reporter that, because the Ivy League doesn't allow postseason competition in football, the Princeton team would "never really know how good they were."

This did not sit well with the Dartmouth football players, or with the undergraduates. Although finals were coming up and few could really spare the time, a bunch of us took the train down to Princeton to see the final game. The father of one of our classmates, a Dartmouth alumnus, had used his seniority to buy a block of tickets, and we sat as a group in the midst of a crowd of older alumni. Palmer Stadium, the grand old structure that has since been demolished and replaced by a smaller modern stadium, was packed.

Dartmouth defeated Princeton that day, a very satisfying victory over an opponent who had been unwary enough to display a bit of hubris on the eve of the final contest. But I've never forgotten the moment at which, when the game was winding down and it was clear that Dartmouth was going to win, an alum sitting behind us, dressed in fall tweeds, gray-haired and distinguished looking, leaned forward and said gently, "It's all right to celebrate, fellows. But don't carry it too far. You do realize, don't you, that a good Texas high school team could beat either of these teams by two touchdowns?"

As it happened, never having been very far out of New England, I didn't realize that. I do now. Still, the point seems to me unimportant in any larger scheme of things. My tendency is to ask precisely why college football shouldn't be played on an amateur, even sometimes on an outright amateurish, level. If it's real, after all, the teams are made up of college kids, young men who want to go on to do other things in their lives than play football.

The contrast between our situation then and that of undergraduates at institutions like Nebraska and Tennessee and Kentucky and Virginia Tech today couldn't be more dramatic. At those schools, the students who go to the stadium, or who sit in the seats in the basketball arena, have no more authentic relationship to the players on the floor than people who buy tickets to see the Jacksonville Jaguars or the Memphis Grizzlies do to the players on those teams.

In fact, the professional franchise has become, in the last twenty years, more and more the model for the relation between Division IA teams and the institutions that sponsor them. It's not an accident that the students who rioted at Ohio State to celebrate a football victory, or the University of Connecticut undergraduates who set fires and overturned cars to glorify a basketball championship, were imitating similar behavior on the part of Oakland Raiders and Boston Patriots fans in recent years.

That's why there's no sound reason for universities to sponsor basketball or football franchises, or to go through the charade of trying to pass off semiprofessional players as college students. People unconnected to a university who want to see top-quality football today have a huge number of professional teams to choose from. It's no trouble at all, for instance, for anyone who lives in the immediate vicinity of Rutgers to get tickets for a New York Giants, Philadelphia Eagles, or New York Jets game. There's no good reason why they should treat Rutgers as a venue designed to provide them with weekend entertainment.

By the same token, people who actually went to Rutgers, or parents who have children at the school, like the students themselves, would get far more pleasure out of watching teams made up of actual Rutgers students than by attending games played by recruited athletes with whom they have no real connection. One of the hardest things to get across to people in the TV age is that alumni and students who go to games played at the genuinely collegiate level—the kind of sports that today survive only in the Ivy League, the Patriot League, and Division III schools—have more fun than the undergraduates who go out to set fires or break shop windows or overturn automobiles after games in places like Columbus, Ohio, or Storrs, Connecticut.

I was thinking about all this as Mrs. D and I sat on the shore of Lake Carnegie, waiting for the lightweight race to start. The atmosphere was very much like that I remembered from my own college football games. The people around us, classmates of the rowers, mothers and fathers and brothers and little sisters, were all there because they had a real connection to the young men in the boats down at the other end of the course. Only a couple of weeks before, as you've heard, there had been a basketball game at which Rutgers students had screamed obscenities at the opposing team, fought in the stands with fans from another school, and gotten so drunk that they had to be carried out of the arena. There were also fights on the New Jersey Transit trains bringing students back to school from the game.

It was impossible to imagine any of that going on there on shores of Lake Carnegie. All of us—the crowd from Rutgers, the Cornell families and friends, the large group of Princeton undergraduates—felt as though we shared something important even while we were there to root against one another's boats. It was real college sports, competition undertaken for the right reasons by people, both athletes and spectators, who realized that athletics is nothing unless you do it for love of the sport.

The race was thrilling. Cornell pulled out to an early lead. Rutgers and Princeton stayed even for what seemed like a very long time, in what looked to be shaping up as a two-boat race for second. Then Princeton began to pull away, moving up a little on Cornell, leaving the Rutgers boat behind by one or two seats. Knowing that both Cornell and Princeton were ranked ahead of us, I resigned myself to hoping for a decent third. I kept my binoculars on the Rutgers boat, trying to get some sense of how they'd shape up in later races this year, and what sort of boat we might have next year.

The Rutgers rowers, though, had something different in mind. About four hundred yards from the finish, they made a move that was almost intimidating in its sense of steady, inexorable purpose. You could tell immediately

"We forget, most of the time, how magnificent college athletics can be."
WCD with students and members of the lightweight crew after Platt Cup race.
Photo: RU1000 Archives.

that this wasn't some kind of last-minute spurt, meant to save a little honor in a race that was already ignominiously lost. They meant to move through Princeton and give Cornell a run for its money.

By now I had my eyes on the Princeton cox, wondering if he understood what was happening. He did. He sat bolt upright, almost as if someone had hit him from shore with a pellet gun, and then leaned forward and started frantically to raise the cadence. To their immense credit, the Princeton rowers responded, and for a tense hundred yards or so it was once again a two-boat race for second. Then Princeton cracked. Rutgers started to move ahead by inches, holding the beat as steadily as when they'd started the move. Up ahead, the Cornell cox was trying to tell his rowers, who at this point thought they had already won the race, that Rutgers was coming on.

As it turned out, Rutgers had come on too late. They lost more because they'd run out of water than because their magnificent move in the end had lost any power or momentum. A Rutgers mom turned to me and said, hoarsely—we'd all been shouting our lungs out during this last few minutes—"If the course had been a hundred yards longer, we'd have taken the race."

I don't know if that's right. Cornell also rowed a splendid race, and Princeton demands all credit for having hung in so bravely against the doomlike inevitability of that last Rutgers sprint, but I do know that to all of us in the Rutgers crowd it felt like a victory.

We forget, most of the time, how magnificent college athletics can be. In an age of sleaze and fraud and commercialization, it's hard to remember what sports are like when the athletes are students who represent the college they compete for. Still, it seems to me that our little group of spectators by the shores of Lake Carnegie were having a more genuine experience of college sports than they could have gotten from a thousand Tostitos Corn Chips Fiesta Bowls or "March Madness" TV spectacles. The rioting students who get drunk and set fires and overturn automobiles after a college sports victory seemed a million miles away, just where one would want them to be, and ideally to stay, forever.

Appendix: The *Rutgers Review* Interview

JOSH SALTZMAN: In his *Targum* attack on you, Athletic Director Robert Mulcahy referred to Rutgers as your "employer." Do you feel that this term accurately characterizes the university's relationship with a professor?

WILLIAM DOWLING: I do think Mr. Mulcahy meant that remark about Rutgers being my "employer" as a zinger: "Hey, this place gives you your paycheck. How dare you challenge the idea that professionalized athletics is good for a university?"

I remember reading that Mr. Mulcahy has seven children. If you raise seven children, there's a strong economic dimension to the relationship. You buy their food and their clothes. You provide housing. You give them allowances. But think of how Mr. Mulcahy's children would have reacted if they'd realized that this was the *only* aspect of their relationship he could grasp: "Hey, junior, I'm your employer, so you'd better do what I say."

I'd expect that in that instance the young Mulcahy would have tried to point out a crucial distinction: "Hey, dad, you're not my employer. You're my *father*."

That's pretty much how I reacted to Mulcahy's description of Rutgers as my "employer." I thought when I read that sentence, "No, Mr. Mulcahy, Rutgers is *your* employer. It's my university. Your whole problem is that you don't understand the difference."

One of the things that saddened me about the recent *Targum* exchanges is that more and more students do seem to be thinking of Rutgers as a "business," education as a "product," and all the rest of it. That's what you might call a Lawrence-Mulcahy effect. Lawrence and Mulcahy are producing a generation of students who see Rutgers in the same terms they themselves do.

The worst thing about professionalized college sports is that, in powerful and indirect ways, it does encourage a notion of education as "commodity." That's why commercial culture has penetrated so deeply into the sports factory schools—TV exposure, skyboxes, Midnight Madness promotions, etc.—to the point that, in many cases, there's nothing left but a hollowed-out shell of the university.

Mr. Mulcahy is a servant of that culture. He came here from running the Meadowlands sports complex, and now, poor man, the only thing he knows how to try to do is to make Rutgers over in the image of the Meadowlands.

SALTZMAN: How do you respond to Robert Mulcahy's labeling of your *Targum* commentary as a "simple-minded argument" unsupported by "any real facts"?

DOWLING: It's the way people like Mr. Mulcahy operate. They don't actually mean "This argument is simple-minded." They mean this: "Listening to genuine intellectual debates, I've sometimes heard people dismiss arguments as simple-minded. I'm not exactly sure what it means, but maybe I could score a point by using it here." So they try it out. To them, saying "simple-minded" is just a form of name-calling.

In fact, the column about which Mr. Mulcahy made that remark pointed out that my own arguments derive from a large body of serious recent work on the subject: books like Andrew Zimbalist's *Unpaid Professionals,* Murray Sperber's *College Sports, Inc.,* Allen Sack and Ellen Staurowsky's *College Athletes for Hire,* and more.

This work is rich in empirical data and highly complex arguments. Andrew Zimbalist, for instance, holds the Robert A. Woods Chair of Economics at Smith College. His book was published by Princeton University Press. There may be arguments against Zimbalist's analysis, but the last thing you'd want to call it is simple-minded.

But I'm sure that Mr. Mulcahy's eyes skipped right over the paragraph where I recommended those books. Mulcahy hasn't read them. He's not interested in them. He's not interested in arguments like mine, which derive directly from them. His main interest is in seeing how many people he can impress by tossing around terms like "simple-minded."

SALTZMAN: How do you respond to the following statement, made by Robert Mulcahy: "For Dowling to attack these students [the women's basketball team] and their achievements leaves me wondering as to what his motives really are."

DOWLING: It's like "simple-minded": borrowed rhetoric. Mr. Mulcahy has heard somewhere that people score points by questioning other people's motives, so he thought he'd try it out here. He has nothing on his mind by using the phrase. It's just another attempt at name calling.

What could my motives be? From the time I was in graduate school, one of my great ambitions was to teach at Rutgers. "Rutgers English" was a legend among my generation of Harvard graduate students: Poirier, Kalstone, Edwards, this tremendous group of brilliant scholars and teachers. It was cutting-edge, glamorous, where everyone with any talent and ambition wanted to be.

When I got to Rutgers, it was even better than I'd imagined. What amazed me—it continues to amaze me—is that Rutgers has a really substantial number of students who are not only bright but intellectually serious, genuinely excited by reading and ideas and argument, eager to learn and discuss and grow. For a professor, it's a kind of Elysium.

Somebody might say: why is it so amazing for students to be bright and intellectually engaged? The answer is that it's not, at some schools: the Ivies, and places like Amherst and Swarthmore and the University of Chicago. But it is very rare—you have no idea of how rare—at state universities, increasingly so. There are a million reasons why: open admissions, deterioration of secondary education, increase of remedial courses at college level—and, it should be said, "professionalized" athletics as an attempt to cover up and compensate for all that.

Rutgers, I suppose for historical reasons, is amazingly different. I don't mean that every Rutgers student is an intellectual. I've heard that there is the usual quota of beer-swilling louts on campus. My students tell me that many undergraduates here have no sense of intellectual community, that they just come for four years, find a parking place, pick up their credits, and leave. And I'm aware that under the Lawrence-Mulcahy administration, the movement is more and more in that direction. But the miracle is that the "old Rutgers" is somehow surviving, that the place still has the characteristics of what Richard Moll, former Dean of Admissions at Bowdoin and UC Santa Cruz, calls the "public Ivy." It's still a place where bright kids from less-than-wealthy backgrounds can come and get a superb education.

In a way, I guess Mulcahy's attempt to be snide has a point. There is a degree of self-interest in my wanting to retain the tradition of the "old Rutgers" that survives, because that's the Rutgers with which my own students tend to associate themselves. It's the Rutgers that makes teaching here such a joy.

SALTZMAN: Mulcahy claims that you have "repeatedly been invited to present [your] views to our Student Athletic Advisory Council, yet [have] declined every time?" Is this accurate? Why did you decline this opportunity?"

DOWLING: I haven't "repeatedly" refused to address the "Student Athletic Advisory Council." I was approached once. I said no. That was it.

To understand why I said no, you've got to understand what I call the machinery of virtue that the NCAA uses to try to legitimize Division IA college athletics, especially in what are called the revenue sports, football and basketball. It's a ceaseless effort at grinding out PR materials meant to throw up a screen between the actuality—the NCAA as the marketing arm of a multi-billion-dollar TV-revenue-driven commercial enterprise—and the myth of "college athletics" that they desperately try to promote.

These "Student Athletic Advisory Councils" are part of the PR campaign. Others are the "Academic All-American" hype, sponsored by commercial corporations, the sanctimonious nonsense about "graduation rates," and the very term "student athlete," which is a kind of Orwellian doublespeak. At a conference I attended recently, it was pointed out that nobody talks about student-musicians, or student-actors, or student-poets. If you have to *say* that the athlete is a "student athlete," that's already a sign that you're trying to promote a lie.

These "student athletic advisory councils," in short, are a sham: it's the athletic department that forms them—by specific direction of the NCAA, by the way—and promotes them.

The usual object is then to make a huge deal about how members of your "Student Athletic Advisory Council" do all this terrific community-spirited stuff, so isn't the athletics program here at Gridiron State just the most idealistic thing you ever saw?

I'm not making this up. Go on the Web. Go to the athletics site of any sports factory school—Florida State, say, or Nebraska, or Ohio State. Keep looking until you find "Student Athletic Advisory Council" and you'll find that the athletes brought in on "athletic scholarships" have been doing just the most wonderful things in their spare time: giving blood, visiting kindergartens, collecting old track shoes to give to orphans in third-world countries, etc, etc. It's all the most transparent kind of hype: the Athletic Department sets it up, delivers the athletes to the kindergarten or the Red Cross blood drive, then grinds out press releases about it. There's a kind of sleazy sanctimoniousness about it that makes you want to throw up.

For the record, I didn't flatly decline. I told the messenger who asked me to appear before the "Student Athletic Advisory Council" that I would be pleased to address any members of the Council who were genuine Rutgers students—that is, the team members who had not been imported on "athletic scholarships" for the specific purpose of performing in a sport. He said he'd report that answer back to the Athletic Department.

Since I never heard again from the "Student Athletic Advisory Council," or from Mr. Mulcahy, I have to assume that they didn't want me to meet with what I consider the real Rutgers athletes—the non-scholarship-players whose presence on a team genuinely represents the school. So Mulcahy is the one who said no, not me.

SALTZMAN: How, ideally, do you see sports playing a role at Rutgers?

DOWLING: The model Rutgers 1000 has always had is the Division IAA non-athletic-scholarship league or conference, like the Ivy League or the Patriot League.

The model is simple. The admissions office accepts a freshman class. Then people who are good at a sport go out for the team, in just the same way as other students try out for the Glee Club or the newspaper or a part in *Mourning Becomes Electra* over in the drama department. Real students playing real college sports, in other words.

The great thing about the model is that it creates what I call an organic relationship between players on the field and students in the stands. When I went to football games as a Dartmouth undergraduate, I cheered on the kids on the team precisely because they lived down the hall from me, sat beside me in classes, in some cases wrote for *Jackolantern,* the Dartmouth humor magazine I edited for my last two years. They *were* the rest of us, so to speak.

The contrast between this and sports factories like Nebraska in football or Kentucky in basketball, where the athletes are imported on "athletic scholarships" and exist as a segregated class employed to perform on teams, couldn't be more dramatic.

At those places, the only point of being a student is to sit in the plastic seats and yowl for a bunch of lower-level professional athletes down on the field. You might as well be at a Giants or Jets game. It's true that the players wear the name of your school on their uniforms, but this has nothing to do with you: it's pure product advertising, name-brand identification for the athletic department.

One of the hardest things to get across to students who have grown up with TV sports is that they don't understand that there is *more* school spirit at colleges and universities where real students play on the teams. The only way to understand that is to go to a school where sports are played at a genuinely collegiate level.

SALTZMAN: One of the biggest concerns of Rutgers 1000 seems to be sports corruption. The past few decades have seen the unmasking of numerous sports scandals in Division IA schools. Is this kind of corruption inevitable for Rutgers as well, assuming it stays on its current track?

DOWLING: The evidence is that you can't run a Division IA program without some degree of corruption. It's built right into the structure of "academic support" for individuals who are brought to campus not because they're top students, but because they're good at throwing something or kicking something or slam-dunking something.

Take the recent Minnesota scandal, for instance, where it came to light that an athletic department "tutor" had ghost-written over 400 pieces of work—papers, take-home exams, homework assignments—for 20 basketball players over a 5-year period.

When the truth was exposed, everybody pretended to be astonished, amazed, shocked: "How could this have been going on at *our* university?" But think about it: what else could happen when you have a "support program" that surrounds these imported athletes with people paid to do nothing but take notes when they're on the road, "help" them with their papers, and coach them through their exams?

Or take Virginia Tech. Tech is in the Big East, the same conference as Rutgers. A few years ago, they decided to go big time, in exactly the way that Lawrence and Mulcahy want Rutgers to do. So they set up the kind of hideaway curriculum that you need to pass a bunch of semi-pro athletes off as college students, invested a huge amount in "academic support" machinery to make sure that the papers would get written and the take-home exams would be passed, and went out to hire the 40 or 50 toughest football players they could find.

But there's a problem. If you have no history of going to bowl games, so that a coach can offer TV exposure and a shot at the NFL to prospective recruits, you have to take really low-level types into your program. They may have tremendous physical gifts, but passing them off as "college students" is very difficult.

The result? About five years ago, Virginia Tech had 19 football players facing felony indictment at one time, on charges ranging from burglary to assault to rape. They'd gone "big time," and they won a lot of games, but they paid a price.

You'd think the price would be too great to pay. If a good private university—Columbia, say, or the University of Chicago, or Princeton—had 19 athletes facing criminal indictment, it would be a matter of such shame that the institution would come close to folding. The best students would stop applying there. Alumni would stop giving money. Faculty would leave in great numbers. It would be a disaster.

At sports factory schools, though, it's just the opposite. The boosters have no loyalty to the university-as-such. What they want is a sports franchise, a winning team. That's what the legislators who pay the bills want. So the effort is to "clean up the program" and "put the past behind us" and get right back to recruiting blue-chip recruits to "give this state a winner."

This last year, Virginia Tech fulfilled its dreams. I'm sure Fran Lawrence and Bob Mulcahy were drooling at the TV exposure Tech got from being in a bowl game.

And if you'd gone to one of the Tech boosters and said, "Um, you know, the way you got here involved having 19 players facing criminal charges at the same time. Don't you think that's a terrible disgrace for an institution of higher learning?" the answer would have been "Why, hell, boy, that was in the past! We've put that all behind us! Point is, we-all is Number One! Woooo Eeeee Tech!"

SALTZMAN: Of the students on the women's basketball team, you said, "Not a single person on Stringer's team was recruited because she was brilliant at philosophy or Greek or math or ancient history. All were brought to New Brunswick for purely physical skills." Do you know this, for a fact, about our women's basketball team?

DOWLING: This is a curious concept of "fact." The point is that a pure concentration on athletic ability is built right into the logic of athletic recruiting. I "know" that C. Vivian Stringer wasn't recruiting Greek scholars in the same way that I know that the Rutgers philosophy department isn't admitting people to its graduate program because they're good at doing overhead slam-dunks.

You have no idea how professionalized this business of Division IA recruiting is. There are magazines like *Hoop Scoop,* and bulletins, and Web sites, that rate every plausible high school football player—and basketball player, male and female—in the country. The boosters at any sports factory school follow these reports avidly.

The only time intellectual ability is ever mentioned in these discussions is when there's a problem about whether some blue-chip recruit can "academically qualify"—that is, meet the ludicrously low threshold (820 combined SAT) that the NCAA stipulates to be given a Division IA "athletic scholarship."

It sometimes does happen that a gifted athlete is an outstanding student.

Bill Bradley is an example. He was a high school basketball star, and over 60 basketball schools offered him "athletic scholarships." He also got into Princeton. But the Ivy League doesn't permit athletic scholarships. Also, since academic scholarships in the Ivies are "need based," and Bradley comes from a well-to-do St. Louis family, they couldn't offer him a penny in financial support. All they could offer was the opportunity to pay his own way at Princeton. Wisely, in my opinion, that's what he chose to do.

So. Suppose C. Vivian Stringer is recruiting a point guard who is genuinely brilliant as well as being a top *Hoop Scoop*–ranked point guard. She not only has 1450 on her SATs and reads ancient Greek, but has published a paper in the *Philosophical Review* as a high school student. While leading her team to an undefeated season.

It seems to me that the solution is obvious. You simply recruit this person as a student. Let people from the Classics department call her and tell her how strong we are in Classics. Let someone from admissions call her and point out that Rutgers has people like Peter Kivy and Colin McGinn to teach her philosophy. Keep C. Vivian Stringer totally away from her.

Then, when the student gets to Rutgers as a freshman, have C. Vivian Stringer visit her and invite her to go out for the basketball team.

SALTZMAN: If division IA sports are so detrimental to the university in so many ways, then why would the administration want to promote such a program?

DOWLING: Well, here you penetrate to the heart of the matter. The problem with Mr. Mulcahy, as I've indicated, is that he's a sports promoter who understands nothing about universities. They're not easy to understand: universities embody a complex intellectual culture going back through the Middle Ages to ancient Greece.

Nothing could be more remote from—or opposed to—the model of commercial or consumerist culture that Mr. Mulcahy represents. At Rutgers, he's just a man who's out of his element. In a way, he's not to blame.

With Mr. Lawrence, the problem is much more complicated. Everyone who's followed the Lawrence administration understands that he's been over his head since the day he set foot on campus.

But about Mr. Lawrence's attachment to sports—which, by the way, is deep and sincere: he actually travels with the teams to away games, like a high school teacher who goes on the team bus—I simply don't understand.

My guess is that, never having spent time inside a really good academic institution, Mr. Lawrence came to Rutgers with a model mainly derived from watching TV sports—Nebraska, say, as you see it on those halftime promotional spots during the Tostitos Fiesta Bowl, or Kentucky or Indiana as you see them on TV during that Final Four extravaganza. I suspect that it's the only model he really has.

The great problem is that Rutgers is being made over in Lawrence's image. We really are becoming Nebraska or Florida State in lots of ways. I hear students complaining, for instance, that Rutgers faculty have no real involvement in undergraduate life. That's true, but it's true because most faculty are so alienated under the Lawrence regime that they simply can't wait to get away from campus at the end of the day.

By the same token, you hear undergraduates complaining that Rutgers has become a "school of last resort" for New Jersey students. Partly, they're right. There's been a terrible slide in admissions standards under Lawrence. When I arrived at Rutgers, for instance, Barron's listed Rutgers College as accepting 38% of all applicants, making it one of the most selective colleges in the U.S. Last year, the same figure was around 60%. From an acceptance rate of around 1-in-3, in short, to one closer to 2-in-3. And keep in mind that Barron's gets its statistics from our own admissions office.

That's a problem, but it's not the whole problem. New Jersey has an applicant pool so rich in talent that even with a relatively low admission threshold you still get a remarkable number of top-notch students. The problem is that "the school of last resort" mentality has produced a very low self-image among Rutgers students. The school is amazingly much better than students here realize it is, but the self-image of the place keeps sinking.

My sense is that Lawrence and Mulcahy both know this. But they have no idea what to do about it. So where a top-notch administration would set about addressing the structural problems—raising admissions standards, putting in place high-powered programs that benefited the most highly motivated undergraduates and acted as a stimulus to everyone else, restoring a sense of intellectual community that would bring faculty back into undergraduate life—the only answer they have is to try to "get a winner" so that the students will be able to see the name of their school on TV. And they honestly believe that this would produce what they call "school spirit," which would be an answer to all their problems.

Here's what they don't understand. At schools where genuine school spirit exists, it exists because students are proud of going to the school. It has absolutely nothing to do with sports.

If God waved a wand tomorrow and made college athletics vanish, for instance, kids who go to Harvard would have just as much "school spirit" as they did before. That's because "school spirit" at Harvard consists simply in pride in Harvard as an institution.

The opposite is true at the sports factories. There, "school spirit" can only be conceived in terms of TV exposure—the college equivalent of the cheap thrill that comes from seeing your Uncle Harold on *The Jerry Springer Show,* one supposes—and brand-name exposure.

So if God waved the wand and abolished Division I A sports, students at places like Nebraska and Kentucky would wake up and find themselves shivering, naked, without anything to call a university behind the smoke-screen of commercialized sports. Take away the Tostitos Fiesta Bowl or the Final Four, and they have nothing left.

Until Mr. Lawrence came to Rutgers, the university was on a rising trajectory toward genuine greatness. We weren't very far away from being the sort of place where, if God waved his wand, nobody would have noticed that athletics had disappeared. The idea of school spirit at Rutgers would have consisted of pride in going to Rutgers, a school with selective admissions, great students, and a top faculty.

If you want to see a symbol of what Mr. Lawrence and Mr. Mulcahy think "school spirit" is, go down to the basement of the Rutgers Student Center. Look for a glass-enclosed display room called the Rutgers Spirit Shop. Take a look around.

I don't know whether the Rutgers Spirit Shop was Mr. Lawrence's inspiration, or Mr. Mulcahy's. Given the general tawdriness of his sports promotions, my money would be on Mr. Mulcahy. But that isn't the point. The point is that the Rutgers Spirit Shop, and what it says about their idea of the university, is a pure image of the only Rutgers that the Lawrence-Mulcahy administration is able to understand. That's where their ceaseless and depressing desire to "get a winner" in the revenue sports comes from. It's an attempt to fill the big emptiness that they themselves have created at Rutgers.

Note on Sources

The books from which I've quoted—e.g., Derek Bok's *Universities in the Marketplace,* Peter Golenbock's *Personal Fouls,* Murray Sperber's *College Sports, Inc.*—are recent and widely available. Since *Confessions of a Spoilsport* has been written as a personal memoir, it has seemed to me best to send it into the world without the elaborate apparatus of footnotes, cross-references, and ibids that are a standard feature of scholarly monographs. By the same token, I've chosen to avoid cluttering the text with parenthetical citations to national publications—e.g., the *Chronicle of Higher Education,* the *New York Times,* the *Wall Street Journal*—or local New Jersey newspapers—e.g., the *Home News Tribune,* the *Newark Star-Ledger,* the *Daily Targum*—from which I've drawn supporting material. As I've found in running my own checks for accuracy, the quoted material is invariably and easily searchable in the online archives of those publications.

One item counts as more or less fugitive. This is "Pagers, Nikes, and Wordsworth," by Martin Scott, the account of teaching remedial students from which I quote on page 15. This appeared in *Profession 2002,* an annual publication of the Modern Language Association.

As I mention in the text, all material relating to Lobogate and the University of New Mexico, including the court transcript of Norm Ellenberger's federal trial in Roswell, comes from the Calvin Horn Collection at Zimmerman Library at UNM. Everything quoted from that collection in *Confessions of a Spoilsport* is in the public domain. I might mention, for those interested in checking details, that the library maintains an analyzed list of items in the collection on its online site.

Quoted e-mail messages and material from Internet sports boards come from files kept during the campaign by the Rutgers 1000 Web team. Some— e.g., the long post from "Paisano" quoted in Chapter 8—were originally featured on the Rutgers 1000 Web site. Though RU1000's files were dispersed when the campaign disbanded, sports board postings quoted in the text have been taken from copies I made at the time for use in *Confessions of a*

Spoilsport. Other Internet and e-mail files—e.g., the e-mail messages sent to Linda Bensel-Meyers by Tennessee football boosters—are taken from copies provided by their recipients. I thank Joshua Saltzman and the editors of the *Rutgers Review* for permission to reprint the interview given in the appendix. Photos included in the text are from the Rutgers 1000 archives, with the exception of the photograph of Norm Ellenberger in Chapter 1, which is reprinted with permission from the University of New Mexico Office of Sports Information, and the photograph of Richard McCormick in Chapter 10, reprinted with permission from the *Home News Tribune*. I'm grateful to Elana Aron for permission to reproduce the photo of Fraidy Reiss that appears in Chapter 6.

In giving accounts of my conversations with students and colleagues—both at Rutgers and elsewhere—I've occasionally altered personal details that would identify individuals who might prefer to remain anonymous. The exception is Steven Rubel, to whom I originally gave another name and whom I had transferring from Rutgers to a different Ivy League university than the one he actually chose. When I sent those pages to Steve to check for accuracy, he wrote back to say that he would consider it an honor to appear in *Confessions of a Spoilsport* under his own name. So the student who appears in Chapter 8 as "Steven Rubel" is, in fact, Steven Rubel. The school to which he transferred from Rutgers was Columbia University.

Acknowledgments

Confessions of a Spoilsport benefited enormously from the suggestions of two acute and exigent readers: Linda Dowling and Jim Barbour. Each read the book in successive drafts, ruthlessly eliminated inessential materials, altered the narrative structure in important ways, and kept me focused on the violated ideal of democratic education that has been so grievous a consequence of commercialized Div IA sports. Barbour, a colleague and close friend from my UNM days, also put in a great deal of time and thought helping me reconstruct the story of Lobogate and the internal workings of the English Department during that period. Two other readers, William G. Bowen and Ronald A. Smith, emphasized the importance of keeping the national background of big-time college sports in view while recounting events at Rutgers. Peter Golenbock was kind enough to answer a series of detailed questions about his grim encounter with the Wolfpack Club at North Carolina State University. Russell Goodman spent hours going through the Calvin Horn Collection at UNM's Zimmerman Library to help me assemble the primary materials on which Chapter 1 is based. Stanley N. Katz, on whose long experience as a leader in American higher education I gratefully drew, provided advice and encouragement early and late. Gordon Gee, president of Vanderbilt University, also gave useful advice.

At Rutgers, my list of obligations is virtually endless. The names of most of the major figures in Rutgers 1000 are given in the narrative, but I want especially to thank my colleagues John Gillis and Norman Levitt for their help and support. As a historian by profession and a central figure in the struggle, Gillis was particularly helpful in allowing me to grasp the story as a whole. Jim Carty, then a sportswriter for the *Asbury Park Press,* taught me many things I didn't know about the inner workings of Div IA sports at Rutgers and elsewhere. Both he and I were surprised, I think, when a relationship that had begun in wary antagonism turned into something very like friendship. Mike Fasano, as indicated in the text, was kind enough to grant permission to include "Sympathy for the Devil" in Chapter 7. Among the Rutgers 1000 alumni, Mark Mattia was especially assiduous in keeping me up to date on developments in the Rutgers Athletics Department and in Trenton politics. Christopher Swasey provided invaluable help in assembling the photographs for the volume.

The earliest version of *Confessions of a Spoilsport* had a chapter on the Drake Group, the one organization that has provided meaningful opposition to Div IA sports corruption at the national level. I was fortunate enough to be present at the original conference at Drake University from which the group takes its name. Today, I regard its members as companions in a struggle that won't end until commercialized college sports are totally eliminated from American higher education. Though I ultimately decided that the Drake Group story needs to be told separately, I've drawn constantly on the thinking of various people—Allen Sack, Murray Sperber, Ellen Staurowsky, Andrew Zimbalist, and, most especially, Jon Ericson, its convener—who attended the Drake conference. The Drake Group member who contributed most visibly to *Confessions of a Spoilsport* is Linda Bensel-Meyers, whose ugly encounter with the University of Tennessee's booster subculture is recounted in Chapter 7. I'm grateful to her for the materials she provided, and to other members of the group for the education they've collectively given me over the years about the consequences of professionalized sports for American higher education.

Index